DISCARDED

THE NEW UNIONISM IN THE CLOTHING INDUSTRY

THE NEW UNIONISM
IN THE CLOTHING INDUSTRY

BY
J. M. BUDISH
AND
GEORGE SOULE

NEW YORK / RUSSELL & RUSSELL

FIRST PUBLISHED IN 1920
REISSUED, 1968, BY RUSSELL & RUSSELL
A DIVISION OF ATHENEUM HOUSE, INC.
BY ARRANGEMENT WITH HARCOURT, BRACE & WORLD, INC.
L. C. CATALOG CARD NO: 68-27054
PRINTED IN THE UNITED STATES OF AMERICA

NOTE

Some readers of this book may miss emphasis on the names of important union officials such as Sidney Hillmann and Joseph Schlossberg of the Amalgamated Clothing Workers of America, and Benjamin Schlesinger and Abraham Baroff of the International Ladies' Garment Workers Union. If we once began to assign credit to individuals, however, the list could not stop with the Presidents and General Secretaries, but would go on through Managers, Business Agents, Delegates, Shop Chairmen, until it had included well-nigh every member of the unions. To write a book about the needletrades organizations without giving due praise to all the able and devoted officials is not to write a Hamlet with the Hamlet left out, for the greatest possible tribute to them is an exhibition of the movement with which they have been associated.

Our thanks is due to the *Survey* for permission to reprint the quotations from Katherine Coman in Chapter IV. For information and criticism we are especially indebted to Joseph Schlossberg and Peter Monat of the Amalgamated Clothing Workers, Miss Fannia Cohn and Morris Zigman of the International Ladies' Garment Workers Union, A. J. Muste of the Amalgamated Textile Workers, Morris Kaufman of the International Fur Workers Union, M. Kolchin, of the Impartial Chairman's Office of the New York Men's Clothing Industry, M. Zuckerman of the United Cloth Hat and Cap Makers, and D. Berger of the United Neckwear Makers.

CONTENTS

CHAPTER I

THE NEW UNIONISM

	PAGE
Success of the Clothing Unions	3
British New Unionism	4
Industrial Workers of the World	6
Hoxie's Classification of Unions	8
Tendencies Toward New Unionism in U. S.	11
Characteristics of the Clothing Unions	11

CHAPTER II

THE CLOTHING INDUSTRY

Magnitude of the Industry	15
Divisions of the Industry	16
History of Men's Clothing Trades	17
History of Women's Clothing Trades	24
Seasonal Character	27
Fluidity of Labor	29
Fashions	30
Power Installation	32
Size and Number of Establishments	33
Contractors and Sub-Manufacturers	34
Difficulty of Controlling Industry	35
Variations in Efficiency	37
Difficulty of Mobilizing Labor	39
Number of Women Employed	41
The Function of the Unions	44

CHAPTER III

THE HUMAN ELEMENT

Assumed Radicalism of the Immigrant	46
Personnel of the Clothing Industry	47
Situation of East-European Jews	49
Culture of the Jews	52
Persecution of Jews in Russia	53
Anti-Jewish Movement in Rumania and Austria-Hungary	55
What the Jews Sought in America	56
Proportion of Socialists Among Jewish Immigrants	57

v

vi   CONTENTS

	PAGE
Development of Socialism Among Jews in the U. S.	59
Italian Immigration	63
Influence of Race and Leadership	66

CHAPTER IV

THE UNIONS—THEIR BEGINNINGS AND GROWTH

The Unions	68
Their History to 1900	70
The United Garment Workers	74
The United Cloth Hat and Cap Makers of North America	76
The International Ladies' Garment Workers Union	80
Backwardness of the U. G. W.	85
The Nashville Conventions	87
The Amalgamated Clothing Workers of America	89
A Needle Trades Federation	93
The International Fur Workers' Union	95
The Journeyman Tailors' Union	96
The United Neckwear Makers	97
The Suspender Makers Union	98
Present Strength of the Unions	98

CHAPTER V

DECISIVE VICTORIES

The Workers' State of Mind	101
A Typical Tenement	102
A Contractor's Shop	104
Specific Grievances	106
New York Cloak Strike of 1910	111
Signing of the Protocol	116
Chicago Men's Clothing Strike of 1910	118
More Recent Achievements	124

CHAPTER VI

COLLECTIVE AGREEMENTS

Community of Interest Between Employer and Employee	126
Conflict of Interest	127
Collective Agreement	128
Operation of Protocol Machinery	129
Friction Under the Protocol	132
Causes of Complaint	134
The Fundamental Conflict	136
Abrogation of Protocol	139
Cloakmakers' Agreement of 1916	140
Agreements of 1919 in Women's Industry	142
Joint Board of Sanitary Control	145

CONTENTS

	PAGE
Hart, Schaffner and Marx Agreements	148
Impartial Machinery in New York Men's Industry	152
Industrial Council in Men's Industry	153
Other Agreements	154

Chapter VII

PHILOSOPHY, STRUCTURE, AND STRATEGY

Power of the Needle-Trades Unions	156
Function of Ideas	158
Origins of Old Unionism	159
Origins of Clothing Unions	163
First Expressions of their Philosophy	167
✓Leadership	171
Structure of the Clothing Unions	173
Strategy of the Clothing Unions	191

Chapter VIII

EDUCATION

Interest in the Unions' Educational Work	205
Educational Function of Unions Themselves	206
Early Labor Education	208
New Conception of Education	212
International Ladies' Garment Workers' Activities	215
United Labor Education Committee	219
New Unionist's Attitude Towards Education	225

Chapter IX

LABOR PRESS AND COOPERATIVES

Growing Power of the Press	229
Bias of the Capitalist Press	231
Union Journals in English	235
Early Jewish Workers' Press	239
The *Forward*	241
Other Journals	243
Clothing Union Publications	245
Cooperative Enterprises	248
A Cooperative Bank	250

Chapter X

TEXTILES

Inter-Relation of Textiles and Clothing	252
The Textile Industry	252

CONTENTS

	PAGE
The Labor Force in Textiles	254
The Older Unions	256
The Lawrence Strike of 1919	257
The Amalgamated Textile Workers	262
Competition Between New and Old Unions	266
Amalgamation with Clothing Workers	269

Chapter XI

THE FUTURE

Speculation About the Future	270
What Remains to be Achieved	272
Wages and Productivity	274
Seasonal Unemployment	279
Workers' Control of the Industry	283
Cooperative Production	285
Revolutionary General Strike	288
Socialization by Political and Economic Action	291
Future Policy of the Workers	295
Interests of the Public	297
Comparative Dangers from Conservative and Radical Unions	299
Necessity of Experiment and Change	301

Bibliography	303
Appendix	307
Index	341

CHAPTER I

THE NEW UNIONISM

THE rapid rise of the unions in the clothing industry is dramatic in itself. The workers who compose them, largely of foreign birth, were for many years notoriously exploited. Their sufferings from overcrowding in the tenements, from occupational diseases, from underpayment, overwork, and seasonal unemployment, formed a favorite theme for the investigator, the proponent of welfare legislation, the social worker. Charity and the law were invoked again and again, without noticeable effect. The periodic revolts of the toilers themselves, spontaneous and well-nigh unorganized, arose with the returning seasons, and spent themselves without permanent gain like furious waves which fall and withdraw again into the sea. For these unfortunate city children there seemed to be no hope. Then came a sudden and unexpected victory. The unions began to flourish. Almost within ten years the clothing workers have come out of the sweatshops and advanced to a leading position in American organized labor.

It is not for their material victories, however, that these unions are worthy of extended study. Other unions also have won good wages and reasonable hours. The needle-trades organizations are typical, not so much of the general labor movement in the United States at the moment, as of aspirations and tendencies which are rapidly gaining ground. It is their philosophy, their methods, their aims beyond wages and hours, their remarkable educational program, which give them a somewhat peculiar significance. They embody what seems to be a new sort of unionism.

As Sidney and Beatrice Webb have pointed out in their "History of Trade Unionism" there have been many revivals in the labor movement to which the term "new unionism" has been applied. As long ago as 1830 the London *Times* was much agitated by a project to form "one big union" of all crafts throughout the nation, and held up *the* Trades Union as a bogy with which to frighten its readers. At that time the innovators favored associations using purely economic action on an ever-widening scale, as opposed to the old-fashioned friendly and benefit societies. In 1842, after chartism had spent its force and the unions had been weakened by frequent industrial depressions, a new unionism arose whose aim was to build cautiously and moderately an enduring structure, with a sounder financial stability. The classic example of new unionism in England, however, was the movement resulting from the dock strike of 1889. For many years organization had been almost the exclusive prerogative of the skilled craftsmen, the "aristocracy of labor." Now came a great and successful strike of the unskilled. Socialist influence showed strongly in the agitation. It was class-conscious, and vaguely revolutionary in aim. The unions were characterized by the absence of benefit funds or any of the vested interests which tend to make labor conservative. They were not exclusive, and were thought of chiefly as instruments of economic warfare. At the same time they welcomed state interference in the form of laws regulating everything except the hours of labor, and looked forward to the time when the workers, as voters, should be the predominant power in the state. Since 1889 the new unionism has been a term in constant use in England; although its precise meaning has varied with almost every change in the aspiration of the more aggressive and radical wing of the labor movement.

The new unionism was revivified in 1911, when another great strike broke out in the port of London. It began with the National Union of Sailors and Firemen, and soon spread to the dockers, the stevedores, the gasworkers, the carmen, the coal porters, the tug enginemen, the grain porters and others. It is estimated that over 100,000 men took part in a parade which aroused the whole city. In spite of the port authorities, this strike was in large measure successful; but the chief of its results was the formation of the National Transport Workers' Federation, an organization of the numerous unions concerned, for the purpose of future industrial action. It is this powerful and radical union which has since joined with the National Union of Railwaymen and the Miners' Federation in the celebrated "Triple Alliance," an inter-industrial body which is probably at once the strongest and most intelligently aggressive organization of labor in the world. With one hand it supports the far-reaching program of the British Labor Party, while with the other it threatens direct economic action for the consummation of national ownership and democratic management of the mines and railways. In maturity, therefore, British new unionism has assumed a well defined philosophy and method. It believes in the fullest kind of industrial and inter-industrial organization for economic pressure. It believes in independent political organization for the use of the franchise. Its goal is a socialized society, operating very much in the manner advocated by G. D. H. Cole and the other proponents of national guilds, if we can judge by the programs of the miners.

In America, too, we have heard the term before. Not many years ago it was applied to the Industrial Workers of the World. The characteristics of this organization have been obscured in the public mind by the propaganda of its enemies, who have succeeded in identifying it with bloody revolt and wanton destruction of property. It arose, however, in much the same spirit as the new unions in England. It was a revolt against the narrow and conservative craft spirit of many of the older unions, it appealed mainly to the unskilled and hitherto unorganized, and it called for a reconstructed society in which the workers, organized by industries, would control production.

The I. W. W. developed along a different line, however, from that taken by the British movement stimulated by Tom Mann and other syndicalists. In Britain, the syndicalists soon gave up the plan of trying to form new industrial unions to compete with the organizations of labor already existing, but rather carried on an agitation for the federation and amalgamation of the old craft and trade bodies. In America the attempt to set up a separate labor movement continued. In England pure syndicalism was abandoned for the use of political action, and for the working out of an adaptation to collectivist theory which is now represented by the guild movement. In America, no compromise with the socialists was attempted by the I. W. W., except in the smaller and less influential Detroit wing. In England, the conscious development of ca' canny, or slacking on the job, did not long continue. In America, the I. W. W. tried to perfect the weapon of the short strike and the strike on the job or the "conscientious withdrawal of efficiency." With the exception of the Detroit group, the American I. W. W. stood for decentralization, and preferred spontaneous guerrilla warfare to the building of a strong organization which, because it had something to lose, might become conservative. Perhaps on account of these policies, the I. W. W. has never secured the adherence of many workers for long, save the casual agricultural and forest labor of the West. Its power has always been overestimated by those who have been afraid of it, and it does not now, if it ever did, offer any such promise as the new unionism in England.

Robert F. Hoxie, in his "Trade Unionism in the United States," contends that unions are not of one or two kinds simply, but assume many forms, according to the function for which they exist. Among these forms he has identified four basic types, to which in some degree all unions in the United States have approximated. *Business unionism,* in this classification, is the kind formed to serve the material interests of its members within the existing industrial structure; its main object is to practice collective bargaining. *Uplift unionism* is characterized by broad humanitarian purposes; its main methods are friendly benefits and mutual insurance; it was prominent during the early stages of union history and was roughly typified during the latter half of the nineteenth century by the Knights of Labor. *Revolutionary unionism* aims to prepare for a new social and industrial order; it is divided into two subsidiary types—socialistic, which lays more emphasis on political action, and quasi-anarchistic, which eschews political action and looks forward to abolishing entirely the state as we know it. The I. W. W. may be taken as an example of the latter. *Predatory unionism* has no large aspirations, but preys on the employer through secret and illegal methods such as blackmail and bribery, sometimes for the benefit of the members, sometimes for the benefit of the dishonest union official. This type flourished twenty years ago in the United States, but has now almost disappeared.

To the present writers it seems that this classification is not wholly illuminating, because it is not based on a sufficiently dynamic conception of the labor movement. The types are not, after all, quite co-ordinate. In the light of the intensification of the industrial conflict which takes place with the growth of the capitalist order, neither uplift unionism nor predatory unionism seem fundamental enough types to set beside business unionism and revolutionary unionism. At bottom the labor movement is one, because it represents a protest, unconscious or conscious, against the status of the wage-worker. Whatever the avowed purpose and policies of the union under consideration, its activities are bound to affect the structure of society to a greater or less degree. Its particular creed and method are dependent on a variety of circumstances. Unions holding to creeds and methods which become unsuited to the advancement of labor tend to disappear as the environment alters. As we have seen, the most revolutionary unions employ collective bargaining; the characteristics of uplift unionism are displayed sometimes by business unions and sometimes by socialist unions; predatory unionism is practiced, if at all, by business unions corrupted by boss politics, or by little cliques in revolutionary unions driven underground through suppression.

The most significant distinction, in our opinion, is

that between unions which are unconscious that their efforts tend toward a new social order and so adapt their strategy solely to the immediate situation, and unions which are conscious of their desire for a new order, and so base their strategy on more fundamental considerations. These two types in turn have many variants, but the nature of every variation bears the impress of the primary type. It is the former type, roughly corresponding with Professor Hoxie's "business unionism" which we have chosen to call the "old unionism," and the latter which we have called "the new unionism." G. D. H. Cole has given this distinction a phrasing which brings out its meaning in an objective way. In "The World of Labor" he writes, "Regarded merely as instruments of collective wage-bargaining, the unions are the most powerful weapon in the hands of labor; if they are in addition the germs of the future organization of industry as a whole, their importance becomes at once immeasurably greater."

In spite of the decline of the I. W. W., the new unionism in other forms is by no means waning in the United States. Various kinds of old unions in the course of their natural development are being forced to approach it by one route or another. The conservative Railway Brotherhoods have little by little been obliged to coöperate with unions of the unskilled; the railway "system federation" is a unit through which craft action has been superseded by industrial action; and the enunciation of the Plumb plan is a long step towards the acknowledgment of the need for a new economic order which can be attained not through collective bargaining but only through combined political and economic action. The United Mine Workers have long been a union industrial in form and practicing industrial rather than craft strikes; socialist influence has been strong within the union, though not dominant in its government. The time is rapidly approaching, as even its conservative officials admit, when no further gains of importance can be made for the members without pressing actively for the nationalization of the mines, a measure already endorsed several times by the convention. Similar tendencies can be observed everywhere in the conservative American Federation of Labor. Thus does the old unionism merge into the new, by force of sheer economic and social pressure.

No strong and important group of unions in the United States, however, has whole-heartedly accepted the new unionism and consciously modeled structure and strategy accordingly, except the unions in the clothing industry. For this reason they may be considered the nearest approach to the pure type now existing in America. They sprang into power about the time of the port strike of 1911 in London, and the course of their development has been much closer to that of the new unions in England than to that of the I. W. W. They arose from mass movements of the unskilled and semi-skilled, carrying the skilled along with them. They have built up a strong and highly centralized industrial structure, but one sensitive at the same time to the will of the rank and file. They skilfully use collective bargaining, not primarily as a means of gaining material concessions, but as a means of solidifying the workers and retaining victories that will make possible further progress along the main highway. While prepared for the most extended economic action, they at the same time take an active part in independent political action. They do not preach sabotage or ca' canny, but on the contrary assist in every sound project that may improve the industrial machine and increase productivity. Upon the cultural aspects of the labor movement—the press, education, and art—they lay great stress. In short, their whole tendency is in the direction of training the workers for assuming control of production, and of accepting the social and economic responsibility which such control involves.

However different in theory and method, all forms of "new unionism" have had one trait in common. They have always come into being during a period in which the labor movement as a whole seemed to have exhausted its resources and was felt to be in danger of decline if not of destruction. They have all represented a divergence from the established practice, and, more significant than that, all have brought to the movement a new breadth of sympathy and vision, a new ideal, and a new hope. An exposition of the new unionism as exemplified by the clothing workers of America may give further light to those who have been stirred by the expressed aspirations of British labor and by the present flux and unrest in the American labor movement, and in particular to those who have seen great promise in the ideal of national guilds.

CHAPTER II

THE CLOTHING INDUSTRY

PEOPLE sometimes think of trade-union problems as if unions sprang from economic theories and flourished in the pure air of a revolutionary or labor movement. Should there be industrial or craft unions? Should they accept collective agreements? Should their strategy be determined by business policy or by faithfulness to the class struggle? These are fundamental questions, but they are not settled, for any particular union, by a mere appeal to metaphysics. Neither is the best answer to them, and to others of similar nature, dependent mainly on the traditions, character, and education of the workers involved. The character of labor organization takes its form from the nature of industry itself. In the case of any group of unions with a special tendency or philosophy it is safe to assume that their characteristics have developed largely from the special industrial environment in which they have arisen. Is it, for instance, pure accident that in both England and America the coal miners, utterly different as they are in races and culture, have industrial unions and demand nationalization of the mines, while in

THE CLOTHING INDUSTRY 15

both countries metal-trade or engineering unions have been built on craft lines, and are now engaged in a difficult struggle for amalgamation? There seems to be at work among the unions a principle of adaptation which in a real sense determines the nature of the survivors. It would be fruitless to attempt an analysis of the labor movement in the needle trades without first studying in some detail the industries in which it lives. It is necessary to understand the problems the unions have to solve to see how they have, not by inspiration or perversity, but by a process of trial and error, hit upon effective methods of solution.

Judged by any standard except capital employed, the group of industries under consideration—that producing clothing—is among the largest in the country. In 1917, according to government estimates made for the military draft, 754,062 persons were engaged in the manufacture of clothing, a larger number than in any other single industry except textiles, and more than in any other general occupation except agriculture, transportation, and the building trades. According to the latest available census figures [1] there were in round numbers 518,000 wage-earners in the ready-made clothing group (including furs), a number surpassed among industrial workers only by those in iron and steel and their products, lumber and its remanufacturers, and textiles. Clothing ranked 7th in wages paid ($256,400,000), 8th in amount paid for materials

[1] Abstract of the Census of Manufactures, 1914.

($696,000,000) and 8th in value of the finished product. ($1,340,000,000). The capital invested was approximately $600,000,000. The number of establishments was about 16,000. If clothing were combined with textiles, the two together would outrank in most respects any other large group of industries.

For our purposes the clothing trades must be divided into two main groups: one, of which we shall speak in this chapter, is that in which the unions originated and developed their strength; the other, of different industrial and social structure, is that into which they are now rapidly making their way. The first group includes [2] men's and boys' clothing (175,000 workers), women's and children's clothing (169,000 workers), cloth hats and caps (7,000 workers), and fur goods (10,000 workers). The second embraces men's shirts (52,000 workers), collars and cuffs (10,000 workers), men's furnishings including neckwear (22,000 workers), corsets (20,000 workers), suspenders and garters (10,000 workers), and millinery. The main distinction is that most of the second group are not so favorable to sub-contracting and small establishments, require a large proportion of capital and have more highly developed machine processes. Overalls are included under men's clothing, but they form a special case which must be discussed separately.

Ready-made clothing was almost unknown before

[2] The figures in this paragraph are from the Abstract of the Census of Manufactures, 1914. These figures are inaccurate now, but they serve to show the relative importance.

THE CLOTHING INDUSTRY

1825. The first factory of which there is any record was that of George Opdyke in Hudson Street, New York City, established in 1831. Neither this nor its successors before the Civil War were, however, factories as we understand the term. The manufacturers merely sold, designed, and cut the garments, and they were sewed in the home, the cheaper grades by farmers' wives, the better ones by skilled city tailors. In no case did the product compete with custom-tailored suits. Its manufacture arose to fill the demand of second-hand clothing dealers for odd sizes to round out their stock, and it was sold principally to sailors who had neither the time nor the money to employ a tailor, and to southern negroes and poor whites. The sewing machine, placed on the market in 1850, gave the industry some stimulus. By 1859 it was estimated that there were 4,000 establishments giving employment to 114,800 workers. The centers were chiefly Boston, New Bedford, and New York, because of their proximity to the mills and to the most numerous supply of cheap casual labor.

Most of the first manufacturers were custom tailors. The busy seasons for the custom tailor lasted but 20 or 25 weeks in the year, and the making of ready-made clothes filled the gap. As the ready-made clothing business grew, some of the larger firms found it profitable enough so that they gave up the custom trade entirely. Before the Civil War, an advertisement appeared in a St. Louis paper announcing sales of ready-made clothing at wholesale and retail, and stating that the goods were made in a New York factory permanently employing 2,000 hands.

Since the spirit of craftsmanship persisted in the tailor, however, and few mechanical processes had been introduced to split the process and make easier the use of unskilled labor, the factory system did not progress here as in other industries. Goods were given out by the warehouse man or manufacturer to the competent but dependent tailors to be done in the home. With the invention of the sewing machine, the participation of the family became easy. The tailor himself did the more difficult sewing and pressing, while his wife and daughters attended to the easier work. This was the beginning of the family system.

At the same time the factories, extending their business, and requiring large quantities of cheap clothing, had to draw into the process semi-skilled workers who could not do good work without supervision. The factory, known as a "warehouse," was already employing a number of skilled tailors as foremen to give out jobs to the home workers, to examine the product and pay for it. The tailors with whom they were dealing were responsible and known artisans, who could be trusted with the goods. There appeared, however, large numbers of persons applying for employment whom the foremen did not know, or did not believe sufficiently skilled or trustworthy. In order to utilize the labor of these persons the contractor was brought into being. The ware-

THE CLOTHING INDUSTRY

houses gave out the goods to the contractor on his own responsibility, and the latter employed the poorer laborers, finding some kind of shop for them. Thus the sweating system developed.

The Civil War laid the basis for large-scale production in the industry. While it cut off the southern market, it substituted government orders for uniforms in enormous quantities, one manufacturer, for instance, receiving a single order amounting to $1,250,000. The natural results were larger establishments, factory buildings erected for the trade, a standardization of sizes, styles, and processes, a greater subdivision of labor making possible the employment of less skilled operators, and more efficient methods of production. The uniform trade furnished the manufacturers with knowledge of the sizes required in quantities and so prepared them to manufacture in advance of demand. When, after the war, soldiers returning to civil life began looking for cheap ready-made clothing, the manufacturers could supply it. Still, however, the making up and finishing of the garment was done in the home or by contractors. Wages were paid usually not to the individual, but to a man and wife. They had risen, on account of the great demand, and without pressure from the workers, a little more than had the cost of living. Whereas before the war a man and wife were paid from eight to ten dollars a week, they now received from twenty to twenty-five. Out of this they had to buy thread, irons, and sundries. Hours, of course, were unlimited, and rapidly growing congestion in the cities was worsening the sanitation and other conditions of work.

By 1869 the men's clothing industry—the women's was of later development—had increased to 7858 establishments. It spent nearly twice as much for material as in 1859, and the value of the product was $148,660,000 as against $80,830,000 a decade before. The number of workers had diminished to 108,128, probably on account of large-scale production, but they were paid almost twice as much in the aggregate.

The decade from 1870-1880 was a flourishing one for the industry. It was a great pioneer period, and immigration both increased the demand and furnished labor. The sale was still for cheap and medium grades, in staple sizes and styles. The fashion factor was unimportant. Jobbers distributed the product to small shops. Long credit was customary. Large capital was therefore necessary and large cutting and merchandizing establishments the rule. Profits were ample. New machinery was invented, notably for cutting. While the number of firms decreased to 6166 in 1879, the average number of workers increased to 160,813, and the product was valued at $209,548,000. Wages, however, remained stationary, the aggregate advancing only in proportion to the number employed. The home and contracting systems of work were almost universal.

By 1889, probably owing to further improvements in process, the number of workers decreased again to

THE CLOTHING INDUSTRY

144,926, and the continued tendency to large-scale production reduced the number of establishments to 4867. The value of the product, however, showed the usual increase, mounting to $251,019,000. Improvements in the manufacture of textiles, with other causes, decreased the amount paid for materials by about two and a half million dollars. Wages were advanced slightly. The conditions of work remained as before, but the heightened competition among the contractors and among the workers under them intensified every evil of the sweatshop. Meanwhile, the industry had shown a large development in Chicago and other mid-western centers.

Through the latter years of the last century the value of the product in the men's clothing industry showed the same steady increase, accompanied, according to the census, by fluctuations in number of establishments and number of workers. These fluctuations are partly due to interaction of the growing demand for ready-made clothing with the improvement of process and the advantage of large-scale production. In part, however, they are fictitious, since different censuses employed different methods of enumeration. The Tenement House Act of 1892 in New York, prohibiting contractors from carrying on manufacture in the home, while it could not be enforced rigidly, was another factor in the establishment of larger shops. It was not until 1895, however, that the first large "inside shop" was established—that is, a shop in which practically all the operations were carried on. The centering of the operations in one building made possible improvements in sanitation, power, and other working conditions, but it did not abolish the contractor. Most of the inside shops continued the sub-contracting system within their walls, dealing only with the sub-contractor and paying him for the finished article or piece. He in turn acted as the employer of the relatives and hangers-on who worked under his direction.

During the first decade of the new century the industry began to undergo changes which further complicated the existence of the workers. It reached out for the trade formerly taken by custom tailors, and to do so it had to diversify styles and materials. Public taste in turn was affected, and many of the staple demands began to cease altogether. It had been the custom, for instance, for men to wear ready-made striped trousers, with a coat of different material. Now the separate trousers business waned rapidly; advertising was not influencing the men who had had their suits tailored as wholes, but was changing the taste of those who had not. With the tendency toward diversification of styles, and the intensified competition in merchandizing, went the gradual elimination of the large jobber and long credit. Goods could not be held over from season to season by retailer, jobber, or manufacturer. They had to be ordered as late as possible, so that the shelves should not be piled with unpopular styles. Tailor-to-the trade houses arose, which made a point, not of carrying stock lines, but of making up suits as ordered through the retailer. All this emphasized the seasonal tendency of the industry and made it still more difficult to avoid seasonal unemployment. It reduced the amount of capital necessary to engage in manufacturing, and robbed the large and medium-sized houses of much of their advantage. The system of small contractors, with all their irresponsibility, was encouraged. And the business became more dependent on general conditions. The panic of 1907 gravely injured the clothing industry, although previous depressions had helped it. Perhaps this indicated that recent panics have affected more people in moderate circumstances, but it is certain that the ready-made clothing industry was now serving more people in better circumstances. While the total of its business had been enlarging as usual, the problems of its workers, and of many of its employers as well, had been much aggravated. It was in this period that the unrest of the workers became acute, and the present labor movement in the industry sprang to power.

In 1909 the men's clothing industry produced nearly one-half the value of the total product of the clothing trades. Its principal center was New York, which turned out 40 per cent of the goods, and contained a still larger proportion of the establishments. Chicago accounted for 17 per cent. Other important centers were Philadelphia, Cleveland, Detroit, Baltimore, Milwaukee, Rochester, St. Louis, Cincinnati, Louisville, San Francisco, and Syracuse.

The following table summarizes its growth:

Year	No. of Establishments	Av. No. of Wage-Earners	Wages	Cost of Materials	Value of Product [3]
			In Thousands of Dollars		
1859	4,014	114,800	19,856	44,147	80,830
1869	7,858	108,128	30,746	86,794	148,660
1879	6,166	160,813	45,940	131,363	209,548
1889	4,867	144,926	51,075	128,846	251,019
1899	5,729	120,927	45,496	145,211	276,717
1904	4,504	137,190	57,225	185,793	355,796
1909	5,584	191,183	89,644	252,522	485,677
1914	4,830	173,747	86,828	230,032	458,211

The women's clothing industry was naturally of later development than the men's. The women whose husbands bought their suits from second-hand or ready-made establishments sewed their own dresses, and the women who could afford custom dressmakers were, on account of the stronger hold of fashions, more conservative in abandoning them. Cloaks were, however, manufactured in quantities before the Civil War. Even in 1860 cloak manufacturers were advertising in New York papers for French women operators. The total product of the New York ready-made cloak business was at that time estimated at about $3,000,000. From the very beginning, the majority of employees were women, especially young girls who did not own sewing machines and worked better in the factory than at home. Home work was therefore not so prevalent as in the men's industry, and "inside shops" were the rule up to the 'eighties.

Working conditions in these shops, however, were no better than in the men's sweatshops. Boston was then a leading center of the industry, and conditions

---

[3] Of course, no deductions can be drawn from changes in money totals without taking into consideration the fluctuations in the value of the dollar.

THE CLOTHING INDUSTRY

there were reported to be better than those in New York. The Boston Labor Bureau in 1871 made a survey which brought out the following facts. The shops were located on the upper floors and were packed so densely that the girls could scarcely move from their chairs; they had no ventilation except from windows at one end of the rooms, and many of the windows could not be opened. Over half the shops had no toilet facilities and no drinking water. In 1872, according to the same bureau, some girls received as little as $1.50 a week, and the highest wage was $18.00, paid to cutters who also acted as managers of entire departments. The usual price for making a cloak was twenty-five cents, and two cloaks a day was the maximum output. The working day was usually ten hours, but as all received piece rates, many took work home at night and sewed from two to three hours in the evening. Some girls lived with their parents but others dwelt in cheap boarding houses, from three to six in a room, the room usually unheated. A few cases were reported of girls dying actually in the presence of investigators "from a death for which it is impossible to find another name than starvation." Others confessed to having eked out their existence by prostitution.

After 1880 the women's garment industry became more diversified and gradually assumed more nearly the character of the men's industry. Suits began to be made in larger quantities, more men were employed in the manufacture of cloaks, and home work and contracting were introduced. Dresses and waists were added to the product in the middle 'nineties. After 1900 a particularly rapid growth was noticeable. House dresses, wrappers, kimonos, skirts, children's and infant's wear, and undergarments of all kinds were produced for the ready-to-wear market. The following table will indicate the strides of the business.

In drawing inferences from this table it should be remembered that here, as with the men's industry, the method of enumeration adopted by the census was not always the same.

Year	No. of Establishments	Av. No. of Wage-Earners	Wages	Cost of Materials	Value of Product
			In Thousands of Dollars		
1859	188	5,739	1,193	3,323	7,181
1869	1,847	11,696	2,514	6,838	12,901
1879	562	25,192	6,661	19,559	32,005
1889	1,224	39,149	15,428	34,277	68,164
1899	2,701	83,739	32,586	84,705	159,340
1909	4,558	153,743	78,568	208,788	384,752
1914	5,564	168,907	92,574	252,345	473,888

Although in 1914 there were not so many wage-earners in the women's clothing as in the men's clothing industry, there were more separate establishments. This is partly accounted for by the greater variety of styles and articles of apparel made, which leads to more specialization. It is an eloquent sign, however, that the contractor is as prevalent here as in any branch of clothing manufacture, and that the small establishment flourishes.

It is worthy of note that the period after 1900, which produced the great diversification of styles,

THE CLOTHING INDUSTRY 27

the intensification of seasonal unemployment, the increase of the small establishment, and consequent labor unrest in the men's industry, was paralleled by an almost identical development in the women's industry. In almost every respect, the characteristics of the women's industry are now similar to those of the men's. It also flourishes in the same centers. The main differences are that the men's industry is steadier and less seasonal than the women's; it contains more large establishments; it employs more men and fewer women workers; and it has more invested capital and mechanical power in proportion to the value of the product.

The most obvious problems of the workers in the clothing industry are caused by its seasonal character. The manufacturers of men's garments begin their busy season in January, and the total number employed is greatest in February and March. After that there is a slow falling-off until November. The 1914 Census figures show that the total of seasonal unemployment reached about 19,000, or over one-tenth of the maximum. In the making of women's clothing, the situation is still worse. There are two busy seasons, one reaching its climax in March, the other in October. Between seasons the number employed shows a disastrous decrease. The maximum in 1914 was 188,526 in March, and the minimum 145,362 in July. Thus if all the operatives thrown out of work could find nothing else to do, there would be in the worst period 43,000 unemployed, or 23 per cent of the total number. Most industries have serious fluctuations, but in no other are there so many jobless concentrated in a few localities. When clothing workers in New York or Chicago are turned on the streets in such numbers, they cannot easily find other employment.

More serious than the case of the actually unemployed, moreover, is that of the majority of workers who, while they do not lose their jobs, are put on part-time during the slack seasons. The full wages received during the busy times do not set the standard of living, but the wages received during the period of lowest remuneration limit it. Savings cannot be great out of even the highest wage paid. It is the current expenses like rent and weekly food bill which determine the standard of life. These must be regulated according to the amount in the pay envelope when it is thinnest. In the dress and waist industry, for instance, during 1912 the average weekly wage earned by all the workers amounted to only 73 per cent of that paid during the busiest week. Census statistics of the cap-makers show little actual seasonal unemployment, but almost all the workers are on part time for some months in the year.

On account of differences in the busy seasons among the various clothing industries, it is possible in some instances for operatives thrown out of work in one industry to find it in another, but this does not appreciably affect the total. Taking all the clothing industries together, the difference between the highest month and the lowest was, in 1914, 76,670 workers. And it must be remembered that this total includes the more highly developed manufactures such as shirts, collars, and corsets, which both on account of their processes and their location do not offer much opportunity of employment to workers on men's and women's garments. A study of selected individuals in the cloak, suit, and skirt industry of New York was made in 1914 by the U. S. Bureau of Labor Statistics,[4] illustrating the usual condition. Out of 29 cutters and 30 pressers, 25 each were out of work at their trade for more than twelve weeks. A conservative approximation of the average period of unemployment for these persons shows that for the cutters it was 18.8 weeks and for the pressers 20.9 weeks. Only five of the cutters and three of the pressers were able to find other work during this period.

The frequency of discharge for seasonal slack work naturally leads to a shifting personnel of the labor force in any one shop. Out of about 15,000 workers questioned in the cloak, suit and skirt industry, the proportion who worked in only one shop during the year from August 1, 1912 to August 1, 1913, ranged from 79 to 57 per cent, according to operation. Some worked in as many as nine shops in that year. This high labor turnover not only adds to the expense of the manufacturer and acts as an economic drag on the entire industry, but it complicates the task of the unions. It is more difficult to keep track of such a fluid labor force, and the frequency of discharge

[4] Wages and Regularity of Employment in the Cloak, Suit and Skirt Industry, U. S. Department of Labor, Bulletin No. 147.

gives the manufacturer many an opportunity to get rid of a worker whom he finds troublesome on account of union activities. After collective agreements were adopted, many of the most vexatious adjustments arose over such questions of improper discharge.

It would be a comparatively easy matter to avoid the worst seasonal fluctuations by distributing work evenly throughout the year were it not for fashions. The total amount of clothing to be sold can be estimated roughly, and if each year the manufacturers could decide on a few staple styles, as they used to do in the last century, they could begin work as early as they liked. But competition has forced them to vie with each other in showing a great variety of samples, some of which are destined to be popular and others not. The public, in turn, has been educated to demand the "latest thing." So the dealers order as little as they can until the season is upon them and they know what is selling. Probably few individual members of the public really want so many styles and so many changes in them, but a spirit of social emulation leads them to accept the process. They blame the manufacturers for the multiplicity of fashions, which they believe are created to increase the volume of clothing sold. The manufacturers, in turn, blame the public for being so capricious and causing them so much extra expense; no individual manufacturer would dare to reduce his styles for fear of losing trade to competitors. He gains no benefit from any possible increased total of clothing sold. The workers suffer in the vicious circle by enduring year after year long hours and rush work in the busy seasons, and semi-starvation in the slack ones. There is no one to make effective the communal will against the individual weakness.

A recent change in the origination of fashions for the ladies' tailoring establishments, or "tailors to the trade" as distinguished from the manufacturers of ready-to-wear garments, has in fact considerably reduced seasonal unemployment in that branch. Whereas fashions used to originate solely in Paris, and American tailors had to wait before beginning large operations until the prevailing fashion for the season established itself, now American capital has invaded the field to such an extent that many of the latest "Paris fashions" are actually produced in New York and are known simultaneously on this side of the Atlantic by most of the important firms. The origination of such fashions is the specialized function of a comparatively few houses, whose income is derived as much from the sale of designs as from the sale of garments themselves. In this way an approach to systematized standardization has been made. It affects, however, only a comparatively small proportion of the clothing workers. The recent lengthening of the seasons has been due in the main rather to the coincidence of a period of prosperity with the absence of immigration; if in the future we should experience a period of depression and an increase in the labor supply, the problem of seasonal unemployment would undoubtedly be as acute as ever.

If it cost the manufacturer more than it does to keep his plant idle or going at low speed, he might make more heroic efforts to break loose from the round of fashions, or to find something with which to fill the slack seasons. In other industries the capital tied up in plant, machinery and power becomes a heavy weight on finances if it is not being used. The average for all American industries was in 1914 [5] an installation of 3.2 mechanical horse power for each worker. In the men's clothing trade there is but one mechanical horse power for every 3.2 workers. In the women's industry there is one horse power for every six workers. The men's industry therefore uses ten times less, and the women's twenty times less power per worker than the average. Over half this power, also, is rented, and represents no investment when not turned on. A manufacturer is concerned to keep engines working steadily because they represent an investment which must be earning dividends, but he can turn man-power off at any time without concern— for that the worker has to pay.

The clothing industry and the employees in it also suffer from changes in the prosperity of the consumer. Clothing in the bulk may be a necessity, but the garments that are actually sold include a large proportion of semi-luxuries, which are cut off in time of crisis. 1914 and 1917 saw greatly slackened pro-

[5] Abstract of the Census of Manufactures, 1914.

duction in women's and men's civilian clothing, although the uniform trade partly filled the breach in 1917.

In most industries the large establishments do the bulk of the business and set the working standards. Once they are controlled by labor, a decisive battle of the workers is won. Not so in the clothing industries. Taking the men's and women's industries together, there were, according to the Census of 1914, 1663 establishments with an annual product of less than $5,000, 3098 between $5,000 and 20,000, 3496 between $20,000 and $100,000, 2129 between $100,000 and $1,000,000, and 101 over $1,000,000. The establishments with a product worth under $100,000 each employed 126,525 persons, more than half as many as those doing a larger business. Their total product was valued at $207,046,000, while the larger houses produced only a little over three times as much—$725,055,000. There were 2,219 establishments employing from one to five persons each, and the number of workers in these shops was 7,553; while there were only 12 establishments employing over 1,000, and the total of their wage-earners was but 22,078. The largest group of establishments (3,901) was that employing from six to twenty workers; 48,415 wage-earners worked in them. The largest total of wage-earners worked in shops employing from 21 to 50; in these 2,443 establishments there were 78,907 employed. The 934 shops employing from 51 to 100 each, accounted for 65,566 wage-earners, the 423 from 100 to 250, 63,509 workers, the 97 from 251 to

500, 32,591 workers, and the 36 from 501 to 1000, 25,235 workers. This condition of small enterprise and free competition may satisfy devotees of laissez-faire economics, but it makes untold trouble for the workers and their unions.

The larger establishments have no great advantage over the smaller, and do not tend to drive them out of business, except in some few lines where a well advertised name can be made to count. The percentage of manufacturing profit to net sales reported from those men's clothing establishments which did an annual business of under $500,000 a year was 4.75, a larger percentage than in any group of establishments except those whose product was valued at $2,000,000 and over apiece.[6] It is the medium-sized firms which make the least.

The same tendency makes contracting prevalent. A few "inside shops" have all the operations performed under one roof, but many give out the work to contractors—either part or all of it. The 1914 Census figures show in the men's industry 124,000 workers in independent factories and 50,000 in contractors' shops; in the women's industry 152,000 in independent concerns and 17,000 in contractors' establishments. Union officials state that these figures grossly underestimate the numbers working for contractors. It is probable that they do, for they are made up from the manufacturers' reports, and many a contractor who aspires to independence and

[6] The Men's Factory-Made Clothing Industry, U. S. Department of Commerce.

perhaps does sell part of his product direct to the retailer will call himself independent. There are also numerous sub-manufacturers—employers dependent for their capital and sales on the larger manufacturers, but each turning out complete garments in shops for whose labor management the larger firms are not responsible. Reports from a representative number of manufacturers show the relation of profits to contracting as follows:[7]

Firms having	Manufacturing Profits on Capital Employed	Net Sales
No operating contracted	12.56	5.66
Part " "	9.79	5.22
All " "	13.04	5.89

There seems to be little advantage to the manufacturer in having all his work performed under his own roof unless he is making high grade advertised goods where direct supervision counts.

This separation of the commercial organization from the strictly producing one is a factor which makes it easy for small firms to arise in great numbers. In most industries the necessity of large-scale merchandizing and the economy of large-scale production go hand in hand, and it is perhaps due to this fact that many writers have failed to distinguish the producing from the merchandizing process, although they are different in many respects. In the clothing industry, however, the distinction is obvious and complete. To compete successfully in the modern

[7] The Men's Factory-Made Clothing Industry, U. S. Department of Commerce.

market, it is necessary to have skilled designers, travelling salesmen, large show-rooms, and expensive advertising. This makes at least moderate size necessary to real success as a merchandizing firm. To produce, however, size is not at all essential. An ambitious cutter or designer has all the knowledge necessary to set up a contracting or sub-manufacturing business of his own, and he needs but little capital. He can rent a loft big enough for a few workers, buy his materials on credit, rent his machines from the sewing-machine manufacturer and his power from the electric company. All he needs is the favor of an independent manufacturer and a few orders. He can pay his expenses out of the first year's turnover. He may be, to be sure, a bad manager; poor accounting and reckless ventures may overwhelm him the moment he tries to expand and secure direct business from the retailer. Every year sees hundreds of little firms drifting into and out of business. The total capital invested in the clothing industries was in 1914, as we have seen (page 16), about 15 per cent less than the amount spent for materials (including power). This shows vividly how little fixed capital is necessary and why no concentration of capital can control the industry. The total of all industries for the country shows, on the contrary, over $22,790,000,000 capital and only $14,368,000,000 spent for materials (including power). The capital for all was, instead of 15 per cent smaller, 27 per cent larger than the sum spent for materials. A further indication of the dom-

THE CLOTHING INDUSTRY

inance of the small establishment in the production of clothing is the fact that in 1914, in men's clothing —including shirts—only 47.1 per cent of the product was made by incorporated firms, and in the women's trade only 29.1 per cent. The average for all industries was 83.2 per cent.[8]

With such a large number of establishments, many of them new each year, there is of course a wide variation in managerial and commercial efficiency. Inefficient firms may lose out in the end, but their constant presence exerts a depressing effect on standards. Few manufacturers have accurate accounting systems, and many cannot tell whether certain styles are being made at a profit or a loss. The multiplicity of styles, with inaccurate accounting, leads to great confusion and divergence in the determination of piece rates. The union, endeavoring as it must to establish uniform minima of wages, is limited by the least efficient employer. The styles sold at a loss create a ruinous competition for the established firms, while on the other hand the majority of firms in an association cannot afford the level of wages that the best managed could pay. A special study of the men's clothing industry[9] furnishes evidence that the level of wages has little to do with the prosperity of the establishment. Of ten establishments showing the highest percentage of manufacturing profit, three had a higher percentage for direct labor than the average for the industry,

[8] Abstract of the Census of Manufactures, 1914.
[9] The Men's Factory-Made Clothing Industry. U. S. Department of Commerce.

and seven had a lower percentage. Of six establishments showing a manufacturing loss, four had a higher percentage for direct labor than the average, and two a lower percentage. A lower percentage for direct labor does not mean necessarily lower wages, but may mean fewer employees and better management. If all establishments were as well managed as the most prosperous, the general level of wages could therefore be far higher than it is. Moreover, the workers suffer in the end from the general economic loss due to the excess of competition. One indication of this is that even some of the best firms carry many styles at a loss in order to present an attractive line and prevent competitors from undermining their custom.

Managerial inefficiency is also reflected in unnecessary unemployment or part-time employment due to a lack of balance between various departments. The failure to provide a sufficient proportion of operatives at one stage of the manufacturing process may cause a congestion there and idleness at other stages. In 1913 in the dress and waist industry, even during the busiest week of the season, a large number of the workers were not fully employed. Although the full working week was 50 hours, 20.9 per cent of the workers were employed for between 40 and 50 hours, 3.7 per cent between 30 and 40 hours, 2.5 per cent between 20 and 30 hours, and 2.2 per cent under 20 hours.[10] Illness,

[10] Wages and Regularity of Employment and the Standardization of Piece Rates in the Dress and Waist Industry: New York City. U. S. Department of Labor, Bulletin No. 146.

THE CLOTHING INDUSTRY 39

tardiness, and other causes leading workers to report for only part of the week must be allowed for in these percentages, but probably the largest factor in them is due to managerial inefficiency. If this is the case during the busiest week of the year, imagine the conditions when there is no particular urgency in finishing the product.

Attempts of the workers to improve their conditions were always hindered by the extraordinary difficulty of mobilizing and controlling the labor in this industry. It has flourished in large cities, and has depended chiefly on the work of immigrants recently arrived, the majority of whom did not know English, but all of whom needed immediate employment. Keen competition among the workers themselves was for long the rule. The fact that much of the work could be done in the home, and was done there for years, prevented the growth of solidarity among the toilers, or any effective regulation of hours, conditions, or wages. Each head of a household might have a separate establishment. His wife and children, and even the boarders, would work for him. Newly come relatives or acquaintances who had no other point of contact with the new world would find at his house temporary employment. Thus they would all work seven days a week and far into the night, in small overcrowded rooms which they rarely had time to clean, often sleeping and preparing their rude meals in the workroom. Much has been written of the sweatshops and the insanitary tenements in the slum. Few, however, have understood that these conditions were not only frightful in themselves, but that they hindered the growth of labor organizations which alone could affect lasting and fruitful improvements. It was not the fault of the homeworker, the contractor or his employees that long hours were the rule. Their competition with each other continually depressed prices and made it necessary to work longer and longer in order to keep soul and body together.

Even after the worst sweatshops were abolished, it was still difficult for the unions to mobilize so fluid a supply of labor. Little skill for much of the work is required, and that is of a type which is usually learned in the home. Every woman knows something about sewing; only the designers and cutters need any special tailoring skill. The unorganized are always in the background, in the masses of the population, ready to drift into the industry. No man can learn to be a toolmaker or a locomotive engineer without undergoing a long apprenticeship in the shop, coming in contact with his fellow-workers, and being educated to union solidarity and discipline. But some woman fresh from a little town in Russia or Poland, unable to read and write, might within a week after her arrival in this country be working in the shop of a garment contractor.

It is a commonplace of the labor movement that women are harder to organize than men. Many of them go to work while they are young and live at home; they accept seasonal employment easily, and they do not intend to stay permanently in the shop anyway. To them marriage is the real career, and wage-work is a mere temporary expedient, to be endured without much thought until the way of escape opens. Motives based on social status and on race or religion are likely to be stronger with women than with men. Many a young woman, forced into industry by the pressure of circumstances, hesitates to admit that she is a member of the working class, and believes that it would cast a stigma upon her to join a union. She prefers rather to maintain her associations with the women who do not have to work for wages, to read and sympathize with the newspapers which support the employers. If she is native-born, she dislikes to link herself with "foreigners," and if she is a Christian, she shares a popular prejudice against Jews. She thinks it unseemly to go to meetings where there are many men who will treat her as an equal, but whom she has not met in a social way, and whom she does not wish to entertain in her home. As a result of these preconceptions, she would rather allow the employer to exploit her than to do anything so unladylike as to affiliate with the labor movement and perhaps be called on strike. Fortunately these remnants of a passing social stratification are now weakening among working women. When organized, their spirit and endurance are often greater than that of men, but it is more difficult to enlist them in the labor army.

This has been an additional obstacle of the needle-trades unions. In 1914 there were more women than men in both the men's clothing and women's clothing establishments, the totals being 147,572 men wage-earners over 16 years of age, and 203,009 women over 16. A special study of representative establishments making men's garments showed only 19.3 per cent of the women workers married, and of these about one-third were in the shop temporarily. The percentage of permanent married workers in the women's industry would probably be even smaller, since it is chiefly the Italians who remain in the shop after marriage, and there are many more Italians in the men's clothing than in the women's clothing establishments.

Unions facing a few strongly entrenched employers such as the manufacturers of iron and steel have their own difficulties, but there at least the problem is clear. It is a test of strength; the workers know that they must organize, and then enforce the conditions they wish. But the character of the clothing industry presents the unions with a confusing entanglement of obstacles. The fluctuations of busy and slack seasons tend to destroy solidarity. For years strikes would occur at the beginning of the busy season, concessions would be won, and then as more and more workers were deprived of employment, competition among them would again arise, standards would be lowered and the concessions lost. The struggle would have to begin anew every year. The union itself would lose members who when out of work could not afford to pay their dues. The large number of small establishments made necessary, not a few great victories, but a thousand small ones. An argus-eyed vigilance was necessary to make sure that agreements were everywhere observed. The manufacturer who himself assented to the union terms might employ a new or irresponsible contractor who obscurely violated them. After associations of employers were formed, the divergence of the members in prosperity, attitude, and ability made negotiations difficult. It was impossible to raise the general level of wages to the point which the best employers would be able to maintain. And it was difficult for the unions themselves to reach and include a controlling majority of the available labor supply.

Here were evident all the worst evils of competition under private enterprise. Words like unemployment, sub-manufacturer, contractor, and sweatshop are symbols which carry to the reader little but a formalized intellectual concept of industrial problems. What they mean in the lives of hundreds of thousands of people, year after weary year, escapes. They really mean the tenements of New York at their squalid and ugly worst, they mean tuberculosis, curved spines, hollow eyes, premature death after an unfulfilled life, sickly children and a stunted race.[11] The important thing to remember is that the problems of the clothing industry have not been simply industrial problems or abstract problems of labor organization, but problems of human life, involving the entire existence of enough people to inhabit a small nation.

[11] See Chapter VI, under Joint Board of Sanitary Control.

The evolution of industry predicted by early socialists took place here only in part. It was believed that industrial establishments would grow larger and larger, that the concentration of capital would become more and more intense, and that eventually the workers, forming the democratic state, could take over industries which were, so to speak, completed products. In the clothing business, capital has been able to approach consolidation of merchandizing, and the bankers control credit, but, in the process of production, competition has persisted as strongly as ever. It has remained for the workers to assume the constructive rôle, and to perform in another way the task which Marx assigned to capital. In order that their lives might be tolerable, some kind of control had to be established. Capital was unable to furnish anything like a monopoly; enterprise and management could not furnish it. There was no single point at which effectual pressure could be applied. The only possibility left was for labor to organize so thoroughly as to provide the necessary cohesive force. Once organized, the workers could not rest on past victories. Since they were the only element of cohesion, the slightest relaxation on their part would allow the industry to relapse into its old anarchic chaos. Furthermore, their task was not only to extract certain concessions from the managements, but in many respects to reshape the entire structure of the industry. No perfunctory type of unionism could help them. The sort of union membership which carries cards and pays dues, but leaves the rest to the devices of business agents and officials, would not have survived—did not survive—their struggle. The union had to go into the daily lives, into the dreams and wills of its members. Its fights had to be fought in thousands of shops, and fought over again in thousands of new shops. Every member had to proselyte without ceasing. And the unions themselves had to be democratically successful, they had to retain the interest and enlist the cooperation of all their members. At the top there had to be vision and leadership, coupled with ability of the most practical sort. It is for these reasons that a particularly strong and self-reliant type of unionism has been developed in the clothing industry. But before relating the history of the unions, it is necessary to say something about the origin and culture of the workers.

CHAPTER III

THE HUMAN ELEMENT

It is a common practice, because it is an easy one, to attribute social phenomena to racial or national causes. Loose generalities of this sort were never more prevalent than now. Observers, seeking to account for the radicalism of the immigrant workers, and particularly of the unions in the clothing industry, point out that the largest single element of these workers is composed of Russian or other eastern Jews and that the next largest racial element has come from Italy.[1] In consequence it is assumed that these people have transplanted to this country a revolutionary socialism which may have been the natural result of the oppression to which they were subjected in Europe, but is out of place in the democratic culture of America. Other observers used to rely on similar generalities to account for other social conditions in this country. Were the slums overcrowded and dirty, and did the workers suffer

[1] No complete figures have ever been compiled. In 1910 the United States Immigration Commission investigated 19,502 wage-earners employed in typical shops in both the men's and women's clothing industry, throughout the country, and discovered the following proportions: Russian Jews, 18 6%, Jews other than Russian, 7 1%, South Italians, 14.4%, Germans, 3 4%, Irish, 0 4%, Swedes, 0.3%. In 1913 the Joint Board of Sanitary Control found that of the 28,484 women in the New York City dress and waist industry, 56% were Jewish, 34% were Italian, and less than 7% were native.

THE HUMAN ELEMENT

from long hours, poor pay, and insanitary conditions in the sweatshops? That was because they were ignorant foreigners, unaccustomed to the American standard of living. Leaders of the American labor movement not so long ago used to accuse the Jewish immigrants of being incapable of organization, and of undermining the standard of living because their over-eagerness for money led them to work for unlimited hours. And in the middle and latter part of the last century, the squalor of the slums used to be explained by accusing the Irish or the German immigrants of uncleanly or improvident habits. The mutual inconsistency of these arguments is enough to show the need for a closer examination of the matter.

When the ready-made clothing industry first grew up, it came naturally into the hands of the custom tailors of the period, who were for the most part native American, English, or Irish. The American, English, and Irish tailors were the owners and managers of the establishments, the manufacturers, cutters, and foremen. From the German immigrants who arrived in numbers during the middle years of the century were recruited the most of the workers. The Jews who were here at that time, most of them of Spanish or German origin, were dominant in the second-hand clothing trade, for which the first ready-made clothing was manufactured. On account of their knowledge of the market, they also took part in the management and ownership of the industry. The period of its first rapid growth was the period of large immigration of Germans and German Jews, many of them tailors in the land of their origin. A few Russian Jews arrived after the Civil War, but they were not numerous until after 1880. Since the bulk of the immigrant tailors between 1860 and 1880 were German Jews, most of the employers were by 1880 of German origin. They did not displace the English and Irish, but filled the gaps caused by the growth of the business.

From 1880 on, a rapidly increasing number of Jews came from a region in eastern Europe having its center of Jewish population in the old Kingdom of Poland. Most of them were from west Russia, but others were from Rumania and Austria-Hungary, originating mainly in the provinces of Galicia and Moldavia.[2] Between 1881 and 1910, there were 1,562,800 Jewish immigrants; of these, 1,119,059 or 71.6 per cent came from Russia, 281,150 or 17.9 per cent came from Austria-Hungary, and 67,057, or 4.3 per cent came from Rumania. During these same years but 20,454 Jews came from Germany. About the same proportions continued until 1914, when the war interrupted mass immigration. In the decade from 1881 to 1890, the Jews formed 3.7 per cent of the total number of immigrants, from 1891 to 1900 they formed 10.7 per cent, and from 1901 to 1910, 11.1 per cent.

Of these Jews a large number were tailors. No figures are available before 1899, but between that

[2] Statistics about Jewish immigration in this chapter, except as otherwise stated, are from Jewish Immigration to the United States, by Samuel Joseph, N. Y. Columbia University.

year and 1910, of the 394,000 Jewish immigrants who had learned trades before arriving, 145,272 or 36.6 per cent were tailors, 39,482 or 10.0 per cent were dressmakers and seamstresses, 4,070 were hat and cap makers, 3,144 were furriers and fur workers, and 2,291 were milliners. Thus nearly 50 per cent were ready to step into the needle trades, and most of them did so. Aside from these artisans, the clothing industry recruited from the large proportion of women who had not been gainfully employed before arriving (those without occupation, including women and children, numbered in these years 484,175, or 45.1 per cent of all the Jewish immigrants) and from the professional men and traders who on account of their ignorance of the English language could not pursue their chosen callings.

The period of great expansion of the ready-made clothing business therefore coincided with the period of mass immigration of Jews from eastern Europe. It was not long before the majority of the wage-earners were Russian Jews, although the Irish, the native-born, and the German Jews for some years provided most of the employers. It is probable that the proportions between the two main groups of Jews are now about the same among employers as among employees.

The region from which this great migration poured is in a primitive state of industrial development. In Russia, before the war, over three-quarters of the population were engaged in agricultural labor, and 85 per cent of the exports were agricultural products.

In such factories as existed, much of the labor was drawn from surrounding peasant communities. Similar conditions persisted in Rumania. Industrial establishments as we know them did not begin to arise until 1887, when the government adopted a policy of fostering them with subsidies. In parts of Austria-Hungary industry was further developed, but not in Galicia, from which most of the Austrian Jews came.

Throughout this great territory the bulk of the non-Jewish population consisted either of peasants cultivating the land, or of the nobility, military, clergy, and bureaucracy—the ruling classes. The Jews, however, were excluded from both these levels. They had never been serfs, and they had been prohibited to acquire land. On the other hand, being regarded as aliens by the law, they could not rise to the higher positions in the state, and of course were unable to penetrate the aristocracy. The result was that they took the place of the middle class. They became money-lenders, traders, shop-keepers, artisans in the home industries, supplying local needs. They handled the sales of most of farm products, dealing in grain, cattle, timber, furs, and hides. Some few were professional men, rich bankers, or stewards of great estates for noblemen. They were in Russia the class which Americans are accustomed to think of as the foundation of a liberal and democratic, but not a revolutionary culture. In business they were independent, self-reliant, ambitious, and inured to competition.

THE HUMAN ELEMENT 51

A few figures will give a picture of their situation. Although they comprised but 4 per cent of the Russian population, they formed 16 per cent of those living in the towns.[3] Over half of them lived in incorporated cities, although three-quarters of the Russian people were rural. Of those Jews gainfully employed, 39 per cent were engaged in manufacturing—as artisans rather than as employees in factories—32 per cent in commerce, and only 3 per cent in agriculture. In Austria-Hungary, the figures were 44 per cent in commerce and trade, 29 per cent in industry, and 11 per cent in agriculture and allied occupations. In Rumania there was a larger proportion in industry than in the other countries, but it is worth noting that although a quarter of the master workmen and employers in Rumania were Jews, only one-sixth of the laborers were Jews. In many cases Jews were actually excluded from employment in factories.

The main industry of the Jews in all these countries was the manufacture of clothing; in Russia the production of wearing apparel supported one-seventh of the Jewish population, and in Rumania over one-third of the garment-makers were Jews. But in this industry the ready-made factory product was unknown. The tailors were independent artisans.

Of the Jews admitted to this country between 1899 and 1909, 29.1 per cent were artisans, 21 per cent were traders, merchants and of miscellaneous call-

[3] After 1887 Jews were not permitted to settle in rural districts.

ings, 20 per cent had no occupation, 8.5 per cent were engaged in the professions, 6.9 per cent were servants, and but 2.9 per cent were common laborers. Of the artisans, besides the 50 per cent in the needle trades, the only other considerable groups were 40,901 carpenters, joiners etc., or 10.0 per cent, and 23,519 shoemakers, or 5.9 per cent. Probably not one per cent of the immigrant Russian Jews were ever wage-earners in factories before coming to the United States.

Their literacy was far above the average. According to the Russian Census of 1897, there were one-and-one-half times as many literate Jews above ten years of age as there were literate persons in the general population. This is again the sign of an urban, middle-class, and ambitious population. With Jews it is a religious duty to educate the boys, and a large proportion of girls also learned to read. They maintained their own educational institutions, some of which were free to those who could not pay.

The culture of the eastern Jews was based on their religious and racial traditions, and was of a conservative nature. They lived apart, wore for the most part a distinctive dress, did not intermarry with the surrounding peoples, observed strictly their religious fast-days and rituals, and held tenaciously to the customs of life which had developed from the Mosaic laws and the Talmud. They spoke, besides the languages of the countries in which they lived, their own language—Yiddish. They believed it a sign of social inferiority to be engaged in common manual labor. They thought it a disgrace for their women folk to work outside the home. This culture was by far the strongest influence upon their mode of thought, and opposed a heavy barrier to the growth of socialism or other radical ideas.

The hostility which led to the persecution of the Jews in Russia was compounded of various motives. The tradition of the ruling classes rested upon the orthodox church and the absolutist state, and the nobility felt a strong affinity for the old feudal culture, which they hoped would resist the penetration of western industrialism and the democratic liberalism which went with it. On all these counts the Jews seemed an undesirable element. To the clericals they represented the lowest type of heretics. This religious prejudice was not under ordinary circumstances shared by the people, who were remarkably tolerant. To the nationalists they were an alien and unassimilable people. For years before active persecution began, the Jews had no more rights under the law than aliens, although the duties of citizens were exacted of them. By the autocracy they were hated as fertile soil for political liberalism. The ruling classes also found them convenient scapegoats on whom to place the responsibility for the troubles of the people.

As a result of this almost universal attitude on the part of the ruling classes, a conscious policy towards the Jews, first of restriction, and later of expulsion, was carried out. When the partitions of Poland took place, the Jews within the district later known as the

Pale, which contained the majority of them, were forbidden to move out of it. There were later expulsions from town to town within the Pale and from without the Pale to within it. There came to be over 1,000 special laws regulating their religious and communal life, their occupations, their military service. Special taxes were imposed upon them. Their education was restricted.

The change from restriction to suppression came with the "May Laws" of 1882. In spite of all the burdens placed upon them, the Jews had measurably prospered, as indeed any trading class would have done through the slow but inevitable spread of commerce and industry. Their competitors among Russian traders were jealous of their success. The whole middle-class was growing, and the occupations in which Jews held supremacy began to seem more desirable to the non-Jewish peoples. Since they were the principal traders in crops and the money-lenders, it was easy to arouse the peasants against them. The May Laws were chiefly economic in nature, and were designed to hinder the Jews in business enterprise. In order to justify this attack upon them, the cry was raised that they were extortionists and robbers of the poor. The religious prejudice and the aversion to western European culture were also played upon. The orthodox Russian then looked upon the constitutional democracies of America, England, and France, and their thriving industrial towns, with about as much horror as that with which the orthodox American, Englishman, or Frenchman recently looked upon Bolshevist Russia.—It was the laws of 1882 which began the mass movements of Russian Jews to the United States.

In Rumania, until the middle of the last century, the Jews suffered under the same disabilities as in Russia. Then, at the instance of the great Powers, liberal laws were passed; but they remained dead letters. In the 'eighties Rumania commenced a policy of discrimination against the Jews more complete even than that of Russia. They were debarred from the artisans' guilds, which exercised a strong control over industry. They were denied the rights of freedom of movement, freedom of work, education, participation in important business enterprises, and employment in the state services.

The anti-Jewish movement in Austria-Hungary is most significant for the present inquiry. There the industrial revolution was felt with greater force than in Russia or Rumania, and the Jews developed not only financial but political power, especially soon after the adoption of the liberal constitution in 1866. The Church, however, in alliance with the nobility, attempted to resist the intrusion of western business methods and culture, deliberately strengthening the survivals of mediaevalism in industry. The most striking of these was the guild, an association of artisans from master workmen down to apprentice, which made its own regulations for the government of industry. Upon the guild basis the Catholics built a party known as the Christian Socialist, which had an anti-Semitic tendency, and denounced the Jews as exponents of capitalism. An alliance between the Christian Socialists and the Catholic middle-class carried on a campaign against the Jews from 1873 on, which reached its height in the 'nineties. Boycotts were organized against the Jewish traders, money-lenders, and artisans, and restrictive laws were passed.

A month after the accession of Alexander III in Russia began the pogroms, which soon extended to 160 places in South Russia. These were semi-organized killing, looting, and burning expeditions against the Jewish quarters, and they did not spare women and children. Pogroms broke out at intervals thereafter, the ruling classes not scrupling to use the Jews as scapegoats for whatever ills the people might be suffering. The Kishineff massacre in 1903, closely followed by that at Gomel, caused thousands of Jews to emigrate through fear of their lives. The Russo-Japanese War, becoming unpopular, was attributed to the Jews' desire for profit. The government, struggling against revolutionary agitation, attempted to divert attention from its own misdeeds by fomenting anti-Jewish attacks. It was not, however, until after the revolution of 1905 that the cry was raised that the Jews were revolutionary socialists.

The oppression, therefore, from which the Jews fled was not the oppression of the capitalist system which forms such a fruitful theme for the Socialist agitator. What they lacked was just the sort of liberal régime out of which modern industrialism has grown. They wanted the freedom of movement essential to the trader and business man, they wanted political liberty, and an opportunity for the development of individual business enterprise. They wanted educational opportunities for their children, and an absence of governmental interference with their religious and social customs. They wanted personal safety. In short, they sought the very institutions for which the American anti-Socialist values the United States. They came to the United States because authentic report told them that here such blessings would be found. Some of them were indeed revolutionists again Tsarism, but their spirit was one ready to be transmuted into fervent allegiance to the government of their adopted country.

At no period of Jewish immigration was any large proportion of the newcomers socialist before arriving at our ports, except perhaps after the Russian revolution of 1905. From the beginning, of course, there were socialists among the intellectuals. There were also anarchists among them, and persons holding other forms of dissentient political faith. In the 'nineties a secret socialist organization known as the "Bund" had grown up in Russia, and it claimed the allegiance of some of the most brilliant Jews. These socialists were, most of them, enthusiastic and active propagandists. On the other hand, there were leaders of conservative thought; any innovation was distasteful to most of the religious dignitaries. The religious community of the Jews played a large part not only in their spiritual but in their practical affairs, isolated as they were from the rest of the population and discriminated against in the laws. Jews would rarely invoke the national law in disputes with each other, but would instead submit to the judgment of the leading member of the congregation. This man as a consequence had great influence, and since he was usually a man of property, his opposition to radical economic doctrine was, as a rule, pronounced. Imagine the difficulty which socialism would have in penetrating a community of devout churchgoers whose leading elder or deacon was not only president of the local bank but magistrate as well. There was little, therefore, in the culture which the Jews brought with them from Russia to indicate that any large proportion of them would embrace radical principles.

The first traces of class feeling in America on the part of the employees as against the employers were of social rather than of economic origin. At the time of the first mass immigration of Russian Jews, most of the clothing manufacturers were German Jews. They had risen appreciably in the social scale, and they had a pride of origin which made them feel that the new arrivals were outsiders. The German Jews in their turn had been a little despised on their arrival by the Sephardic Jews from Spain and Portugal who were the first immigrants of Semitic blood. Thus the Jews were no exception to the other seekers of opportunity in America. We are a nation of immigrants and the children of immigrants, and yet each migratory group, as soon as it becomes acclimatized, looks down upon the newcomers because they are "foreigners."

The Jewish charities, upon which fell the first responsibility of alleviating the misery of the slums, were in the hands of the Germans, and most of the relief was given to the eastern Jews. This fact again formed a barrier, for in spite of all the merit there may be in charitable institutions, they seldom increase goodwill between the givers and the beneficiaries. In this case the United Hebrew Charities seemed to emphasize the social and economic distinctions between the German and the Russian Jews. Now and again, when the workers were on strike in some shop, the employer would notify the charitable institutions that he was in a position to offer jobs to the needy, and newcomers would be sent him without any inquiry as to the purpose for which they were to be used. To the unions this practice, innocent as it was on the part of the charities, seemed like deliberate strikebreaking.

Later the Jewish workmen, following a rapidly growing practice in this country, attempted to eliminate the need for charity by forming mutual benefit associations. This was the origin of the "Workmen's Circle," which has had a large share in increasing the feeling of solidarity on the part of the workers, and has helped them out of many a difficulty.

Separated as they were from employers of their own race, the Russian Jews had no other point of contact with the community. Their ignorance of English kept them apart, while the fact that they had their own religious institutions prevented them from mixing much with the immigrants of other nationalities, such as the Irish, Italians, and Poles, who at least had the Catholic Church in common. Owing to their concentration in separate trades they did not come in close touch with the American workmen even in the workshop.

The socialist intellectuals had little opportunity to pursue their chosen professions in a strange country, and many of them consequently entered the clothing shops. They were the only thinkers whose philosophy led them to cultivate the workers as such; and the great majority of the immigrants were and remained employees. Socialist editors started newspapers in Yiddish, and they attained large circulations. Socialists organized trade unions; they brought the workers together, furnished halls for them, and introduced the only community spirit that seemed to fit the new environment. Yet it took years for the radical view of affairs to take hold and develop. The unions remained small and ineffectual. Some of the newspaper readers accepted socialism, but they accepted it only as an affair of ideas, because they still did not understand the modern industrial system and the concentration of capital. Many of them cherished the hope of starting independent businesses and laying up fortunes; some of them, in fact, did so. Others even expected to accumulate money and go back to the land of their origin when a more auspicious time should come.

How far the people were from unity in thought

may be inferred from an early article by Henrietta Izold on "Elements of the Jewish Population in the United States."[4] "At present," wrote this author, "by reason of their tendency to break up into groups, the Russian Jews are looked upon by their patrons and by their own leaders as the most unorganizable material among the Jews, who at best are not distinguished for the quality of being organizable." A person interested in organization is likely to think that any kind of human material is unorganizable, and yet such testimony is not without its significance. The Jewish immigrants did not for a long time cast off their tradition of competitive individualism. Industrial friction was prevalent, and strikes occurred; but the strikes were rather spontaneous rebellions against the awful conditions of life and work than planned battles of a class war. At one time, during the early 'nineties, the anarchists had a considerable influence among the workers, although they opposed trade unions, as palliatives and substitutes for spontaneous action.

Almost from the very beginning of the mass immigration, more Jews brought their wives and children than did immigrants of other races. The sense of permanent American residence grew appreciably among the Jewish settlers as the years went by. There has been much fluctuation in the comparative numbers of men and women immigrants, but the highest proportion of men among the Jewish

[4] Included in "The Russian Jew in the United States," by Charles S. Bernheimer.

newcomers was reached in 1886, when male arrivals made up 67.5 per cent of the totals, and the highest proportion of women came in 1909, when the percentage of females rose to 46. Among immigrants of all nationalities from 1899 to 1910, the percentage of females was but 30.5. From 1908 to 1912 only 8 Jews departed for every 100 admitted, while of all immigrants 32 departed for every 100 admitted. The only immigrants during these years who showed a greater permanency of residence were the Irish.

It was only after a sense of permanency as employees became general among the clothing workers that unionism received their consistent support. They had become, as it were, acclimatized, they understood better the peculiar difficulties with which they had to contend, and the futility of attempting to avoid them or to contend with them as individuals. At first, for one reason or another, they had accepted the hardship of the slum and the sweatshop as temporary evils, from which an escape might shortly be found. For some the hope of escape took the form of the ambition to become employers, independent store-keepers, or agents, for others it was a vague intention to return to Russia, for still others it was merely a pious faith that some day a beneficent power outside themselves would provide the remedy. But most of the workers never saw any of these doors open, and the promise of the Socialist trade-unionist was the only one which retained any measure of reality. They gave up hope of leaving the country, and they gave up hope of being anything but wage

THE HUMAN ELEMENT

earners. As soon as the Jewish workers accepted the facts and conditions of America as they were, they became unionists. For them, the process of Americanization was itself the process of accepting the Socialist union.

The wave of Italian immigration began somewhat later than that of the eastern Jews. According to the census of 1890, there were not then 200,000 residents in the United States of Italian birth, and many of these were transients. Between 1890 and 1900, 655,888 Italians arrived, and in 1900 the resident Italian population had increased to 484,703. After 1900 the numbers of Italian immigrants rose rapidly. During the years immediately preceding the Great War, a little over one-sixth as many Italian tailors and dressmakers arrived as Jewish, the former averaging about 2,500 a year, and the latter 12,500.[5] Besides these artisans, however, many unskilled Italians, particularly women, have entered the clothing shops.

Most of the immigrants from Italy, like those from eastern Europe, knew nothing of factory labor before arriving in this country. The modern industries have developed in the northern part of the nation, whereas by far the greater part of the immigrants have come from the South. Most of them are classified as common laborers, farm laborers, or servants. Of the skilled artisans, the largest group were, for instance during the fiscal year of 1903, tailors, seamstresses, and dressmakers, and over nine-tenths of

[5] Annual Reports, U. S. Commissioner of Immigration.

these came from the South of Italy. A recent investigation of Italian women workers in New York[6] showed that of the cases examined, most had never done factory work in their home country, although 93.9 per cent were working in factories here. Of these over half were engaged in making men's and women's clothing.

The motive behind this immigration was in almost every case the desire to make money. Inequitable and annoying taxes, combined with oppressive landlordism and the lack of prosperity at home, have caused the great Italian migration. It was far less stable than the Jewish, even during the last decade. In 1912, for instance, 26,443 persons arrived from the North of Italy and 13,000 returned to it, while 135,830 came from the South, and 96,881 returned.[7] At the beginning of the period there were at least four times as many male immigrants from Italy as female. Many of the immigrants from the South of Italy were illiterate—in 1913-14 the proportion was, of those 14 years of age and over, 47.4 per cent.

All these facts go to show that not many of the Italian immigrants were Socialists before their arrival in this country. The stronghold of Italian Socialism is in the northern industrial regions, where there is a large population of literate factory and mine workers. But the artisan or home-worker who comes from the South with the intention of laying up out of American wages a competency with which he

[6] Italian Women in Industry. By Louise C. Odencrantz. N. Y. Russell Sage Foundation.
[7] Annual Reports, U. S. Commissioner of Immigration.

can later set up his little shop at home, is not likely to take seriously the prospect of a social revolution in the United States. Because of their greater impermanency and lower literacy, the Italians have not been quite as strong a factor as the Jews in the needle-trade unions, proportionately to their numbers in the industry. The radicalism of the unions certainly cannot be traced to the land of their origin. Yet the increasing numbers who have come to regard themselves as permanent residents of America and workers in the clothing trades are as ardent and faithful unionists as any.

So it is with the smaller groups—the Bohemians, who concentrated mostly about Chicago, and the Poles, Slovenians, Russians, Finns, Lithuanians, and others who have found work in the garment shops. No matter what the culture and the traditions various groups of immigrants brought with them, all nationalities and races who have been subjected to the same industrial and social conditions here have embraced the same hope and method of altering those conditions.

Once the trend of their development in America was established, the national characteristics of the Jews had something to do with the strength and effectiveness of their organizations. Whatever lack of unity they have at times exhibited, the tradition of unity is deep within them. After the unions became powerful, they were recognized as among the accepted institutions of the people. A scab became, not only an unfair competitor, but a social outcast.

The alliance of unions known as the United Hebrew Trades has provided not only much practical help, but a strong morale to the workers' organizations at many a critical time. And the establishment of collective agreements with the employers was certainly furthered by the fact that the Jewish community is educated to arbitrate its own disputes rather than to seek outside intervention, and to accept the impartial arbitrament of its prominent men. But these influences merely cluster about the central fact that the industrial and social experience of the Jews in the United States have led them to accept a radical economic philosophy. The same racial traits would have been no less active in promoting social cohesion if the energies of the workers had turned toward any other form of organization.

It would be unfair to underestimate the influence of personal leadership such as that of Morris Hillquit, who himself began as a worker in a shirt factory, or Abraham Cahan, the editor of the Jewish *Forward,* or of other politicians, journalists, and the numerous outstanding figures among the union officials. Without the brilliance and devotion of such leaders, the radical unions would not be what they are. Yet these men would be the first to point out that to separate a leader from the mass tendency of his time is to create an artificial distinction. They were leaders on account of the very fact that they were able to perceive which way the current was flowing, and because they were able consistently to express that which the masses recognized as truth.

In the radical unions, furthermore, leadership plays a less important rôle than in the conservative ones.

The economic attitude of the workers in the clothing industry, in short, cannot be accounted for by any accident unrelated with their social and economic experience. The oppression which they endured in the countries of their birth made them not less, but more ready to accept the prevalent régime in the United States. Their racial heritage was as conservative in its influence as it was helpful to radical institutions after such institutions had become the objects of conservation. Their isolation in this country gave an opportunity to the Socialist "agitators," but what could be made of that opportunity depended not so much on the agitators as upon the pragmatic truth of what they had to say. The former social and national separation between employer and employee gave at least as much promise of blind group hostility as it gave of economic analysis. It is necessary to examine the labor movement itself in order to discover why the socialist theory assumed reality in the mind of the clothing workers; suffice it here to say that without successful unions the worker had no hope, and that only unions built upon and adhering to the principles of the new unionism—the socialist unionism—could overcome the extraordinary difficulties to organization inherent to the needle trades.

CHAPTER IV

THE UNIONS—THEIR BEGINNINGS AND GROWTH

The history of a labor union, if fully told, would be as complex as the history of a nation. There is, in the first place, the outward formal history of dates, names, numbers, and crises. There is also the history of political philosophy, structure, and laws. There is the cultural history, and the economic and social one. The present chapter, in order to make comprehensible any further discussion, must confine itself chiefly to the formal history of the clothing trades unions.

The unions now existing are the International Ladies' Garment Workers Union, having jurisdiction over all branches of ready-made women's and children's garments, the Amalgamated Clothing Workers of America, which embraces the majority of workers in the manufacture of men's and boys' clothing, the United Garment Workers of America, which officially has the same jurisdiction as the Amalgamated, but exercises actual control only in the overall industry, the United Cloth Hat and Cap Makers of North America, which in addition to those specified in its title includes a large number of millinery workers, the International Fur Workers' Union of the United States and Canada, whose title is self-explanatory, and a number of locals of men's neckwear makers. All these unions are affiliated with the American Federation of Labor, with the exception of the Amalgamated Clothing Workers, which was organized after a conflict within the United Garment Workers, and is regarded as an outlaw body by the officials of the federation. To these might be added the Journeymen Tailors Union of America, because, although it consists mainly of employees of custom tailors, the line between the custom tailoring house and the clothing manufacturer is often dim. The Fancy Leather Goods Workers Union should perhaps also be included, since they are mainly needle workers in a trade similar in structure to the others, and they are racially and psychologically similar to the rest of the group. A few minor trades, such as suspender makers and garter makers, will complete the list of the unions.

These unions grew up and are strongest in the branches of the clothing industry where immigrant labor was chiefly employed, and large-scale production has shown the least development. They have thoroughly organized the makers of cloaks, suits, skirts, dresses of all kinds, waists, overcoats and the like. They are waging a heroic battle for the makers of shirts and collars. They are just beginning to be successful with the corset-makers. There are practically no unorganized makers of cloth hats and caps, but still a good many non-union workers in the millinery trade.

Not one of these unions existed before 1890, and only one—the United Garment Workers—has been in continuous existence since before 1900. Strikes occurred long before the Civil War, and after 1880 small unions were repeatedly organized and disappeared again. For a union to have a dues-paying membership above a thousand or so was unknown. The leaders and the intellectuals never gave up the attempt, and perennial conditions offered them frequent opportunities to renew the agitation. But to make permanent gains for the workers seemed like trying to fill a bottomless pit. A strike at the beginning of a busy season would win concessions, for then every worker was needed. Gradually as the work decreased, the concessions would be withdrawn, and any toiler foolhardy enough to protest would be replaced by another, already out of a job and fearful of starvation. There was no machinery to apply the concessions universally, and the highly fluid competition acted to break down standards. Union members would drop off during the slack months, because they could not afford to pay their dues. And eventually the union itself would vanish, only to be replaced by another when a new rebellion against the employers broke out.

As Abraham Cahan, editor of the Jewish Daily *Forward,* put it in an address to a recent convention, "In those days when our movement gave birth to a child, somehow or other the child did not live. No

UNIONS—BEGINNINGS AND GROWTH

sooner was it born than it died and then a new child would have to be born and the same thing would occur. But now the situation has entirely changed. The children are beginning to thrive."

The history of the individual unions before 1900 is therefore the history of scattered and mostly unsuccessful, though persistent efforts at organization. Like all small and ephemeral bodies, they never developed a consistent policy and were often at odds with each other. First one faction would obtain control, then another. But no faction exerted a considerable influence on the main body of workers. During the 'eighties the Socialists and the Anarchists waged a petty warfare over them. Then the American Federation of Labor, with its conservative influence, began to grow stronger, and the radicals fought to keep the unions out of its hands. The anarchists soon disappeared in the unions, but the Socialists carried on a campaign to affiliate the workers with the old Knights of Labor. This was not so much through a love for the Knights of Labor as through a desire for some unifying influence. After that organization became plainly obsolescent, a separate central body was formed, known as the Socialist Trade and Labor Alliance. During the second half of the 'nineties, after the split in the Socialist Labor Party, that parent body would not recognize unions affiliated with the American Federation of Labor, while the seceding Social Democrats made no distinctions. All this time the United Hebrew Trades was striving for unity of the

Jewish unions on a consciously socialist philosophy, and was fighting corruption wherever it appeared.

For corruption did appear. The great mass of the workers, never having been educated to union discipline or to consciousness of their democratic property in the union, did not feel that it was theirs, that they could make what they liked out of it. They regarded unions rather as outside agencies which could be paid to conduct strikes and negotiate settlements. Trading on this feeling, and on the recurring unrest, strike promoters arose, irresponsible persons whose names and achievements were obscure. Calling themselves union officials, they would circulate notices in the shops that a strike was on. Dues would be collected, the workers would walk out, and then a settlement would be announced. During the rest of the year the promoter would live on the proceeds. As a result of the unions' lack of victorious prestige, of their transient character and quarrels with each other, and finally because of the prevalent corruption, there came a time in the 'nineties when many self-respecting socialist workers, fully in sympathy with the labor movement, would not belong to a union. And yet all this time spontaneous strikes periodically arose in a futile attempt to better conditions.

In 1890 the cloakmakers won a lockout-strike for higher wages and the right to belong to a union, but by 1893 the union had only a formal existence. In 1894 another successful strike was followed by the disappearance of the union. In 1896 a victorious

UNIONS—BEGINNINGS AND GROWTH

strike so exhausted the union that it perished. In 1898 the Brotherhood of Tailors, which was affiliated with the United Garment Workers, suffered the same fate. Thus the conservative unions as well as the radical were ineffectual. Although at the beginning of the decade thirty-three organizations were affiliated with the Jewish labor movement, the number later dropped much lower. Extravagant hopes alternated with despair. The spirit of organized effort would lift its head for a moment out of the confusion in which the industry existed, only to sink back again into the morass. Life was battling for its birth in chaos. Little experiments, tiny nuclei, formed themselves out of the constantly renewed instinct for order, and were swept away again in the whirl of nebulous forces. Many of the very leaders who today are at the head of the strong and successful unions were then attempting the seemingly impossible, and they never gave up hope. Patiently the Yiddish press and the socialist intellectuals strove to educate the masses to their true interest, and built little by little the basis for the only kind of morale which could endure such disruptive forces.

Many of the early locals were composed of cutters, they being at the time the more highly skilled craft. At the beginning of the 'nineties, however, organization spread among operators, basters, and pressers. The decreasing differences in the amount of skill required in the various operations made the industrial form of organization, favored by the radicals, the natural one. This led in 1891 to the formation of the first national union—The United Garment Workers—which held its initial convention on April 18th in New York. Thirty-six tailor delegates were present from New York, Boston, Chicago, and Philadelphia. These delegates elected a group of American-born non-socialist officers, since it was thought on account of their superior knowledge of the language and customs they could better handle the affairs of the union. At the same time socialist resolutions were passed, the new officers acquiescing in them to gain the support of the radical tailor delegates. The union immediately affiliated with the American Federation of Labor. It was not long before the officers, relying on the support of the conservative element in the union—for the most part native skilled craftsmen—began a warfare on all socialist activities, and ever since then the United Garment Workers has been anti-socialist.

In the big clothing markets this union was no more successful during the 'nineties than any of the others. Its membership never grew large, and it remained in existence simply because there was always a group which clung to the A. F. of L. charter. Its policy was and has remained that of the old unionism. Basing its strength on the craft spirit of the skilled, it has striven to improve the condition of its members by limiting the supply of labor and by cultivating cooperation, wherever possible, with the employers. Peculiar conditions made this policy effective in one respect. Some of the cheaper ready-made suits, and a large proportion of the overalls, are bought by union labor. By developing among these union men a demand for the union label, the United Garment Workers were enabled to bargain successfully with certain manufacturers. The union label gradually became not only an inducement for recognition by manufacturers, but a means of discipline within the union. No label is authentic except that endorsed by the American Federation of Labor, the label is protected by United States registry, and as long as the Federation supports the officials of the garment workers' union, these officials can, by granting or withholding the label to manufacturers as they please, maintain almost a personal monopoly of the labor supply. Wherever, as in the case of overalls, such a monopoly is effective, it may be used either to benefit or to restrict the workers, but in any case it obviates the necessity for more democratic methods of building up union strength, and tends to minimize the need for conscious solidarity on the part of the workers. So complete has become the reliance of the United Garment Workers upon the union label that the principal association of employers with which it now negotiates collective agreements is entitled the Union Made Garment Manufacturers' Association. This association consists chiefly of overall manufacturers employing largely native-born operatives in the smaller cities throughout the country, and includes almost none of the manufacturers of regular ready-made clothing in the great clothing markets.

The membership of the United Garment Workers

remained small in the large centers until the New York strike of 1913. Up to this time the union had not retained a membership of over 4,000 in New York, although the International Ladies' Garment Workers had become powerful and negotiated the famous "Protocol" as early as 1910. It was soon after the strike of 1913 that the split in the men's tailoring union gave birth to the independent Amalgamated Clothing Workers.

Next to the United Garment Workers, the oldest international union in the needle trades is the United Cloth Hat and Cap Makers. One of its locals, Cap Cutters, Local 2, has been in continuous existence since 1880. An attempt to form an international was made in 1886 by representatives of New York and Boston unions, and at that time the name was adopted. The present organization, however, was not effected until 1901, when delegates from nine locals, three in New York and one each in Chicago, Philadelphia, Boston, Detroit, Baltimore, and San Francisco, met and established it. The first convention enunciated a radical policy, and voted to remain independent, taking no part in the conflict which was still being waged between the Socialist Trade and Labor Alliance and the American Federation of Labor. Yet the young international soon was forced into a controversy with the American Federation of Labor, which had taken under its protection a few outside locals of cap makers. As a result the General Executive Board, in conjunction with delegates from some of these outside locals, decided in 1902 to amalgamate and affiliate with the American Federation of Labor. The charter was granted on June 17th, and for a long time the Cap Makers held it without difficulty, although they have always remained faithful to the socialist movement. They have consistently represented the radical attitude within the Federation, and have frequently been in opposition to its larger policies.

The international immediately opened a fight against long hours, home work, and sweatshop conditions. In 1902 and 1903 general lockouts took place in New York and Philadelphia. In December, 1903, the largest manufacturer in New York attempted to safeguard the open shop by a lockout which precipitated a ten-weeks' struggle, ending in victory for the union. This was the signal for general organization on the part of the manufacturers, which led to a national onslaught on the union during the winter of 1904-5. The New York strike lasted thirteen weeks, and there were general strikes or lockouts in Chicago, San Francisco, New Haven, Cleveland, Detroit, Cincinnati, and almost every other town which the union had penetrated. The battle was decisive, resulting in the establishment of the union shop and a greatly enlarged membership. This was the first lasting success won in the needle trades.

In the meantime the union had begun to turn its attention to the millinery trade, which employed many young women and was so closely associated with the manufacture of caps that it was impossible fully to control the one without organizing the other.

Application was made for jurisdiction over the millinery workers, and in 1903 this was granted, first by a unanimous vote of the Executive Council of the American Federation of Labor, and later by the Boston Convention. The victory of 1905 cleared the way for aggressive organization of the millinery workers as well as for constructive improvements in the condition of the cap makers.

Just at this time, however, the Industrial Workers of the World came into active being and began a campaign for the allegiance of A. F. of L. unions. The Cap Makers, because of their radicalism, were naturally one of the first points of attack. The I. W. W. had not at that time adopted the weapon of sabotage, and stood for constructive revolutionary industrial unionism, therefore it enlisted some support among the membership. The union, however, decided not to abandon their regular affiliation, and an ugly quarrel resulted, which was not terminated until 1907. The dual unions which arose during this internal struggle naturally made the conflict with the manufacturers more difficult, but in the end the Cap Makers reestablished their complete jurisdiction. With this difficulty out of the way, the union began its progressive effort for the betterment of conditions.

Near the end of 1909 separate locals were established for millinery workers and in 1910 an intensive organization campaign was begun among them. In 1915 this campaign had become so strong that the manufacturers did not force the issue, and after one-tenth of the millinery employees had been out a short time a collective agreement was negotiated with the Ladies' Hat Manufacturers' Protective Association.

Up to this time the United Hatters, having jurisdiction over makers of felt hats, derbys, etc. had maintained friendly relation with the Cap Makers, and had never made any attempt to organize the girl millinery workers, who were excluded by their constitution. In 1915, however, after the successful milliners' strike, the United Hatters altered their constitution to admit the women's straw hat makers and applied to the American Federation of Labor for jurisdiction over them. The Executive Council of the Federation, reversing their decision of 1903, granted the application. The 1917 and 1918 conventions of the Cap Makers both decided that it would be against the best interests of their members to comply with this decision, and the conventions were supported by a referendum vote of the membership, 7011 against 19. As a result the union remained for a number of years suspended by the Federation. Nevertheless, wishing to avoid another division in the labor movement, the Cap Makers proposed a compromise in the form of an industrial amalgamation between themselves and the Hatters. This suggestion was rejected by the Hatters, and not considered by the A. F. of L. officials or convention in 1918. In 1919, however, the Executive Council of the Federation took it under advisement.

The United Cloth Hat and Cap Makers now consists of 46 locals in 25 towns, with a membership of about 15,000. They have attained a 100 per cent organization in the cloth hat and cap trade, being the only union in the clothing industry which has succeeded in establishing a universal closed union shop. In the millinery trade their organization is strong except in the custom retail shops. The strike of the Cap Makers in 1919 won every demand made upon the employers, including the forty-four hour week, and the substitution of week work for piece work. A millinery strike, however, was not so successful, in part on account of the jurisdictional dispute with the Hatters.

Local unions of women's cloakmakers were among the transitory organizations which were born and died so frequently in the early years of the labor movement in the needle trades. A lockout-strike for recognition in 1890 is on record. In 1894 some of the cloakmakers joined the United Garment Workers, but withdrew in 1895 and continued an agitation which they had been conducting for a national union of workers on women's garments. The other unions concerned did not respond enthusiastically, however, until the end of the 'nineties, when the cloak manufacturers began to use the injunction to prevent strikes.

On June 3rd, 1900, the International Ladies' Garment Workers Union was organized at a convention at which there were present delegates from New York, Philadelphia, Baltimore, Newark, and Brownsville. Soon afterwards the Chicago and San Francisco workers joined. The International, adopting a socialist constitution, immediately affiliated with the American Federation of Labor and has retained this affiliation ever since, although, like the Cap Makers, it has often disapproved of the policies of the Federation officials.

The original plan of the union was to duplicate the success of the United Garment Workers with the union label—this, if nothing else, made affiliation with the A. F. of L. necessary. Between 1900 and 1907 it struggled along in a vain attempt to establish its label, relying for direct gains only on the old method of sporadic strikes against individual manufacturers at the beginning of the busy season. No organizers besides regular officials were kept in the field and financially the union lived from hand to mouth.

In 1907 an event occurred which changed the whole outlook of the membership. The reefermakers, led by refugees from the Russian Revolution of 1905, went out in mass and stayed on strike for nine weeks, showing such common determination and spirit that they won most of their demands and put courage into the rest of the workers in the needle trades. For the first time in years it seemed possible to win direct results through strong organization and fighting tactics. Although the financial panic of 1907 severely affected industry and threatened the union with extinction, the stimulation of this success endowed it with new resolution; the members held together and soon undertook a great organizing campaign. With the recovery of business in 1908 and the rapid expansion of the women's ready-made clothing industry, the union grew quickly. It was also during this period that a definite negative decision was reached regarding a proposal to amalgamate with the United Garment Workers. The latter organization not only rejected the proposal, but advised the International to surrender its charter. The current of events was bearing the two organizations farther apart rather than closer together.

In 1909 another surprising mass movement gave proof of the workers' heightened morale. The small local of waist and dressmakers in New York called a strike, expecting about 3,000 to respond. Instead 30,000 went out, including workers of all races, except a few native-born women. No such strike of women had before been known or thought possible. It aroused the public as never before to the sufferings of the needle workers. The more liberal churches and newspapers gave it much attention, and many of the purchasers of fine garments that were made under such frightful conditions felt a twinge of conscience. Substantial gains were made, and the local succeeded in retaining for some time afterwards a membership of 12,000.

This strike stimulated the cloakmakers to renewed activity; they rushed to join the union and repeat the success of the waistmakers. Enthusiasm ran high, and on July 8th, 1910, the great strike [1] was called

[1] For a description of this strike, see Chapter V.

UNIONS—BEGINNINGS AND GROWTH

which aroused the whole city, lasted for ten weeks, and resulted in the establishment of the first collective agreement in the ready-made clothing industry —the so-called "Protocol" which is discussed in detail in Chapter VI. After this the union maintained nearly a one-hundred per cent organization of the cloakmakers. In 1913 another general strike of the waistmakers brought about a collective agreement in that trade as well, and the permanent membership grew correspondingly.

The Protocol remained in force for five years, the workers achieving under it progressive concession in material conditions. Nevertheless friction was constant and increasing, there being an element among the manufacturers who desired complete independence and hoped to destroy the union, and an element in the union which was too radical to be anything but restive under a compromise with the employers. There were many points of conflict also which the divergent interests of both parties made inevitable. On May 20, 1915, the manufacturers abrogated the Protocol, charging that the union had not lived up to its provisions. Soon thereafter eight leaders of the cloakmakers were indicted on various charges including murder, all these charges dating back to the strike of 1910. The accusers were, for the most part, characters of the underworld. The eight men were brilliantly defended by Morris Hillquit; the charges against some of them were dismissed by the court, and the rest were acquitted. These events aroused intense feeling among the workers, and convinced them that the manufacturers had embarked upon an attempt to destroy the union by fair means or foul. A strike was temporarily averted by a Council of Conciliation appointed by Mayor Mitchel under the stress of public opinion, but the award was abrogated by the manufacturers in the spring of 1916. On April 30th the 400 members of the employers' association ordered a lockout. The result was a bitter general strike lasting fifteen weeks, during the entire slack season. It ended by a victory for the union, and the establishment of a new agreement modified in their favor. This agreement was for the period of three years, and its conclusion was marked by another successful strike.

These repeated victories stimulated the organization not only in New York but throughout the country, and resulted in the acquisition, since 1907, of more than 75,000 members outside the New York cloak trade. The union is one of the few in the country until very recently which has been able to organize women in large numbers. The Waist and Dressmakers Union of New York, Local 25, is the largest single local of women in the country, and is strong and progressive in every respect. Dozens of conflicts with the employers have added to the ranks of the International not only cloakmakers and waistmakers throughout the country, but workers on house dresses and kimonos, white goods, raincoats, embroidery, corsets, etc. In the spring of 1920 the International officially reported a paid-up

UNIONS—BEGINNINGS AND GROWTH

membership of 102,000. In 1919 it was the sixth largest union in the American Federation of Labor, being surpassed only by the United Mine Workers, the Carpenters and Joiners, the Machinists, the Electrical Workers and the Railway Carmen; all these organizations were greatly aided by the war, although the war created a depression in the women's garment industry. If the Ladies' Garment Workers had included those not in good standing because in arrears through unemployment at the time of computation, the total would probably have reached 150,000.

Seeing the success of the makers of women's garments, the workers in the men's clothing industry became more and more restless during the years between 1907 and 1913. They had not made parallel gains, and the United Garment Workers, which held official jurisdiction over them, seemed to them inactive and impervious to the spirit of the times. A general strike in Chicago in the fall of 1910 resulted in a satisfactory agreement with the large and progressive house of Hart, Schaffner, and Marx, which already had about 6,500 employees, but in New York no appreciable gains were made. Agitation was continuous, however, and in December, 1912, a strike referendum was finally submitted to the union members in New York and overwhelmingly carried. The referendum showed the membership to be not over 5,000. Yet about 50,000 walked out within a few days of the strike call. Repeated efforts at a settlement were rejected by votes of the determined strikers, who were resolved to achieve their full demands. A final proposal to submit the controversy to arbitration was accepted without a referendum, by the President of the United Garment Workers, who on his own responsibility declared the strike at an end. Some of the workers refused to go back to the shops until the decision of the arbitrators should be announced, but the action of the President effectually broke the strike. On this account ill feeling against his administration was intensified. The award, when finally published, contained substantial concessions, but made no provision for peaceable settlement of future difficulties.

Dissatisfaction with the existing régime in the union was prevalent also in the other great clothing markets, and a movement was launched in the Yiddish press and among the clothing workers in the large cities to capture the offices at the coming convention. In the ensuing controversy many heated charges were made on both sides which, if related at length, would demand far more space than a book like this could possibly devote to the matter. No full and impartial investigation of these charges has ever been made, but it is important to note that the specific charges were but the occasion of a split which was really the result of a fundamental difference of philosophy and spirit between the radical workers and the conservative officers.

The radicals charged that the officers misused the union label and employed their power to make money for themselves, that they had private understandings with the manufacturers and deceived the membership, that, in order to maintain themselves in power, they designated far-away Nashville as the convention city and fabricated unwarranted bills against the opposition locals in order to disfranchise them. The officers charged that the radical movement was promoted by outsiders and intellectuals for their own benefit, that it was founded merely on race prejudice and aimed to secure an exclusive control by the Jews, that it was from the beginning a conspiracy to found a competing union, and that with this end in view the opposition locals withheld percapita taxes which were rightfully due.

The ill-fated convention met on October 12th, 1914, at Nashville, Tennessee. As had been expected, most of the delegates from the large cities were not seated by the credentials committee. A hearing by that committee after the first day of the convention failed to smooth over the difficulty. On the second day the convention attempted to go ahead with business, but those few radicals who had been granted seats insisted that a complete report of the credentials committee was first on the order of business. When they were overruled, they left the hall amid a turmoil, and with the unseated delegates proceeded to hold a convention of their own in another hall, which they claimed was the only rightful convention of the union, and to which they invited all the delegates.

A comparison of the official reports of both conventions, and of the subsequent first convention of the Amalgamated Clothing Workers, reveals the following figures:

	Delegates	representing Locals
Seated by United Garment Workers....	184	147
Of these, left for insurgent convention..	19	11
Remaining with United Garment Workers	165	136
Present at insurgent convention.......	110	54
Absent from both conventions.........		91
Of these, represented at first convention of Amalgamated		16
Present at first convention of Amalgamated	130	68

It thus appears that the radical element did not have a majority of the delegates, even if all had been seated. There was a decided inequality, however, due to the fact that the larger locals in the big cities did not have anything like a proportional number of delegates. The claim of the insurgents to represent a majority of the membership was probably just, since they included almost all the delegates from these large locals in New York and Brooklyn, Chicago, Boston, Rochester, Baltimore, and Philadelphia, besides a few from Syracuse and Cincinnati, whereas the loyal delegates were from small locals in scattered towns, and in great part represented the workers in overall factories controlled by the union label.

The insurgent convention elected its own officers and adjourned after transacting whatever business it could. A series of legal skirmishes followed, which resulted in the establishment of the right on the part of the original organization to retention of its title and the union label, and the right on the part of the insurgent locals to retention of the funds in their treasuries. Toward the end of December, 1914, the insurgents held a second convention in New York, adopted a democratic constitution and the title of the Amalgamated Clothing Workers of America, and united with the Tailors' Industrial Union, formerly known as the Journeyman Tailors' Union. Later, however, this organization withdrew and renewed its original title and its affiliation with the American Federation of Labor.

The insurgent convention in Nashville had elected delegates to the coming convention of the American Federation of Labor. The Credentials Committee of the Federation, after hearing in private the claims of the rival groups, forthwith decided not to recognize the insurgents. Their decision was sustained by the convention. Repeated attempts to bring about a reconciliation have been rebuffed by Mr. Gompers and the other officials of the Federation, solely on the ground that secession cannot be tolerated in the labor movement. The attitude of Mr. Gompers in this matter, as fully expressed before the United Hebrew Trades, is an interesting one. There is no room in one country, he said, for competing labor movements; unity is the first requirement of strength. Yet the labor movement has no police power, no army and navy, to prevent the setting up of secessionist bodies. The only way it can do this is by using discipline. It must insist, first of all, that all differences of opinion and policy be settled within the existing organizations. The general administration cannot look back of the official and regularly registered decisions of these organizations. Therefore, no matter how many just grievances may underlie the disaffection of the Amalgamated Clothing Workers, these grievances can not be investigated or relieved unless the insurgents shall first submit themselves again to the jurisdiction of the parent organization.

It is easy to see the force of this principle of legitimacy, and yet it has not sufficed to make the men's tailors surrender or to prevent the growth and success of the Amalgamated. To Mr. Gompers they reply that they see perhaps even more strongly than he the need of unity, and that they will eagerly be accepted by the Federation as soon as their basic principle, the principle of democracy, is recognized and practiced. They inquire how a majority faction, wishing to change the policy of a union and the personnel of its officers, can do so if by the rules of that organization and the tactics of the officers the majority is not allowed to express its will. They assert that, if while frowning upon secession the Federation does not exert its disciplinary powers to make sure that honesty and democracy exist in its component unions, secession is made necessary rather than discouraged. They point to their own existence as the pragmatic proof of their position.

Mr. Gompers might reply that the insurgents who founded the Amalgamated Clothing Workers did not represent a majority of the United Garment Workers, and that their charges of dishonest administration are untrue. But to do so would be to raise at once a question of fact, and to admit that an impartial investigation of facts is necessary before a fair decision in the matter can be reached. That is just what he refuses to do.

In any case it is too late now to heal the breach by an appeal to ancient history. The officials of the Federation, in conjunction with those of the United Garment Workers, were evidently animated by the belief that if the new union were effectually outlawed and fought with every available weapon it would be weakened and discredited, and its members would individually return to the fold. Such a policy, at least, they have attempted to execute. In Baltimore, for instance, the local representative of the Federation, even made an alliance with the I.W.W. against the Amalgamated. He engineered a small strike of sub-contractors against a manufacturer who had just abolished sub-contracting in compliance with the demand of an overwhelming majority of the workers. During this conflict actual violence arose, a pitched battle occurring in the shop and in the street outside. Again and again, when members of the Amalgamated have been on strike, officers of the old union have negotiated an agreement with the employers, declared the strike at an end, called the workers back into the shop under their own jurisdiction, and if the strikers refused to return, attempted to fill their places with strikebreakers from the "official" union. The American Federation engaged in a long controversy with the United Hebrew Trades, endeavoring to force the Jewish central body to expel delegates from the Amalgamated, on pain of being itself outlawed by the general labor movement. For a time the United Hebrew Trades resisted this pressure, but eventually the Amalgamated withdrew of its own accord in order to save its fellow unions embarrassment. Still, however, the United Hebrew Trades refused to accept delegates from the United Garment Workers as long as the rival union was not represented. James P. Holland, President of the New York State Federation of Labor, attempted to direct again the Amalgamated the popular hostility to "Bolsheviki," and gave testimony before the State Legislative Committee investigating Bolshevism which might easily have caused trouble for the union. Apparently some officials of the Federation and their close followers, relying on the anti-secessionist principle, have believed that all means of battle were fair against the outlaw. At any rate they have fought it with a persistence and bitterness seldom shown against employers.

The other needle-trade unions, however, have taken no part in this campaign. The fact that in philosophy and method they are sympathetic with the Amalgamated, and that this union in a closely related industry, in spite of all persecution, has grown powerful, make it necessary for them not to oppose it, but to strive sincerely for an end to the quarrel. The fight in the United Hebrew Trades against exclusion of the Amalgamated was led by the delegate of the International Ladies' Garment

Workers. When, during the war, a depression in the women's clothing industry was accompanied by a great demand for military uniforms, the two unions negotiated an agreement to share equitably between their respective memberships the jobs available. The International introduced into the 1918 convention of the American Federation of Labor a resolution calling for the establishment of a clothing trades department, similar to the metal trades and mining departments, to coordinate the various unions concerned, with the idea that such a department might facilitate the return of the Amalgamated. This resolution was supported by all the needle-trades unions except the United Garment Workers, but was defeated on account of the hostile attitude of the Federation officials. The culmination of this movement towards unity, fostered as it was by the philosophy of the unions concerned, was the proposal in the spring of 1920 for a Needle Trades Federation, to be consummated if need be without regard to the American Federation of Labor. This proposal seems about to bring together all the radical clothing unions for joint action. The prevailing sentiment among the clothing unions seems to be that it is not worth while to persecute thousands of fellow-workers and widen a breach in the labor movement solely for the sake of the anti-secessionist principle. This feeling is strengthened by the consciousness that the historical basis of the division has never been candidly examined, and by a strong suspicion that the supporters of regularity are animated not so much by a desire to preserve labor discipline in general as by a desire not to weaken the prestige and power of the existing conservative administration of the American Federation of Labor.

The jurisdictional warfare with the United Garment Workers has, however, been little more than a distressing incident in the life of the Amalgamated. The large associations of manufacturers were forced to deal with it. A collective agreement in New York was signed in July, 1915, providing machinery for the adjustment of disputes. The formal agreement was later destroyed, but informal arrangements were substituted for it. A spirited general strike in December, 1916, gained the 48 hour week for all members of the union in New York; this struggle, involving nearly 60,000 workers, was the first in the history of the clothing trades to be financed entirely with funds raised from the locals concerned. Successful strikes in Baltimore, Toronto, Montreal, Chicago, Boston and other centers kept the morale high and increased the membership. The union took a prominent part in the agitation against sweatshop conditions which began to crop out in the manufacture of army clothing, and assisted the government to put an end to them. Without any missionary work on its part, shirtmakers' locals of New York and Boston came over to it from the United Garment Workers, the occasion being orders from the higher officials of the United Garment Workers to assist in breaking strikes called by the Amalgamated. Early in 1919 the Amalgamated established

UNIONS—BEGINNINGS AND GROWTH 95

a precedent in the American labor movement by gaining the 44 hour week, being one of the first unions in the country to win this concession.

The Amalgamated now has a membership in good standing of over 150,000, and if it should include those members who are in arrears through unemployment the total would probably be close to 200,000. The United Garment Workers pay to the American Federation of Labor a per-capita tax on 46,000 members. Their total membership can hardly be larger than this, since there are, on a generous estimate, not 46,000 overall workers in the country, and the remainder of their locals, scattered among shirt makers, raincoat manufacturers, and custom tailors, cannot include a numerous membership.

The International Fur Workers Union of the United States and Canada, though the youngest of the group, has been highly successful. A club of German fur workers, most of them cutters, existed in 1882 and continued until 1913, but it exhibited few of the qualities of a trade union, being chiefly a social organization with fraternal benefits. Attempts to form unions failed in 1882, 1893, and 1902. An international union was founded in Washington, D. C., and affiliated with the American Federation of Labor in 1904, but it did not grow large, and in 1911 the charter was surrendered. In 1907 a new organization was formed in New York, but a lockout destroyed it. The union was revived in 1910, and limited itself to propaganda for two years. By June, 1912, it had a membership of about 600, and on that date it called a general strike which lasted for nearly twelve weeks and ended in complete victory. An agreement was arrived at, although the manufacturers would not enter the same room as the union representatives, and carried on negotiations through a third party. The agreement was renewed, with progressive improvements in conditions, in some cases after strikes, in 1914, 1917, and 1919. The union is now recognized, has a 44 hour week, and a remarkably high scale of wages. It embraces about 80 per cent of the workers in both fur goods and dressed furs, having a paid-up membership of 10,800, and about 1,200 more in arrears. Of the members, 3,500 are women.

The Journeymen Tailors' Union as at present constituted was formed in 1883. Tailors' strikes had occurred spasmodically ever since the beginning of the century, and previous attempts had been made to found a national union. The organization had many ups and downs, but has never experienced any such dramatic leap to power as the unions in the ready-made clothing industry have known. Indeed, since it consists of custom tailors, and the ready-made industry has been steadily sapping the strength of the custom-tailoring houses, it has been forced to work against strong handicaps. It has been affiliated with the American Federation of Labor since 1887, and has, with a few interludes, adhered to conservative policies. One of the chief difficulties of the Journeymen Tailors' Union has been the constantly recurring jurisdictional disputes with the unions in the ready-made industry. This has led recently to an agitation to amalgamate once more with the Amalgamated Clothing Workers.

The men's neckwear industry has for a long time remained without a national organization. Although there are between eight and nine thousand workers in the trade throughout the country, the unions are still locals affiliated as federal locals directly with the American Federation of Labor. There is a local of cutters in New York, and another union for the rest of the workers in the city known as the United Neckwear Makers. About 70 per cent of its members are women. Other locals exist in Boston, Chicago, San Francisco, and St. Louis. Cleveland and Philadelphia are entirely unorganized. The total membership in these unions is about 3,200. They feel strongly the need of national unity, but an application for a national charter was refused by the Executive Council of the American Federation of Labor, at the 1917 convention. The locals have retained their membership in the Federation solely because they wanted the privilege of using a union label, but even in this respect the Federation has failed them, because the paper label supplied cannot be conveniently used on neckwear. As a result of these unfavorable conditions, the neckwear makers are not abreast of their fellows in the needle trades. If they do not soon achieve a national union within the Federation, they will undoubtedly do so outside it.

The first attempt to organize the suspender

makers was made in March, 1890. After a four weeks' strike, the union was destroyed. Repeated attempts to reorganize were made in 1892, 1894, 1896, and 1897. During these years many long strikes were conducted, of which the last continued for 16 weeks. Eventually the union won recognition and several closed shops. It also introduced a label. In 1901 the Suspender Makers Union affiliated with the American Federaton of Labor as Federal Local 9,560. In 1903 and 1905 two long and bitter strikes ended in total failure. The crisis of 1907 still further hampered the progress of the organization. But since 1909 it has entered upon a more successful period, and has won many concessions. In 1910 the union had a jurisdictional controversy with the United Garment Workers, who argued that suspenders must be considered an integral part of trousers. The Executive Council, however, did not sustain this bit of logic. Since then the progress of the organization has been slow and steady.

In spite of their comparative youth, the clothing trades unions are now, from any point of view, among the strongest in the country. Wages, hours, control in shop, and morale of the membership, will be discussed in succeeding chapters; we are here concerned with size alone. In the men's clothing industry, the 1914 census figures place 174,000 wage-earners, or if we include shirts, collars, and cuffs, 236,000. The combined membership of the Amalgamated Clothing Workers and the United Garment Workers is at the moment 196,000. Of the trades

UNIONS—BEGINNINGS AND GROWTH

in which they are well organized they therefore include nearly 100 per cent; of the whole industry over which their jurisdiction extends, 83 per cent. There were in 1914, 169,000 wage-earners in the women's clothing industry, and although this figure decreased during the war, we may now take it as the basis of a rough computation. The 150,000 members claimed by the International Ladies' Garment Workers would compose 88 per cent, or if we add the 20,000 corset workers over whom they have jurisdiction, 79 per cent of the total. The Fur Workers have 80 per cent of their possible members. The Cloth Hat and Cap Makers control 100 per cent of the workers indicated by their title; it is difficult to estimate their percentage of the millinery workers, since in the census these are grouped with the lace makers; but a very conservative estimate would be 25 per cent. The census indicates 22,459 in the men's furnishing trades; these include the 8,000 neckwear makers of which the various locals have 3,200, or 40 per cent. There are 9,646 makers of suspenders and garters, of which perhaps a quarter are organized.

Let us take the figures which will give the most unfavorable result. Let us take the total of 518,000 wage-earners in all branches of the ready-made clothing industry, and place against it the total of paid-up membership in good standing shown by the unions, or 305,800—excluding the Journeyman Tailors and the suspender makers. These figures show 60 per cent of the industry organized, whereas the whole American labor movement has not much over 15 per cent of the nation's wage-earners. According to the American Labor Year Book of 1917-18 only one industry—the breweries—had a higher percentage, 88.8. This figure has since become nearly meaningless.

On the other hand, let us take the more favorable figures. Let us take the total of wage-earners in those branches of the industry where the organizations grew up and were first effective—men's ready-made clothing, women's ready-made clothing, furs, cloth hats, and caps. This omits those trades where the unions are now doing their missionary work. It gives us 360,530 wage-earners. Setting against that the full membership claimed by the unions, it is evident that these trades are virtually 100 per cent organized. Considering the fact that this membership is not held together so much by control of large establishments or other direct means as by the democratic allegiance of the workers themselves under extraordinary difficulties, it is a remarkable achievement.

CHAPTER V

DECISIVE VICTORIES

A REPORT of a strike usually enumerates a list of grievances, as formulated by the union or by investigators, and sometimes adds to them a statement that there is "general discontent." The reader receives the impression that there are certain well-defined goals which the workers have in view, and that with these attained, the processes of work will go on smoothly, as if the grievances were foreign bodies which had to be removed from the industrial system by skilful surgery. Such a conception of a strike may be helpful to analysis, but it is over-formal, and does not give a real picture of the worker's state of mind. His daily life is to him a continuous process; he knows when it becomes burdensome or unbearable, but he does not often pick out a single minor cause for that condition. Some things, to be sure, irritate him more than others, but his dissatisfaction is usually a general and cumulative one, and is only dulled by the adjustment of grievances. Not until the whole course of his life is altered for the better does he feel any appreciable difference.

So it is with the issues which have assumed importance in the many struggles of the needle-trades unions. They have been in themselves important, but to understand their significance to the workers it is necessary to think of their lives as a whole.

Dr. A. S. Daniel, speaking before the annual meeting of the National Consumers' League early in 1901, described a tenement which he said was typical of the thousands in which home work was being done on the East Side of New York. "The apartment consists of three rooms, two opening on an absolutely dark air-shaft; the other on a narrow yard; at midday only does any light from the outside penetrate this apartment, and then only the outer room, for a short time. At other times kerosene oil lamps or candles are used. Two families (consisting of eight persons) occupy this apartment, for which is paid $9.00 rent. One of the men has consumption, and both men, heads of the two families, assort lemons, which one peddles, or they assist their wives in finishing trousers at 1½c each pair. Their hours are as long as they can hold their heads up or they have any work to do. . . . It requires two hours for one person to finish a pair of trousers, and by their combined efforts they earn 30 to 50 cents a day, or rather in twenty-four hours. The children have become rachitic, the elders will succumb to the first severe malady that attacks them. . . . I have seen women in the last stages of consumption, propped up in bed, finishing trousers until nature could stand it no longer, and the work stopped

DECISIVE VICTORIES 103

from absolute exhaustion, or death mercifully put an end to their suffering."

Dr. John H. Pryor, testifying before the Tenement House Commission on Nov. 16, 1900, stated, "In New York City alone there are in the tenement houses constantly 20,000 consumptives." Dr. Hermann M. Biggs testified that the dust in such houses was infectious, and that experiments had shown that it produced tuberculosis in animals. Mrs. Frederick Nathan, President of the New York Consumers' League, on the same day testified, "The clothing industry is one of the most degraded, if not the most degraded of all the industries." Such conditions were not peculiar to New York, but existed wherever clothing was made. Overcrowding was discovered for instance in Baltimore through a special investigation by the Maryland Bureau of Industrial Statistics in 1901. They visited 247 tenements containing clothing sweatshops, and found in the small rooms used for work, an average of over five persons to a room. Among them were a large number of boys and girls under fifteen. The number of persons both living and working in these houses amounted to a little over two to a room, counting as rooms cellar, garret, kitchen, toilet, and hall rooms.

Much has been written about the evils of the sweatshop, but this is enough to give a hint of what "home work" means. As for the folk-ways of the contractor's shop, they can be suggested by quoting in part the story of an Italian girl, taken down verbatim by Prof. Katherine Coman of Wellesley College during the Chicago strike of 1910, and published in *The Survey* of Dec. 10, 1910.

This girl applied for work, and when she showed that she was experienced the contractor hired her as forewoman for the other girls in the shop, whom he described as "greenhorns." She asked him why he did not employ more experienced people, and said she had some friends who might do. The contractor replied:

"Experienced girls? Not in my shop." "Why not?" He said: "I want no experienced girls. They know the pay to get. I got to pay them good wages and they make me less work, but these greenhorns, Italian people, Jewish people, all nationalities, they cannot speak English and they don't know where to go and they just come from the old country and I let them work hard, like the devil, and those I get for less wages."

The contractor then told her she must make the girls finish ten coats a day.

"Well those people were all married women, they all had families of small children, some had husbands that were sick, and there was a woman there that had a husband that was blind for two years and besides he was sick in bed, and she was in that condition she could not work, but she had to work in the shop to get fifty cents a day to support her and her husband. So I said, 'Well you must finish up ten coats a day.' Those people started to cry. They said: 'How can we support our families if we have to do ten coats a day, because we could not do a coat in an hour and a half.' . . .

"So I went to the boss and I told him, I said: 'The people are not satisfied. Ten coats a day, an hour and half on each coat, you ask them to work fifteen hours a day.' He said, 'If they cannot finish ten coats a day, let them finish up just as much as they can in the day time, and the rest of the coats they bring home and make them in the night time, so they can do one day's work.'"

The workers, seeing that at their existing wages, paid on the basis of ten coats a day, they could not hold body and soul together, asked for piece-work rates. The contractor offered thirteen cents a coat. The forewoman said this was too cheap, since if they worked ten hours a day they could only make 50 cents. "I can get all the greenhorns I want to do the work," replied the boss, "and I can get them cheap." The women therefore accepted this rate. A little later he came to the forewoman and told her he had to turn out the work cheaper to keep his trade, and therefore would have to lower the rate to twelve cents.

"'If you would lower the price down to twelve cents they cannot make it.' He said: 'If they cannot make it, here is the window and here is the door. If they don't want to go from the window they can go from the door, and if they don't want to go from the door, they can go from the window. I have lots of greenhorns. I got to make my own living.'"

This price was also accepted. The boss then

made himself obnoxious by walking about the shop and insulting the girls because they were not working fast enough. At length the forewoman asked to be relieved of her job and put at work with the others. He made an arrangement with her for basting, but demanded impossible performance. "You know that these coats must fly like the leaves on a tree, that is the way you must make the work fly," he would say to her. He blamed her for not doing her part of the work quickly enough to keep the others busy, but he would employ no one else to help in her operation.

"Of course, he was insulting me every day and the other people too. So I knew they were striking in all the other shops, so I told all our girls, I said: 'The first whistle we hear in the window, that means for us to strike. You cannot work for twelve cents a coat, and I cannot baste thirty-five coats a day, and we will all go on strike. So one day, it was dinner time, a quarter after twelve, and we hear a big noise under the window and there were about 200 persons were all whistling for us to come down and strike, so I was the first one to go out and get the other girls to come after me."

This story illustrates a number of the grievances which on various occasions became the subject of negotiation. The suggestion that the girls take the work home is reminiscent of the "black bag" which was for many years the symbol for this practice in the needle trades. Tired workers could be seen going home in the evening with large shapeless bags filled with unfinished garments to be sewed as long as they could keep awake at night. Children's express wagons, baby-carriages, and pushcarts were also used for this doleful freight. The need for standardization of wages and hours is evident. It was not only a matter of securing fair rates from individual employers, but of making sure that those rates were uniformly upheld throughout the trade, so that competition would not immediately depress them. The demand for the abolition of the contractor, or for a guarantee of wages on the part of the "inside shop" is also explained. The boss's constant insistence that he could do what he liked because he had "plenty of greenhorns" shows why a strong union was necessary, why it had to insist on recognition, and on some form of the union shop.

There were other causes for complaint. Owing to the fact that the industry had grown up from the custom tailoring trade, and that the first workers had been independent artisans, it was for a long time the practice for the operators to supply their own sewing machines and their own thread and sundries. The fact that the worker had to move his machine whenever he changed his job practically bound him to one employer in spite of any abuse he might receive. Many of the strikes in the 'nineties had among their objects the furnishing of machines by the employer. Later, the fatigue from using foot-power all day long led the workers to demand electric power, and many employers installed it simply on account of its superior efficiency. Still, however, the cost of the power was charged against the worker, and deducted from his wages. When the employers began to furnish thread and sundries, they also charged these against the wage account. The inevitable result was such a reduction of wages —often a reduction out of all proportion to the actual cost of power and thread,—that the employees revolted against it.

The Italian girl's story takes no account of seasonal unemployment (see Chapter I). The effort of the unions to mitigate this has taken various forms. At first it was an insistence that all their members should be employed the year round. Such a demand was rarely successful, and where it was granted, the light work in the dull seasons led to such a reduction of wages that it was of little avail. The constant struggle for a reduction of the working week was largely based on the theory that if overtime were made expensive enough for the employer during the busy season, he would try to find some way of distributing work more evenly throughout the year. An indirect method of this sort, however, is at best unsatisfactory. Recently, since the unions have grown more powerful, they have begun to demand an average minimum wage based on a full number of weeks in the year. This measure is really effective, since although it puts pressure on the manufacturer to equalize the seasons, it does not allow the worker's livelihood to depend on success in that attempt.

Abolition of unsafe and insanitary conditions in

DECISIVE VICTORIES

the shops and tenements has also been an important factor in improving the life of the workers. An account of the progress in this regard will be found in Chapter VI under the Joint Board of Sanitary Control.

It is impossible to trace the conquest of any one of these evils separately, to say that on such and such a date the undesirable condition was eliminated. Home work, for instance, gradually disappeared as the union grew stronger and was able to enforce its demands wherever clothing might be made. If the unions should be dissolved tomorrow, as much clothing might soon be made in insanitary tenements, in spite of anyone's desire to the contrary, as in 1890.[1] The amount of actual home work is largely

[1] A demonstration of the ineffectuality of legal measures to control home work is furnished by an article in *The Survey* of February 4, 1911, which shows that in spite of tenement house and factory laws, 13,000 tenement houses in New York were licensed by the Bureau of Factory Inspection of the State Department of Labor, and that these licenses were issued merely on the basis of a perfunctory sanitary inspection once a year. The number of families occupying the houses was not taken into consideration, and there was no law to prevent children under fourteen from working in the tenements. In 1918, during the war with Germany, Professor William Z. Ripley of Harvard University, in an address to the convention of the International Ladies' Garment Workers, stated that the United States arsenal at Schuylkill, Pennsylvania, gave out work in bundles to be done in the homes of about five thousand women in neighboring cities. Said Professor Ripley: "Here is a home in Philadelphia where a man died of tuberculosis, while his wife was working on shirts. . . . The Board of Health had been asked to fumigate the house several weeks before, and had apparently forgotten to do it. Shirts went on being made day after day in those unfumigated premises." . . . Another case was of a colored woman who wished to do work for the government and applied for the necessary inspection. "She got her inspection. Why? Not because anybody came to her tenement, but because the Board of Health of the city of Philadelphia was pleased to report that some years before they had inspected another tenement in the block and found it all right. And in that house there were both measles and whooping-cough, and those shirts were going out to the boys on

dependent on the general level of wages. The same is true, to a limited extent, of hours. A collective agreement may specify a maximum number of hours, but if the union is not strong enough to see that this provision is carried out in small and independent shops as well as in the shops of the manufacturers' association, if it cannot keep wages up to the point where home work after hours is not indispensable, the provision as to hours soon becomes a dead letter. It is even impossible to quote general figures on the rise in wages, except of the roughest sort. Such a large proportion of the work has been done at piece rates, and those rates vary so largely with the many different operations, all of which change with the changes in styles, that no complete figures have ever been compiled. Even where minimum rates are specified in collective agreements, it is impossible to compute average weekly earnings for the year without taking into consideration the slack work in the dull seasons.

The condition of the workers, given the same basic economic conditions, depends finally on the organic strength of the unions, upon their control over all the wage-earners, and their vigor in every shop, small as well as large. The unions are like an advancing army. Their main object is not to find provender, to win this or that position, to defeat this or that opposing corps. Their purpose is to win the war; all the rest is incidental. With

the other side." When the War Department took measures to supervise the sanitary conditions under which army clothing was being made, it had to rely largely on the assistance of the unions.

DECISIVE VICTORIES

power and victory, the incidentals follow. And this truth corresponds with the worker's actual feeling about the industrial struggle. He is interested not so much in the recording of concessions on paper as in the general engagements and victories, the morale and effectiveness of the whole force of which he is a member.

The first great strike in the clothing industry which resulted in substantial and permanent gains was that of the New York Cloak, Suit, and Skirt Makers in 1910. The grievances included almost all the evil conditions against which the unions had fought for two decades. The workmen objected to subcontracting within the "inside shops," to low wages and long hours, to home work, to individual contracts which bound the employee to the manufacturers at disadvantageous terms, to irregular payment of wages and charges against wages for materials and power.

As an example of the result of subcontracting, one shop has been cited which employed 500 operatives, but paid directly only fifteen. These fifteen had two series of subcontractors under them, with the result that actual wages were very low, the helpers at the bottom of the system receiving only from $3.00 to $6.00 per week. Aside from subcontracting, however, even the highest paid workers, the sample makers, received but $18.00 weekly during the busy season in the best shops, the cutters and skilled operators averaged in the neighborhood of $15.00, the pressers $14.00, the finishers, including their earnings from night work, $12.00. This meant in terms of average weekly earnings throughout the year, a starvation wage. During the busy season the hours were eleven daily, and only after this exhausting period was the extra rate for overtime paid. The union asked for a forty-nine hour basic week, with a maximum of two and one-half hours of overtime daily during the busy season.

The principal demand of the strikers, however, was for the status which would safeguard whatever gains they might win. Long experience had taught them that strikes, no matter how extensive and how successful for the time being, were fruitless in the long run if the industry were to be allowed to relapse into the old chaos as soon as they went back to work. They therefore placed most emphasis of all upon the "closed shop." If they could wring from the employers an agreement to employ none other than union members, all other concessions could be retained, and the foundation laid for future advances.

Before the strike the Cloakmakers' union had about 20,000 members, but the response to the strike call, issued on July 6, 1910, was almost unanimous among unorganized as well as organized workers, 45,000 in all going out. Approximately 1,800 establishments were affected. With a strike on such a vast scale, by poorly paid workers most of whom were unaccustomed to union tactics and discipline, a tremendously difficult problem of administration was presented to the union. The first step was to organize the strikers about the unit of the shop. The workers in each of the 1,800 shops elected their own chairman and their own picket committee, and held separate meetings daily. To provide places for these meetings, a Hall Committee of the union was appointed, which hired fifty-eight halls. A corps of speakers, experienced and widely known union members, was organized by a Speakers' Committee to address the meetings. Understanding the large part which public opinion plays in the settlement of strikes—the public has perhaps shown a more marked interest in the clothing strikes than in the workers' struggles in any other industry—a Press Committee was appointed. A Law Committee took care of the legal difficulties which always accompany a great strike.

About 5,000 workers, one-tenth of the entire number, did not at first answer the strike call, and picketing was undertaken to win them over. The workers in each shop had the duty of picketing that shop, since they knew thoroughly the location and characteristics, and the employees in it. Picketing had to be carried on day and night, in four-hour shifts, since all the shops which attempted to keep open were naturally working overtime to fill their orders, and strikebreakers were often imported at night. The result was that practically every striker did picket duty. In order to advise the pickets as to their rights and duties, to fill in where a preponderance of women strikers made help necessary in the night picketing, and to guard shops which employers moved elsewhere in the city or out of town, a General

Picket Committee was formed at union headquarters.

In the second or third week, it was necessary to begin paying benefits to the more needy members. At first about five to ten thousand had to be relieved, and the number grew as the strike continued. To undertake this duty a Relief Committee was organized. Its work was performed with admirable method and promptness. Applications for relief were first signed by the chairman of the shop, who knew the workers and their circumstances. They were then countersigned by the various hall chairmen—the men in charge of the halls, who knew the shop chairmen and could guarantee their signatures. The applications for the day were totalled and compared with the available funds for that day. If the funds were not sufficient, a pro rata reduction was made. Every cent collected and expended was accurately accounted for by a corps of bookkeepers. It was the duty of the Relief Committee also to help in collecting the funds.

The general officers of the union were occupied in supervising the work of the various committees, in making speeches, in raising funds, and in carrying on negotiations with the employers. Strike headquarters were as busy as the headquarters of an army in the field. It is worthy of remark that these responsible administrative tasks were performed successfully by men receiving little more than the ordinary wages of the average workmen.

As a result of the efforts of the Press Committee, and of disinterested members of the general public

DECISIVE VICTORIES 115

—like members of the National Consumers' League which had long been trying to abolish the sweatshops—wide public interest was aroused, and general sympathy for the strikers was expressed. Prominent men like Mr. Louis Brandeis and Mr. Louis Marshall became interested and assisted in the negotiations. The owner of a retail store in Boston, an important buyer of clothing, Mr. A. Lincoln Filene, exerted his influence with the employers in behalf of a just settlement. In spite of all pressure, however, it was long before an approach to an agreement was made.

On the closed shop issue the union would not surrender, and the manufacturers, although willing to make other concessions, would not meet the demand of the strikers on the vital one. Twice negotiations were broken off on this account. A manufacturers' association, including seventy-five of the largest employers, was formed, and resolved to resist the closed shop to the end. As the deadlock wore on and became more costly to the manufacturers, many not in the association surrendered to the union. At length 600 independent establishments, employing 30,000 persons, had settled. The payments from these working members increased the strike fund. A few weeks before the close of the strike Judge Goff issued a remarkable injunction forbidding union members to picket in support of the demand for the closed shop. The New York *Times* characterized this injunction as "the strongest decision ever handed down against organized labor." As an answer to the injunction, $18,000 was poured into the union treasury in one day from its members, and in one evening 85 pickets were arrested for defying the order. This was proof enough of the support for the closed shop among the rank and file.

At length a happy suggestion, the authorship of which is usually attributed to Mr. Brandeis, brought a settlement nearer. For the "closed shop" as ordinarily understood was substituted the "union shop," or the preferential shop, that is, a shop in which union conditions were to be adhered to, and in which, when engaging an employee, the employer should give preference to a union member. The first draft of the proposed agreement used the words, "union shop as distinguished from the closed shop," and specified that of two applicants of equal ability, the union member should be given the preference. It left hours and wages to arbitration, and did not recognize the shop chairman as the representative of the employees in negotiations about the piece prices. On these accounts the strikers rejected it. They contended that the explicit distinction between the closed shop and the union shop would serve only to make trouble, that the phrasing of the preference clause made the employer the sole judge of ability and would lead to evasion, and that to insure justice the shop chairmen must be recognized.

After ten weeks, on September 2, a final agreement was reached and the noted Protocol signed. It was almost a complete victory for the union. It urged the installing of electric power and abolished charges against employees for power and material. It forbade the giving out of home work, abolished sub-contracting within the shops, and ordered the regular weekly payment of wages in cash. It raised the pay of workers by the week from 25 to 100 per cent, and established the 50 hour week, with a maximum of two and one-half hours extra during the busy season only, and with double-time rate for overtime. Piece rates it left to be adjusted between shop chairmen and individual employers. It established the Joint Board of Sanitary Control.

What was to the union the most important clause was that establishing the union shop, which read as follows:

Each member of the manufacturers is to maintain a union shop, a "union shop" being understood to refer to a shop where union standards as to working conditions, hours of labor, and rates of wages as herein stipulated shall prevail, and where, when hiring help, union men are preferred, it being recognized that, since there are differences in skill among those employed in the trade, employers shall have freedom of selection as between one union man and another, and shall not be confined to any list, nor bound to follow any prescribed order whatever.

Since at the close of the strike there were not more than 1,000 strikebreakers working in the shops, and many of these immediately joined the union, the clause was as effective, for the union's purpose, as if the full closed shop had been adopted. Ever since this settlement the cloakmakers have retained in their organization practically all the workers eligible.

The Protocol departed from all previous collective agreements in specifying no date for its termination, although, like an international treaty, it could be terminated at any time by the decision of either party. It established a Board of Arbitration with an impartial chairman, before which future disputes should go, before a strike or lockout could be declared. A subordinate committee on grievances was set up. Much attention has been directed to these sections of the agreement, which some prophets expected would establish permanent peace in the industry; but future events proved such expectations exaggerated. The arbitration provisions undoubtedly did prevent petty and unwarranted strikes and lockouts, but their main function was not so much the ambitious one of preserving permanent peace as of seeing that the provisions of the agreement, while it lasted, were honestly carried out. A discussion of the arbitration machinery will be found in the next chapter.

After the settlement independent manufacturers who had already granted the closed shop were allowed to substitute the Protocol for their original agreements, and join the association. Many did so, and the Protocol soon became the ruling basis of the industry.

The first great strike in the men's clothing industry began in the early part of October 1910, in Chicago. It was a spontaneous outbreak, beginning with twenty workers in one shop, and spreading rapidly until 40,000 were out. The grievances were long hours and low pay, deductions from wages through fines and charges for material and power, amounting in many cases to 15 or 20 per cent of the total wages, overbearing foremen, and the absence of any way to adjust disputes. Demands were formulated only after the strike had become general. They included the closed shop in the cutting and manufacturing departments, a forty-eight hour week for cutters and trimmers, and a fifty-four hour week for tailors, with time-and-a-half rates for overtime and double time for holidays, and the adjustment of local misunderstandings between the employer and the shop steward of the union, with a third impartial party as arbitrator if they failed to agree.

A settlement was soon negotiated between the manufacturers and the officers of the United Garment Workers. It provided for an arbitration board to decide the questions at issue, but excluded from consideration by that board all questions relating to the recognition of the union and the closed shop. The open shop was to be retained, and was not to be considered a grievance. This settlement was signed by the officers of the union, but was overwhelmingly defeated by a referendum of the strikers on the same day.

A large citizens' committee was then formed to investigate the dispute. The chairman was Emil G. Hirsch, and among the members were the Rev. Jenkin Lloyd Jones, Judge Julian W. Mack, Jane

Addams and Alice Hamilton. This committee reported that sweatshop conditions had been carried over into the factory, that the employees were underpaid and overworked, and that they were subjected to innumerable petty tyrannies. It recommended some form of organization within the shop in order that the employees might have adequate representation and a voice in the conditions under which they were working. To all demands of the strikers and appeals of the public the manufacturers replied by a general denial of bad conditions, stating that the strike was simply the result of agitation and that they had nothing to arbitrate.

Meanwhile the spirit and determination of the strikers became firmer. Unorganized as they had been, they needed assistance, and this was furnished without stint by the Chicago Federation of Labor under John Fitzpatrick and the Women's Trade Union League under Mrs. Raymond Robbins. A strike organization was perfected similar to that of the New York Cloakmakers. The Chicago Federation recommended that its affiliated locals assess themselves to help the tailors, and many unions did so. The Teachers' Federation, liberal churches, and public leaders gave assistance. On November 28th the Board of Aldermen resolved to mediate, and appointed a committee which suggested a conference. The large firm of Hart, Schaffner and Marx and a few others consented to this plan, but most of the manufacturers held to their original position.

As the strike continued through the winter it was

estimated that the daily loss in profits and wages was over $100,000. The strikers naturally were threatened with tragic destitution, and relief for them was organized on a large scale. Rather than pay cash benefits, the strike committee made its resources go farther by buying supplies in bulk, and rationing them out. To supply the families four stores were set up in various parts of the city, one for the Poles and Lithuanians, one in the Italian settlement, one for the Bohemians, and one for the Jews. Five hundred numbered tickets were issued for each store, for each of the six week days. A ticket entitled the head of a family to a week's rations. Thus 3,000 families were supplied weekly by each of the four stores. The tickets were given out by the shop chairman to the individuals known to be needy. In this way twenty-two carloads of food and 200,000 loaves of bread were distributed. For unmarried workers 3,000 meal tickets were supplied by the Jewish Labor World and the Jewish Workingmen's Conference; the Women's Trade Union League opened a free lunch room for girls. A special milk fund for babies was provided by a public committee, and 2,000 quarts of milk were distributed daily for two months. The Women's Trade Union League sent coal where it was most needed, but many strikers had to go without this luxury. A special committee was formed to deal with rents and evictions, and it succeeded in moderating the action of the landlords. Many hospitals gave free care to the sick. One volunteer committee furnished layettes for the expectant mothers. On Christmas Day 1,200 Christmas baskets were sent out, but many of the more radical strikers politely declined them, on the ground that they did not wish to accept charity. The settlement houses contributed old clothing and shoes.

In all, nearly $100,000 was spent for relief, and of this sum all but $25,000 was contributed by working people.

The conference between representatives of Hart, Schaffner, and Marx and the strike committee had meanwhile arrived at a basis for settlement which omitted the objectionable features of the former offer. A board of arbitration was to consider all questions at issue without exception, its decision was to be binding, and all strikers were to be taken back to work except a few who had been convicted of violence during the bitter struggle. On December 24 this proposition was submitted to the Hart, Schaffner, and Marx employees, but they refused to benefit by a peace which did not affect the people in the other shops. As a proof of comradeship they rejected the proposed settlement unless it should be extended to all the strikers. This decision naturally was regretted by those who had negotiated the agreement, since they felt that the heroic struggle could not continue much longer. It showed, however, how strongly the spirit of solidarity had entered the workers who but a few weeks before had been for the most part unorganized. This spirit was given emphasis, when, on a cold winter day, 20,000 strikers marched to the deserted baseball park and held a mass meeting, being addressed in small groups by hundreds of speakers in half a dozen different languages.

At length, on February 3, this cold and hungry army, unable to hold out longer, capitulated without conditions and went back to work. An agreement similar to the one previously rejected had in the meantime been accepted by the Hart, Schaffner, and Marx employees, but the rest had to be satisfied with the subjective victory of having learned that they could conduct a strong campaign. Further operations were merely postponed. The struggle broke out again several times during the succeeding years, and was never relinquished until the majority of the employers signed a collective agreement in the summer of 1919.

The decision of the arbitrators in the Hart, Schaffner, and Marx case granted better wages, hours and conditions, cleared the way for the presentation of complaints, and established a permanent board of arbitration. It did not, however, provide for recognition of the union or for the union shop. Successive improvements were made in it without an actual break in relations, so that today the preferential union shop exists, and the agreement is in other respects among the most satisfactory in the country. It was in this establishment that light was first thrown upon the extraordinary abilities of a young leader, Sidney Hillman, who later became the first General President of the Amalgamated Clothing Workers of America.

The two strikes of 1910 were not only dramatic events in themselves but they served as the foundation for the rapid progress of the unions. They were models for the conduct of future battles; they gave the workers a confidence in themselves unknown before, and the agreements which arose out of them established the minimum necessities for sound growth. Future struggles were undertaken for the establishment of similar agreements in other branches of the industry or in other cities, for the preservation of gains won in these agreements, or for still better agreements.

Subsequent controversies raged about higher wages and shorter hours, the right of the worker to security in his job, improvements in the machinery of the agreements, measures for alleviating seasonal unemployment, and further uniformity in wage rates. Most of these, on account of the spirit of the workers, the strong form of industrial organization, and the democratic efficiency of the unions, have been won by them. More detailed discussion of these victories belongs with the chapter on collective agreements.

The present situation of the workers in the well unionized branches of the ready-made clothing industry is as favorable as that of any group of American trade-unionists. Most of them have the forty-four hour week. Their unions have full recognition, and the union shop, in one form or another, prevails. The cruder forms of suffering, such as those inseparable from home work and the sweatshop, have been virtually abolished. Organized control within the shop has been achieved through the shop chairmen and price committees; it was well developed before the advent of the shop committee movement in other industries, of which we have heard much since the war. General averages of wage-rates, for reasons explained before, it is impossible to quote, but the minima specified for the best paid workers are in the neighborhood of $45.00 weekly, and the average is probably well above that of industrial wage-earners throughout the country, which still, in the fall of 1919, lingered about $20.00.

To say this is not to say that the unions have no difficult tasks before them. There are large branches of the clothing industry in which the workers are still without the full benefits of the union. The seasonal character of the trade is still unconquered; it causes much unemployment and reduces the yearly wage level unduly. Where they are strong, the unions have reduced to extremely narrow proportions the margin between what they have won and what it is possible to win from the industry in its present character and under its present régime. But the possibilities for the better organization of the industry and its more efficient conduct are great. It is to the development of these possibilities that attention must now be turned if further advances are to be made. For this reason the most solid achievement of the unions is not to be measured in terms of any material gain, but rather in terms of their power and intelligence, of their internal fitness for further victory.

CHAPTER VI

COLLECTIVE AGREEMENTS

THE collective agreement is sometimes regarded as a means of putting an end to industrial strife. Strikes are obviously clumsy instruments with which to settle controversies. They bring hardship to the workers, they are annoying and costly to the employers, and by interfering with production they increase the cost of living and cause inconvenience to the public. Cannot all parties come together on a fair basis and agree to arbitrate future difficulties? This is a view frequently expressed. There is a measure of truth in it. No union wishes to strike for a concession which can be gained by peaceful methods. Wise unions wish to obviate strikes for trivial reasons, strikes which do nobody any appreciable good and could be avoided by a little negotiation. Employers, on their side, are willing to pay a price for industrial peace. In an industry still subject to competition, the most progressive employers, who wish for the sake of efficiency to treat their workmen well, are glad of the assistance which a collective agreement offers in bringing recalcitrant competitors into line. In a sense and to a degree there is a real community of interest between the enlightened employer and the progressive union.

Upon this community of interest can be built agreements calculated to minimize controversy.

It is not true, however, that the chief interest of either the employer or the employee is to maintain peace. The employer desires above all else to retain control of the productive process, and to use that control primarily for the benefit of the capital invested—secondarily, perhaps, for the benefit of the public and the employee. The union, on the other hand, whatever its conscious philosophy, finds the reason for its existence in the desire to benefit its members. To benefit them it must sometimes encroach on the productive control of the employer. Here is a fundamental conflict of interest. The conflict is often far from the surface, but even with the most amicable intentions on both sides it crops out on occasion and creates a situation in which both sides would rather incur the expense of a strike than submit to compromise.

Another popular belief with regard to collective agreements is that the agreement itself is the source of the benefits which labor wins, as if it had been established by a sort of divine edict. This is taking the appearance for the reality. The agreement is but a symbol of the power and successes of the union, it simply records the gains the union has been able to make. It would be a dead letter if the union were incapable of enforcing its provisions. In many cases it is abrogated or turned into a dead letter the moment the employers feel strong enough to defeat the union.

In other words, the collective agreement represents the point at which the power of the union balances the power of the employer. It is not law founded upon some abstract rule of justice or bill of rights, but is merely what its name implies, a document specifying the conditions under which both parties are willing for a specified time and considering all the circumstances, to live in peace. This remains true even if, as in the clothing industry, the agreements have become highly evolved constitutions regulating in much detail the relations of employer and employee. The only circumstances in which it could be permanent would be those in which the relative power of employer and employee should remain forever unchanged and there were no important changes in the characteristics of the industry itself. Such circumstances are of course hardly conceivable. It might be continually altered by conciliation or arbitration, without strikes, if neither party ever deemed itself stronger than it was. But it is hardly likely that two parties with opposing interests would forever deny themselves the actual test of strength. It is difficult even for impartial observers to determine where the balance of power lies at any given moment, to say nothing of the contestants themselves.

An analysis of the collective agreements in the clothing industry will illustrate in part what an agreement can and what it cannot do. The first and best known, the Protocol of Peace in the cloak, suit, and skirt industry of New York, signed on September 2, 1910, had several functions. In the first place, it recorded the concessions made to the union as the result of the strike, concessions which may be considered the organic law of the agreement. Under this head come the regulations regarding mechanical power, the abolishment of home work, the abolishment of subcontracting, the hours and wages of the workers, the preferential union shop, etc. In the second place it established a judicial system consisting of a Board of Arbitration, whose decision was to be accepted as final on all future controversies, and a Committee on Grievances to deal with minor disputes. In the third place it founded the Joint Board of Sanitary Control, containing representatives of employers, employees, and the public, to establish sanitary standards and see that they were carried out.

In this system there was no sharp division of functions. The Board of Arbitration, consisting of a representative of each side and a representative of the public to act as chairman, was not only a final court of appeals to give interpretations of the established law, but it could actually change the fundamental law—that is, it had the legislative power to revise wages and hours, or settle any other dispute which might arise. The joint Committee on Grievances, consisting of representatives of each side with no impartial chairman, could not only decide minor disputes, but it could devise legislation to guide its own procedure and to help make effective the basic law. The Joint Board of Sanitary Control combined legislative, judicial, and executive functions. In a sense, the union and the manufacturers' association had executive duties, since they were morally bound to see that their respective memberships adhered to the agreement and the decisions under it.

It is clear that the framers of the Protocol, building on a hope that there was enough community of interest between the contending parties to make permanent peace possible, tried to frame an organic law which could grow naturally as conditions changed. Otherwise they would have made a sharper distinction of function. If they had recognized that there was, besides a temporary community of interest in maintaining peace under this agreement, a fundamental conflict of interest which would tend to destroy or alter it, they would have created a system of machinery to interpret and make effective the agreement as long as it should last, but they would not have expected this same machinery to enact new organic laws. Nevertheless, the system was fitted to endure as long as an effective community of interest existed.

The Committee on Grievances, at first consisting of two representatives from each side, was soon enlarged to five from each side, and worked out a technique of conciliation. Its name was changed to the Board of Grievances. Two chief clerks were appointed, one for the union and one for the manufacturers, to oversee the investigation of disputes. The chief clerk for the union was also the manager of the protocol department of the union, and the chief clerk for the association was also the manager of its labor department. A number of deputy clerks were appointed for each side. Whenever a dispute arose, the first attempt at conciliation was directly between the shop chairman and the employer concerned. If this failed, a complaint was filed. When a complaint was filed by a union member, it went to the union's chief clerk; when it was filed by an employer, it went to the Association's chief clerk. The chief clerk in question forwarded the complaint to his confrère, and if either side was clearly in the wrong, the matter was settled by a few words from the labor manager to the employer, or from the protocol manager of the union to the shop workers. If the case was not clear, an investigation in the shop was at once undertaken by two of the deputy clerks, one for each side, acting in concert. They reached a decision if possible, recommended the action to be taken, and reported in writing the disposition of the case. If they disagreed, the two chief clerks made a reinvestigation, and settled the case if they could. If they in turn disagreed, the dispute went before the whole Board of Grievances, and if that was deadlocked, the matter came before the Board of Arbitration, where the representative of the public held the deciding voice. This arrangement worked in such a way that clear cases of violation of Protocol law or precedent were disposed of by subordinate representatives of the two parties to the agreement acting in concert, whereas more complex disputes, or those involving new issues, went before higher bodies.

Between the date of the creation of the Board of Grievances, April 15, 1911, and October 31, 1913, 7,656 complaints were filed. About 90 per cent were adjusted and dropped by the deputy clerks, nearly 8 per cent were adjusted by chief clerks, 2 per cent were adjusted by the Board of Grievances, and 1 per cent were decided by the Board of Arbitration. Apparently, therefore, the system was working well. It would seem as if the rank and file should have been satisfied with the settlements, since their deputy clerks—otherwise known as business agents—were democratically chosen. The method of election was as follows. Each of the local unions nominated candidates. These candidates were subjected to an examination by the New York Joint Board—the elected executive of the local unions. The candidates were rated as a result of this examination in four grades, a, b, c, and d, and were then subjected to a general vote of the entire membership. This election chose business agents. From the business agents the Joint Board chose four or five for chief clerk and deputies. The Joint Board, however, sometimes appointed as chief clerk a man not elected by the membership.

Nevertheless, friction existed and was increasing. Although at first Protocol law was admirably enforced, it was not long before the union requested the right to send inspectors into shops where no complaints originated, on the ground that workers might by intimidation be prevented from complaining. This request was ruled upon by the Board of Arbitration, with the result that a joint investigation of any shop was authorized upon the written request of any member of the Board of Grievances. Of the cases which on account of deadlock had to go to arbitration, one-third arose in the first two-thirds of the period mentioned above, and two-thirds arose in the last third of the period. At length the union, claiming that it did not receive justice from the Board of Grievances as constituted, and alleging undue delay in reaching decisions, requested a change in the machinery by which, if the Board of Grievances could not agree, the question was to be submitted to an impartial arbitrator, to be chosen on each occasion from a number of designated representatives of the public. The arbitrator was to render a decision within 48 hours after the submission of the evidence, this decision to be final.

An intensive investigation of the working of the machinery for adjustment resulted from this request.[1] The investigation established the facts quoted above as to the small proportion of cases which were referred to the Board of Grievances, and the still smaller proportion in which they were unable to reach a decision.

It seemed at the time that the system must be reasonably satisfactory because in only nine cases out of 7,658 complaints did the Board of Grievances

[1] Industrial Court of the Cloak, Suit and Skirt Industry of New York City. Bulletin of U. S. Bureau of Labor Statistics, No. 144.

remain in deadlock. The report further pointed out that the Board had never deadlocked on questions of fact, but only on questions of law or motives. An examination of the actual cases in which no decision was reached did not seem to reveal anything particularly menacing. Three of them were complaints of manufacturers against shop strikes, two were complaints of employees against discrimination, two were against irregular price settlement, one was against a shop lockout, and one—involving twelve separate cases—was against non-payment for a holiday (the holiday happened to fall on Saturday). It did not seem to occur to the investigators that the heat generated by these few cases was entirely out of proportion to their specific importance, and must be due to unsatisfactory conditions of a more general nature.

The investigation showed that the rules of procedure were fair and adequate, that the facts were fully ascertained and presented, and that investigations and decisions were reasonably prompt. Among the cases brought before the Board, no discrimination against the union was apparent. The following table shows their disposal.

Disposition	Per cent.
Compromised	29.58
Dropped	25.13
In favor of unions	17.90
In favor of association	12.30
Disagreement	11.18
Withdrawn	3.91

COLLECTIVE AGREEMENTS

The large percentage compromised or dropped seemed to show the success of conciliation. The cases dropped were those in which the contending parties came to an understanding before the investigation, those in which the nature of the complaint was too trivial to be considered, those in which there was insufficient evidence to establish the charge, those in which the union did not press for a solution, or those between employees, in which the employers were in no way involved.

A classification of the cases according to the nature of the complaint is more enlightening, in view of future events. The two most frequent complaints by the union were discrimination against individuals (22.1 per cent) and alleged wrongful discharge (17.3 per cent). The most frequent complaint of the Association was against the shop strike or stoppage of work (75.5 per cent). Although the union secured favorable adjudication of minor complaints in over 61 per cent of those against underscale payments and 50 per cent of claims for wages due,— it received favorable decisions in only 18.5 per cent of cases against discrimination and in only 19 per cent of cases of alleged wrongful discharge. In minor complaints the manufacturers' association received a high percentage of favorable decisions, but in complaints against shop strikes their share of success was only 20.9 per cent. It is highly significant that in the complaints most frequently presented, decisions satisfactory to the complainant were least frequent.

These major complaints on both sides had to do with questions of control of the productive process. They were not primarily questions of material conditions. It might have been expected, by those who conceive the chief conflict between employer and employee to be that about wages, that most of the disagreements would concern piece prices, which the Protocol had left to be settled between the shop price committees and the individual employers. Disputes in price-making gave rise, however, to only 5 per cent of the complaints filed.

The union representatives, reflecting the sentiment of the rank and file, were especially on their guard against cases of discrimination or discharge, which they suspected the worker suffered as a result of legitimate union activity. Some discharges followed shop strikes, which the letter of the Protocol prohibited; but the union contended that the remedy against the shop strike was not discharge, but an appeal to the judicial machinery in the Protocol.

On the other hand, the manufacturers were especially jealous of their "right of discharge," which they maintained was absolutely essential to discipline and to efficiency. When the workers protested against such discipline, by means of shop strikes, the employers pointed to the fact that strikes were forbidden by the Protocol, and that the judicial machinery was open for appeals against unjust discharge.

Yet when, in either case, the Board of Grievance

was appealed to, the union representatives were reluctant to outlaw and discipline shop strikes, and the employers' representatives were reluctant to limit in any way the right of discharge. The consequence was that in these complementary grievances an increasing tendency was manifest to disregard conciliation and to appeal to direct action. It was a fundamental conflict cropping out—the deep seated conviction of the worker that he has a right to his job, opposed to the deep seated conviction of the employer that he has a right to unlimited authority in his shop. In just this fundamental conflict effective community of interest began to break down, and the Protocol was violated.

A significant commentary on this struggle is furnished by the fact that by far the greater number of complaints filed by the union arose during the dull seasons, when discharges were necessarily frequent and the small amount of work available gave opportunity for unfair distribution. Here technical complaints of injustice often masked the natural interest of the worker in holding his job. A union member was discharged, let us say, when work began to fail. He had been active in gaining concessions for the workers. The employer claimed that he was less efficient than the people retained. Was the discharge a result of discrimination? Such questions are difficult to decide. Owing to the difficulty of analyzing motives, the arguments about unjust discharge took on a metaphysical and hair-splitting nature. It can hardly be doubted, however, that the ruling and unconscious desire of the workers was not so much to maintain technical justice under the Protocol as to establish a fundamentally just condition in which all workers should retain their means of livelihood. This desire was intensified by the character of the industry itself—by its seasonal fluctuations.

The request of the union for a change in the machinery and for greater promptness in decisions was merely a blind attempt to break away from the difficulty; the basic cause of the trouble was not at the time fully understood by any of those concerned. In an attempt to satisfy the request, the Board of Arbitration on January 24, 1914, created a Committee on Immediate Action, to consist of the two chief clerks and a third impartial person. This committee was empowered to decide all questions submitted to it by the chief clerks except those involving Protocol law. It could not consider cases in which a stoppage of work existed until the striking workers returned to their jobs. An appeal from its decisions could be taken direct to the Board of Arbitration, without first passing through the Board of Grievances. What this ruling did, therefore, was merely to substitute a smaller and less unwieldy body for the Board of Grievances, and to outlaw shop strikes.

The new committee of course did not solve the problem. The questions regarding the right of discharge and the shop strike constantly grew more contentious. Among other things, they involved the

COLLECTIVE AGREEMENTS 139

interpretation of the preferential union shop plan,[2] and its application in dull seasons. The *New Post*, a journal published by the New York Joint Board of the union, discussed them at length, and the rank and file became increasingly restless. The friction gave encouragement and power to those employers within the association who were most strongly anti-union and cherished the hope of escaping from any form of joint control. The association attempted to fix the blame for the friction upon the chief clerk of the union, refused to work with him any longer, and presented a demand for his resignation. Although this action was in itself a violation of the Protocol, the union for the sake of peace permitted him to resign.

Meanwhile the manufacturers came to feel that they were in a more advantageous position than at the time of the signature of the Protocol, because a depression in the trade incident to the war had caused much unemployment. Piece prices went down steadily. The Board of Arbitration was trying to find a way out of the confusion, but without waiting for its final action the manufacturers' association abrogated the Protocol on May 20, 1915, giving as a reason the recurring shop strikes. This followed soon after the trial of the cloakmakers' leaders for unproved charges growing out of the strike of 1910.

Public opinion set strongly against the manufacturers, and as a last attempt to preserve industrial

[2] See Chapter V.

peace Mayor Mitchel appointed a Council of Conciliation consisting of prominent citizens. After more than three weeks of public hearings the Council handed down a decision raising the scale of wages, renewing the Protocol, and granting the right of review in all cases of discharge. The decision was at once accepted by the union, and was afterwards reluctantly ratified by the association. During the next year the fundamental conflict became intensified. On April 30, 1916, the manufacturers, after again abrogating the Protocol, declared a lockout. They charged that on account of the shop strikes the Protocol was a failure, and that they were fighting a battle of principle—a battle for the "right of discharge," without which they could not remain masters in their own establishments. They stated that they could not allow " outsiders "—the representatives of the public in the Protocol machinery —to determine whom they might and whom they might not employ.

The result was a bitter general strike which lasted for fourteen weeks. The test of strength proved that the union was, even in the unfavorable circumstances of the moment, too powerful to be destroyed. Both sides debated the issue at length in newspaper advertisements. Finally the President of the union, Benjamin Schlesinger, issued a statement which became the basis of negotiations. He wrote: "We are willing to concede to the employer the right to increase or decrease the number of his employees to meet the conditions in his factory and to retain such of his employees as he may desire on the basis of efficiency. This concession is made honestly without modification or limitation. It is of course understood that the workers retain their right to strike against any employer who will exercise the above power arbitrarily or oppressively or use it as a weapon to punish employees for union activity. Neither the workers in this industry nor in any other body of free American workers can exist without this right." The negotiations resulted in a new agreement embodying certain specific concessions to the union. A 49-hour was substituted for the 50-hour week, minimum piece rates were agreed upon, the preferential union shop was retained and further defined, sub-manufacturers to whom the inside shops gave out work were to be registered so that union conditions could be made uniform, the association guaranteed to enforce the conditions of the agreement on its own members, and price committees were recognized as before. The judicial system of arbitration under the Protocol, however, was not renewed. The agreement was limited to three years. The employer was to retain the right of hiring and discharge, and the union was to retain the right to strike in individual shops.

This agreement recognized the realities of the situation. In matters where a relatively lasting balance of power had been reached and community of interest existed and could be enforced, it established legislation. In the matters where the fundamental conflict might break out at any time and could not be adjudicated, it left the issue to tests of strength by direct action. It did not pretend that permanent peace could be maintained.

To say this is not to say that ensuing relations of the manufacturers and the workers were any more happy than before. The conflict was not abolished; it was frankly thrown into the arena, and the strain of attempting to settle it was removed from the agreement itself. Unjust discharges, or discharges which the workers felt were unjust, still occurred. Shop strikes were called, about these and other matters. The recurrence of the dull seasons still impressed upon the workers a sense of injustice in losing their jobs or in having their work cut down. The general lack of order in the industry, and the wide variations in wages, made constant trouble. Some shop committees were stronger than others and could enforce greater concessions. Some manufacturers were conciliatory, others recalcitrant. The anti-union manufacturers seemed to hold their ascendancy in the association, and gave every sign of trying to break down the agreement, and in their own good time, engaging in another battle to destroy the union.

The battle came early in 1919. The union made it the occasion, not only of preserving itself and its former gains, but of improving its position. Strikes in both the cloak industry and the dress and waist industry were brought to a successful termination. The 44-hour week and increased wages were gained, but the chief victories concerned the points of contention left open by the previous agreement. Since that had permitted shop strikes and local stoppages, it had interfered with the standardization of wages throughout the market; the strongest locals had won all they could extract from the employers while the weaker ones had been left behind. The remedy for this inequality was two-fold. In the first place, week work with minimum rates was in many cases substituted for piece work. In the second place, where piece work was retained, standard minimum rates were worked out by the "log" system—one which had been adopted earlier, but had not been systematically and universally applied. This consisted in establishing a minimum hourly rate as a basis, and then figuring the piece rates from it by observing how long it took for an average group of workers to perform the operation in question.

A method of reviewing discharges was also adopted.[3] Any worker discharged after his first two weeks in the shop had a right of appeal. His case was first reviewed by the chief clerks or their deputies, and if they were unable to agree, by an "impartial chairman"—a new office created as a substitute for the old and somewhat ambiguous "representative of the public." The impartial chairmen were paid by both sides, and were chosen for their familiarity with industrial problems, and their neutrality of outlook.

[3] The method here described existed in the dress and waist industry. Procedure in the cloak and suit industry was not outlined in such detail, as may be seen from the agreement, printed in full in Appendix.

An employee discharged before he had worked four months for his employer, if his discharge was found to be "unfair, arbitrary, or oppressive," had a right either to reinstatement or to a money payment fixed by the reviewing body; the choice between the two methods of redress being left to the employer. If he had been employed more than four months, the redress was the same, except that the Impartial Chairman rather than the employer had the right to choose which method should be applied. No discharge whatever was to be permitted for union activity in the case of a member of a Price Committee. The size of the Price Committees was limited.

This provision, if fairly carried out, of course goes a long way towards settlement of the discharge issue in favor of the union. It is one of the most remarkable instances on record of the tendency towards diminishing control over production exercised by the employer. Under it the old "right of discharge," so bitterly defended as a fundamental necessity, is punctured. It must be noted, however, that the provision does not establish the right of the worker to a job. There may still be contention about what is "unfair, arbitrary, or oppressive." And far greater measure of control over the industry than this must be achieved before the union can abolish seasonal fluctuations, which are at bottom responsible for most of the discharges. The provision is chiefly valuable in clearing the air, and in tending to demonstrate the more fundamental cause of dissatisfaction, which had previously been obscured by the demand for formal justice.

With this issue settled, shop strikes were forbidden, and it was thought possible to renew part of the machinery of arbitration. A Grievance Board was established, with the Impartial Chairmen holding the deciding vote, to pass on disputes under the agreement. The duration of the agreement, however, was limited.

The Joint Board of Sanitary Control established by the original Protocol was composed of two representatives of the union, two representatives of the manufacturers, and three representatives of the public. Its function was "to establish standards of sanitary conditions to which the manufacturers and the unions are committed, and the manufacturers and the unions obligate themselves to maintain such standards to the best of their ability and to the full extent of their power." Both parties have contributed an equal amount to its support.

The abolishment of home work in the making of women's clothing had at one stroke removed the greatest menace to the workers and the public, but much remained to be done. The tenements still stood, and those who lived in them continued to be abnormally subject to disease. The work itself, requiring intense concentration and a stooping position, produced favorable conditions for tuberculosis and sub-normal vitality. Many of the shops were not in modern buildings; they lacked adequate ventilation, were not fire-proof, had insufficient stairways and fire-escapes, were not kept clean, had insanitary toilet facilities, used dim artificial light or did not protect eyes from the glare of improperly shaded lamps. The fire in the Triangle building, in which young girls were burned to death or were crushed in jumping to the pavement, had shocked the public conscience, but laws and their perfunctory enforcement did not prevent similar fire traps from continuing to house clothing shops.

The industry employed about 60,000 people in about 2,000 separate establishments; new shops were being constantly opened. In 1913 the Protocol in the dress and waist industry added 40,000 workers and 700 factories to those under the supervision of the Board. One of the first inspections (August, 1911)[4] showed 63 shops in buildings with no fire-escapes, 236 with drop-ladders lacking or useless, 153 with entrances to fire-escapes obstructed, 25 with doors locked during working hours, and 1,379 with doors opening in. Although over one-third of the workers were in shops above the sixth floor, all these shops had flimsy wooden partitions, were littered with inflammable materials like cotton and woolen scraps and pine packing boxes; only 128 had automatic sprinklers and but 15 practiced any sort of fire drill. In lighting and sanitation an even worse condition appeared. Medical examination of 800 workers chosen at random (March and April, 1912) showed that only 298 were free from any disease

[4] Third Annual Report of the Joint Board of Sanitary Control, December, 1913.

whatever, and the rest suffered from one or more diseases. Of the 800, 21.7 per cent had anaemia, 21 per cent digestive trouble, 13.7 per cent respiratory diseases, 13.9 per cent nervous diseases, and 1.6 per cent suffered from tuberculosis. This does not by any means exhaust the list.

Improvement of these conditions could result only from the co-operation of those immediately concerned. Here, if anywhere, an effective community of interest existed. The Joint Board of Sanitary Control went to work with admirable system and energy, sometimes relying on existing law, and sometimes setting up its own standards in matters which the law did not touch. Its constant vigilance and its pressure upon the backward employers, heartily supported both by the union and the better elements of the employers' association, succeeded in reducing hazards to life and health. The direct and easily aroused interest of the public in these affairs, not obviously connected with the industrial struggle, helped the work to be effective. Of course, any such agency can do little more than mitigate the worst evils necessarily incident to overcrowding in a great city.

In addition to inspection and encouragement of better conditions, the Board conducts educational work of preventive nature in safety and sanitation, has established cooperative medical and dental clinics for the workers in the two industries, and has assisted the union in founding a tuberculosis sanatorium. Both dental clinic and sanatorium are supported entirely by the unions. Progress in safety is naturally much easier and more rapid than in the health of the workers.

The best proof of the usefulness of the Board of Sanitary Control is that when the Protocol was abrogated it continued to function with the consent and financial support of both union and employers.

The first important agreement in the manufacture of men's clothing was that reached in Chicago in 1910 by Hart, Schaffner, and Marx and their 6,500 employees. Although in some respects this document is similar to a collective agreement, since the firm, having numerous shops, consented to bargain collectively with its employees, it is not a collective agreement in the sense usual in the clothing industry—that is, an agreement between the union and a group of employers.

The agreement in its original form did not recognize the union, but it established a Board of Arbitration which should have the final word on all disputes during its life, recognized the right of the presentation of grievances through a democratically chosen "fellow-workers," and specified that the employer should establish a labor complaint department to entertain such grievances. It was found that the labor complaint department, representing the disposition of the firm to adjust disputes from above, did not prove satisfactory to the workers, and that an increasing number of cases was referred to the arbitrators. Many of these cases concerned discrimination and discharge, and could not

COLLECTIVE AGREEMENTS

be decided by people who did not have an intimate technical knowledge of the trade, and so could not pass on questions of efficiency. On April 1, 1912, a Trade Board was therefore established to investigate and attempt to settle disputes before they were referred to the Board of Arbitration. The Trade Board corresponded to the Board of Grievances in the New York Protocol, and like it was composed of an equal number of members from each side. The union members had to be employees of the firm. Unlike the Board of Grievances, however, the Trade Board had an impartial chairman. It was empowered to appoint chief deputies and deputies, corresponding to the chief clerks and deputy clerks in the Protocol machinery.

As in New York, the deputies succeeded in adjusting most of the grievances, and the Trade Board most of the others. Only a few ever came before the arbitrators. As in New York, by far the greater number and the hardest fought of the employees' grievances concerned discharge, and the employer seemed to be most bothered by shop strikes. When, in the spring of 1913, the agreement was about to terminate, prolonged negotiations failed to result in its renewal, and a strike seemed imminent. The union asked for shorter hours and higher wages, but its chief demand was for the closed shop, which it believed was necessary to protect its members against discrimination. There was a feeling among the workers that the small proportion of non-union employees not only profited by the gains of the union without sharing in its burdens, but were favored by the company in distributing work or cutting down the force in the slack seasons. At the last moment peace was preserved by the adoption of the preferential union shop. The right of review of discharges by the Trade Board was granted. The powers of the Board of Arbitration were enlarged so that it might adjust wages. With these and some minor additions, the agreement was renewed for three years.

The rules for the application of union preference were carefully formulated in detail, to minimize disputes. Later the company, wishing to eliminate the discharge grievance if possible, worked out an admirable technique in the matter. Foremen were not allowed to discharge, but after several warnings they might suspend. Discharge could come only from the labor complaint department. The result was that this means of discipline was exercised sparingly. Only 21 per cent of the employees suspended were discharged, and of these over half were reinstated by the Trade Board on review.

The comparative success of the Hart, Schaffner, and Marx agreements in avoiding general strikes is due to a number of factors. Here the union was dealing with one firm engaged in quantity production, making a good quality of clothing, and having a high standing in the trade. Its product was assured a relatively steady sale through advertising. The employer was therefore able to maintain conditions constantly a little in advance of those ruling throughout the industry, and to eliminate many of the inequalities which cause trouble when the industry as a whole is considered. The full force of seasonal fluctuations was not felt in his shops. Furthermore, he was wise enough to yield point after point as the union gained strength and consciousness of its desires, so that the equilibrium of power between the organized workers and the employer was constantly expressed in their formal relations. In a small degree and to a limited extent, the conditions in these shops indicate what might be the conditions throughout the entire industry, if some force could control and regulate it efficiently. To say this is far from saying, however, that there is no fundamental opposition of interest in the shops concerned, and that a point may not sometime be reached when this opposition will assume precedence over the effective community of interest which has been organized and in force since 1910.

The agreements in the clothing industry were among the first to recognize in theory that the public has a legitimate interest in adjusting disputes. To their boards such distinguished "representatives of the public" as Justice Louis D. Brandeis of the Supreme Court, United States District Judge Julian W. Mack, and Rabbi Judah L. Magnes have been called. Such men have given conscientious and valuable service. Yet after all it is little more than a matter of form to call them representatives of the public in anything like the sense in which the other participants are representatives of employer and employee. "The public" is still a vague and unanalyzed term. It may mean the people in their capacity of consumer, or the community in its exercise of police power for the general good, or the middle classes as distinguished from organized labor and organized capital. No representative of the public in any specific sense can be added to arbitration boards until organized consumers, the state, or some other functional body elects them to safeguard specific interests. The "representatives of the public" who have previously been appointed are rather men selected as impartial chairmen, chosen on account of their reputation, authority, probity, and wisdom.

In New York the Amalgamated and the manufacturers of men's clothing for several years have had no formal agreement. During the war, the War Department established a Board of Standards, and later an Administrator for army clothing, who adjusted disputes where government orders were involved. A strike broke out late in 1918, and was finally submitted to the arbitration of an "Advisory Board" consisting of experts in industrial relations. This board granted the 44-hour week and wage increases, recommending that the concessions be applied throughout the country. It later submitted supplementary reports,[5] based on the Hart, Schaffner, and Marx experience, and advised the appointment of a labor manager for the employers in the New York market, and an impartial chairman for the review of discharges and the settle-

[5] See Appendix.

ment of other disputes. The aim was not to write a formal agreement, but to build a basis on which the law of the industry could grow by decisions of the impartial chairman, just as public law grows by successive decisions of the courts. It should be noted that the absence of a formal agreement allows the question of wages and hours, as well as other issues, to be brought up at any time, rather than at some date previously set for the expiration of an agreement. This arrangement corresponds more flexibly with the realities of the economic situation.

Subsequently a National Industrial Federation of Clothing Manufacturers was formed by the employers' associations in New York, Chicago, Baltimore, and Rochester, the chief centers of the men's clothing industry. Each association appointed an industrial expert as its labor manager, and the four labor managers were united in a board to work out uniform policies. Finally, in the summer of 1919, a joint industrial council to cover the nation was formed by the National Federation and the Amalgamated union. This council has remained temporarily dormant, but there is a chance that it may be revived.

Whether this ambitious undertaking will lead to permanent industrial peace, as some of its founders hope, remains to be seen, but at least it is an advance in systematic regulation of the industry comparable only with the advance made when the unions ceased dealing with the separate manufacturers in one market, and resorted to collective agreements with an association. It clears the ground for the consideration of some of the larger possibilities, such as the mitigation of seasonal fluctuations through unemployment insurance. It is the first joint Industrial Council, the parties to which are a national association of manufacturers and a national industrial union, to be consummated in the United States.[6] The new experiment in the men's clothing industry is therefore one of the greatest significance.

The latest agreement of the Cap Makers, consummated in July, 1919, has three interesting innovations. One is the provision that the schedule of wages shall be readjusted every six months to meet the changes in the cost of living. This provision was included in a number of awards by the government during the abnormal conditions of the war, in cases where the employer was protected by the fact that he was working on a government contract providing for his reimbursement in the event of his being forced by the award to grant higher wages. Few such provisions, however, have ever before been included in a wage agreement between a union and a manufacturers' association dependent on the open market. A still more remarkable passage reads: "No manufacturer shall give out work to be made

[6] The coal miners and coal operators developed a somewhat similar organization several years ago, but on a basis not recognizing, as does this arrangement, the latest achievements of labor's control in the shop. An Industrial Council in the book and job printing industry includes, on the employees' side, not one industrial union, but several craft organizations typical of the old unionism, and came near being wrecked by a quarrel between conservative officials and radical locals.

for him in non-union shops, or buy goods from such shops. No manufacturer shall sell goods to a concern at a time when there exists a controversy between the Union and the concern." This clause furnishes a suggestion of a new means of extending union control.

The agreements whose operation we have described in some detail are merely typical of others set up in other branches of the industry and in other cities. Most of them have undergone much the same process of development, modified of course by the experience gained in labor management, conciliation and union tactics, and by the peculiar circumstances in each case. In every trade and city in which the clothing unions are now strong, some such agreement exists with a manufacturers' association including the most firmly established and largest producers. Similar agreements with individual independent manufacturers cover the remainder of the industry in question. The tendency is for the manufacturers' associations to extend over an increasing proportion of the industry. They are also acting with greater unanimity throughout the nation. It is quite possible that the next general strike or lockout in the clothing trades may be a national one, and it is even within the range of vision that a strike may cover various branches of the industry at the same time.

CHAPTER VII

PHILOSOPHY, STRUCTURE, AND STRATEGY

THE rapid rise of the unions in the needle trades, contending, as they have, against enormous disadvantages, accounts for the keen interest, both friendly and hostile, which they have aroused in the public and the labor movement. On the one hand they are put forward as shining examples for the rest of organized labor, and on the other they are denounced and persecuted as "Bolsheviki" to be shunned by the "bona-fide" unions. Large employers who for some years have dealt with these organizations praise them in the highest terms and are satisfied with existing relations, notwithstanding the fact that they know many of the members of the unions concerned are in opposition to the whole wage system.[1] Yet there are still leaders of organized labor who believe it their duty to cleanse the movement of the influence of these radical bodies. To the observer both these attitudes, strange as they may seem, must give evidence of the power which the needle-trades unions have developed; to

[1] Ray Stannard Baker in the *Evening Post*, N. Y., of February 18, 1920, gives opinions of employers concerning the labor situation in the clothing industry.

him the primary question would be, not whether they are "good" or "bad," but what sort of thing are they, and wherein lies the source of their success? How were the workers employed in industries with such a chaotic economic structure able to build such strong organizations?

The strength of these unions lies primarily in the type of unionism they have developed—a type which binds their members in a fraternity of ideals, and is based on a sense of solidarity in a tireless struggle towards a new system of society. It is a common consciousness that makes it possible to knit together workers of the most divergent trades and varied standards into a united army, always responsive and ready for concerted action. This spiritual brotherhood, based upon a common aspiration—a thing which the old unionism so badly lacks—made it possible for the needle workers to create more powerful and cohesive organizations than could their employers. The supremacy of organization gives the workers their firm hold in the industry and explains in large measure their achievements. History here has repeated one of its frequent paradoxes. The very weakness and backwardness of the industrial structure in the manufacture of clothing, the very difficulties which the labor organizations had to face, forced them early in their struggle to embrace principles which gave them their ultimate power.

The fundamental differences between the old and the new unionism lie not so much in the form of organization as in the attitude toward the methods and purposes of the labor struggle. The gulf is to be found in ideology rather than in structure. The fact that the old unionism so obstinately clings to the remnants of craft or trade organization, while the new unionism strives towards complete industrialism, is merely the sequence of that difference in attitude which makes the former seek its power in a kind of bargaining partnership with capital, while the latter looks for its strength primarily to the solidarity of the working class, with a resulting disbelief in the ultimate necessity of profit-making capital. The old unionism has no quarrel with the fundamentals of capitalist society. It does not question the right of private property to control production. In any case, it acquiesces in this right; it recognizes the "reasonable" profit and dividends on honest investment. The very conception of the class struggle is barred from its dictionary. Its hostilities are directed merely against "those employers who refuse to understand modern industrial conditions and constant needs for advancement of the working people."[2] It fully and unreservedly endorses the primitive theory of competition as the only reliable incentive of human endeavor and progress.

The old unionism therefore struggles only for the immediate betterment of the condition of the working people, while the new unionism thinks of imme-

[2] This and succeeding quotations on the old unionism are from the testimony of Samuel Gompers, President of the A. F. of L., before the Industrial Relations Commission, May, 1914.

diate improvements merely as a means toward a larger end. The old unionism concentrates all its efforts on here and now, on the problems of today, on those proximate difficulties which vary from trade to trade and from industry to industry. "It works along the line of least resistance," and this line is different according to circumstances. Not merely has it no vision, no announced program, no dream of its own, but it wishes none; more than that, it believes every vision or dream or comprehensive program a serious danger, which may divert the attention of the workers from the struggle for immediate betterment. Though zealously protecting its right to strike as a safeguard against "bad" employers who refuse their workers a voice "in determining the questions affecting the relations between themselves and their employers," the old unionism looks to collective bargaining to bring the sentiments and views of the employers "in entire accord with the organization of the working people." The old unionism appeals to the business or trading consciousness, while the new unionism makes its chief appeal to the desire for ultimate economic emancipation.

The old unionism was not so much the result of plans of leadership as it was the result of adaptation to conditions. Taking the line of least resistance may be repugnant as a social philosophy; it is likely to be, however, the course pursued in the early stages of any human institution. Well considered programs, aims, and methods based on a broad social view, are always of later origin. They come, for the masses, only when the initial progress along the line of least resistance has led to a point where greater freedom of action and choice are possible, or when all lines of resistance reveal so many obstacles that to hew out the highway of a great ideal becomes indispensable for making one's way at all. It would take us too far if we were here to make a complete historical analysis of the old unionism in this country, but a few suggestions might not be amiss.

With inexhaustible resources of free land, with many opportunities to acquire property, with an apparently unlimited political equality, the American working people did not for a long time develop much class-consciousness. The whole attitude of the nation was one of individual "getting on," and this conception of affairs was always sustained by literature, the press, and public education. Early unionism was frequently of a welfare nature. Mutual assistance in need, cultural self-perfection, vague "uplift" common to the whole people without distinction of class or position, were its main characteristics. Political movements of the workers were usually directed toward increasing the opportunities for individual advancement rather than toward improving the status of wage-earners as a whole. The free-soil parties, for instance, were of this nature. When small groups of workers began to combine for strictly economic betterment, their field of activity was naturally confined to the exclusive possessors of skill in a given handicraft. Machinery had not become a widespread substitute for the skilled craftsman, and, in the industries which machinery had conquered, organization was slow. The line of least resistance led to manipulation of demand and supply in the labor markets. The opportunity of improving the conditions of the skilled worker by limiting the supply of labor and eliminating competition within the group was considerable.

The labor market of each trade at this stage was still little influenced by the labor market in other trades. The more skill a trade demands, the less it can depend on a surplus of labor elsewhere. Every effort to minimize competition and so improve bargaining conditions could naturally count on far greater success when limited to a trade than when extended to an entire industry. For practical achievement, for immediate betterment, the craft union was the best form of organization. The methods it worked out were those calculated to create the most favorable conditions in bargaining with employers. Long and strictly regulated apprenticeship, limitations on the admission of new members, undisputed jurisdiction over the workers concerned, detailed regulations for accepting or leaving a job, rules limiting the productivity of the worker, the so-called "permit system," and the union label, were all intended to put craft groups on a better footing when it came to bargaining with their several employers. This was the goal of the craft union; if it attained recognition and the closed shop, it could rest at its ease.

The results accomplished by these methods were in the early stages obvious. The difference between the high status of the skilled and organized workers and the misery of the unskilled and unorganized was so striking that there was no doubt that the craft union "delivered the goods" to those whom it was formed to serve. This led to the further strengthening of the craft union, and to a large measure of complacency. The result of early necessity was, in the minds of leaders and of many working people themselves, converted into a principle. The program of no program, the policy of no policy, and the philosophy of no philosophy, were themselves transmuted into a set of eternal and ideal doctrines. Even long after industrial conditions had radically changed, after craftsmen had been almost all replaced by machinery, after competition itself ceased to be such an important factor and the lines of demarcation between trades had become most vague, after, in the natural course of development, the trades union had supplanted the craft union, and even the industrial union—such as the United Mine Workers—had come into existence within the fold of the American Federation of Labor, this ideology still retained its firm hold upon the official labor movement. The old unionism is distinguished now not by its structure, but rather by a lingering craft interpretation of life, and by a narrow attitude toward the aims and tasks of the labor movement.

PHILOSOPHY, STRUCTURE, STRATEGY

Entirely different conditions surrounded the growth of the labor movement in the needle trades. The distribution of free land had ceased to be such a strong influence by the 'eighties, when these industries absorbed the immigrant hordes—and the Jews were not accustomed to living on the land in any case. The immigrant was handicapped in experimenting, in pioneering, and in advancing his commercial fortunes, by his lack of knowledge of the language and customs of the country. Even the apparent political equality did not embrace him for several years after his arrival, and then only as the result of exceptional effort on his part. Our system of public education and press had little or no influence on him. While the intolerable conditions of work in the clothing shops and the low wages barred the great masses from the wider aspects of life, there was from the beginning a considerable nucleus of cultivated socialist intellectuals who had through force of circumstances become manual workers, and who naturally took the lead in every effort towards organization.

A far more important factor, however, was the utter impossibility of accomplishing results by following the policies established by the American labor movement. Competition in the labor markets of the needle trades, at least in the formative period of the unions, could not be limited. The flood of immigration increased every year, and most of the operations did not demand much skill. With the single exception of the cutters, the period of apprenticeship necessary for acquiring average ability in the needle trades is too short to create much of a barrier around the crafts. It is easy to pass from any one of the trades to another. The conditions in any one of the trades affect too directly those of all others to permit separatism.

The cutters, who were the first to organize, did pass through a development similar in some respects to that of the general labor movement. At an early period, when the passage from the cutting craft to the employing class was somewhat easier, they practiced the welfare type of unionism, with benefits, vague idealism, ceremonials, etc. Later they had craft locals, businesslike, conservative, and aloof. Even after the internationals were formed they retained a certain separatism within the organization, considering themselves a sort of aristocracy. As the large unions grew, however, they became more and more dependent on the majority of their fellows. Recent innovations in cutting machinery, which eliminate some of the skill of the old handicraftsman, hastened the process. But perhaps what had more effect than anything else was that in some cases they were actually outdistanced in wages and conditions by other crafts who whole-heartedly accepted the new unionism from the beginning. The cutters now have little particularism.

The large number of small and transitory firms, the keen competition among them on the one hand, and among the workers on the other, and the highly seasonal character of the industry, made all conditions so unstable and fluctuating that it seemed impossible for most of the workers to hope for material improvement without abolishing the capitalist régime. The evils of competition were so apparent and abhorrent that the workers could not think of it as a valuable incentive to human endeavor and progress. The business-like method of the old unionism,—entrenching in the separate crafts, making a gain here and there, and extending the organization bit by bit,—was evidently inapplicable under these conditions. A strike in a single prosperous shop or group of shops could bring only ephemeral gains. The proprietor of the struck shop would transfer his work to outside sub-manufacturers or contractors, or would entirely reorganize his establishment a few blocks away, with a new staff. Concessions granted at the height of the season would be taken away, often with interest, as soon as the slack season set in. While in the general labor movement partial gains occurred before large organization, the process in the needle trades was the reverse. Almost a complete organization had to be accomplished before any lasting improvement could be brought about. Organizers who held out promises of immediate betterments through partial action could not arouse the interest of the workers after many years of hopeless struggle. The labor movement in these industries had to build its organized strength upon a class consciousness looking towards complete economic emancipation.

The creation of this consciousness and hope was,

however, a Herculean task. It took decades of incessant agitation and education to coalesce the human atoms scattered over such an endless number and variety of shops into a solid, living organism. During these decades the union were growing in potentiality, in the common consciousness of the workers, rather than in tangible form and achievement. To the outsider the needle workers seemed unorganizable; even the insiders, the group of devoted leaders, were ready to despair of their own ability to accomplish results. The leadership of the old unionism seemed to be infinitely more successful. It was this appearance which, at the first convention of the United Garment Workers in 1891, led the radical delegates, imbued though they were with the principles of the new unionism, to elect as officers a group of conservative unionists, and to affiliate immediately with the American Federation of Labor, which was in bitter opposition to socialism.

But this attempt to take a leaf out of the book of old unionism has now shown conclusively how ill adapted its methods are to the clothing industry. The failure of the United Garment Workers is not chiefly a failure of persons, it is a failure of method. As soon as this method changed, as soon as the majority of the members came over to the new Amalgamated Clothing Workers, it became possible to create an almost one-hundred per cent organization in the same men's clothing industry in which the United Garment Workers never succeeded in gaining a firm foothold.

When the preliminary process of agitation and propaganda was at last completed, when a common consciousness had become rooted in the minds of the working people, a single stroke was enough to give the potential organizations tangible shape, and to endow them with a deeper solidarity and a firmer control over their members and industries than the old unionism could ever attain. This explains their dramatic appearance on our social surface and their sudden success. The appeal to organize for immediate betterment failed not merely to bring any organization but also to achieve any betterment. The appeal to organize for the ultimate emancipation of the working class, disregarding immediate advantages, brought about not merely an almost complete organization, but also very substantial betterments.

The philosophy of the new unionism, like every vital philosophy, was not born complete, and is being enriched continually. It does not exist in a formal way even in the minds of the working people adhering to the organizations that exemplify it. It will be found rather as a mental attitude, an imperfectly expressed interpretation of events. Yet a movement based primarily on the conscious views of its adherents, as the new unionism is, was bound to attempt at an early period to formulate its philosophy as concisely as possible. As previously stated, the first convention of the United Garment Workers adopted a radical constitution, declaring for the recognition of the socialist newspapers, the *Arbeiter Zeitung,* the *People,* and the *Volks Zeitung,* as the official organs of the union, and for agitation among its membership in favor of participating in the political activities of the socialists. Of course the action of the officers quickly made these provisions dead letters. The next oldest international in the needle trades, the United Cloth Hat and Cap Makers, formulated its social creed in the following preamble to its constitution:

"Recognizing the fact that the world is divided into two classes, the class that produces all wealth—the working class—and the class that owns and controls the means of production—the capitalist class;

"Recognizing the fact that the concentration of wealth and power in the hand of the capitalist class is the cause of the workingmen's economic oppression; and

"Recognizing the fact that only through organization and by united effort can the workers secure their right to enjoy the wealth created by their labor;

"Therefore, we, the workers of the Hat and Cap Trade, have formed this organization under the name of the UNITED CLOTH HAT AND CAP MAKERS OF NORTH AMERICA, in order to improve our conditions and secure by united action our due share of the products of our labor; to establish a shorter work day; to elevate our moral and intellectual standard and develop our class consciousness by means of propaganda and the press; to cooperate with the national and universal labor movement for the final emancipation of the wage earner and for the establishment of the Cooperative Commonwealth."

The preamble to the constitution of the International Ladies' Garment Workers Union, while of the same nature, defines more clearly the method of attaining the final emancipation of the wage-earner. It announces as its aim, "to organize industrially into a class-conscious trade union" in order "to bring about a system of society wherein the workers shall receive the full value of their product." In the above preambles all the elements of the new unionism were already contained. Further development, however, was necessary to expand these elements into a complete system. These preambles are vague with regard to the method in which the "Cooperative Commonwealth" or the "system of society wherein the workers shall receive the full value of their product" is to be brought about. The Cap Makers see this method as cooperation with the national and universal labor movement; the Ladies' Garment Workers refer to "cooperation with workers in other industries," but from the context it appears that they put much more weight upon political representation of the workers "on the various legislative bodies by representatives of the political party whose aim is the abolition of the capitalist system."

The constitution of the Amalgamated Clothing Workers, as the latest in the series and also as one created in direct opposition to the old unionism, gives a fuller and more definite expression of faith. Says the preamble:

"The economic organization of Labor has been called into existence by the capitalist system of production, under which the division between the ruling class and the ruled class is based upon the ownership of the means of production. The class owning those means is the one that is ruling, the class that possesses nothing but its labor power, which is always on the market as a commodity, is the one that is being ruled.

"A constant and unceasing struggle is being waged between these two classes.

"In this struggle the economic organization of Labor, the union, is a natural weapon of offense and defense in the hands of the working class.

"But in order to be efficient, and effectively serve its purpose, the union must in its structure correspond to the prevailing system of the organization of industry.

"Modern industrial methods are very rapidly wiping out the old craft demarcations, and the resultant conditions dictate the organization of Labor along industrial lines.

"The history of the Class Struggle in this country for the past two decades amply testifies to the ineffectiveness of the form, methods and spirit of craft unionism. It also shows how dearly the working class has paid for its failure to keep apace with industrial development.

"The working class must accept the principles of Industrial Unionism or it is doomed to impotence.

"The same forces that have been making for Industrial Unionism are likewise making for a closer inter-industrial alliance of the working class.

"The industrial and inter-industrial organization, built upon the solid rock of clear knowledge and class consciousness, will put the organized working class in actual control of the system of production, and the working class will then be ready to take possession of it."

The philosophy of the new unionism has molded the structure, and still more, the strategy of these organizations. Deriving their strength from the class consciousness of their membership, they must depend upon intelligent appreciation by the rank and file of their problems and policies. It is necessary that every member shall identify himself with the organization, shall think of it as an embodiment of his own aspirations and will. The leadership in these organizations, regardless of the manner of election, must therefore be of a somewhat different nature from the leadership in the old unionism. This difference cannot be adequately expressed in any constitutional provisions with regard either to the selection or the authority of the officers. The methods of election in the unions of clothing workers are not uniform and do not differ materially from those practiced by the organizations of the business type. The general officers of the Ladies' Garment Workers and the Hat and Cap Makers are elected by their biennial conventions; the general officers of the Amalgamated Clothing Workers are nominated by their biennial conventions and elected by a referendum vote of the membership. The same methods are employed by the old unionism. The fundamental difference lies rather in the attitude of the leadership toward the rank and file and of the rank and file toward the leadership.

The old unionist is inclined to think of the union as a business concern. His attitude toward it is similar to the attitude of a stockholder toward a corporation. As long as the directors of a corporation keep it solvent, as long as dividends are paid regularly, the stockholders have no further interest in the affairs of the concern and are ready to leave it entirely in the hands of the management. They do not want to be bothered by detailed consideration of methods or policies. Results are all they ask; the rest they are ready and anxious to forget. On the other hand, the directors hold themselves accountable to the stockholders only for immediate results; they are likely to consider it an intrusion if any but the large stockholders attempt to interfere in the policies of the business.

The business consideration is to the new unionist only secondary; he is mainly interested in the organization itself as the expression of his aspiration to control the industrial system. The immediate gains are, both to the members and the leaders, a by-product derived in the process of work on the main task, the preparation of the workers for actual control of production. This attitude makes methods and policies far more important than immediate results accomplished. Consciously and unconsciously, the rank and file imbued with the spirit of the new unionism will always look behind immediate advantage to that higher goal to which they have dedicated their efforts. Their revolt against being arbitrarily ruled was their original motive for organization, and they cannot be expected to submit long to boss-rule in their own communities. Neither will they be over-anxious to give undue authority to their representatives.

The leadership in these unions therefore has more the character of spiritual guidance in a voluntary fraternity somewhat like the church communities at the beginnings of Christianity, than of authoritative control even by democratic rulers. The rank and file look to their leadership for enlightenment, advice, and counsel, but they consider the will of the people as the superior wisdom and expect their leaders to abide by it. The leaders see the mainspring of power of the organization in the mass volition of the membership. They are therefore extremely reluctant to use arbitrarily their authority or discretion. To undertake any important step, however advisable, before the rank and file has come to will that step would be to undermine the only power that could make it successful. It cannot be said that the legal safeguards against abuse of authority are much stricter than in the more advanced organizations of the old type. But there is the safeguard of an always alert public opinion, of mutual confidence and respect, of a common ideal to serve as a criterion in the shaping of policies.

The structure of these organizations cannot be fully outlined on the basis of written constitutions or by-laws; it contains numerous extra-legal institutions which play a decisive part in their life. Furthermore, the practices are not rigidly fixed. Regarding the processes of society themselves as constantly in flux, the unions readily change their practices to meet changed conditions. But in all changes the supreme consideration is to make it possible for the organization to have behind its every action the comprehension and resolution of the membership.

The supreme authority in each of the clothing unions is concentrated in the industrial unit, representing the entire membership in the United States and Canada. The will of the membership as a whole constitutionally finds its expression in the periodic convention, in the General Executive Board and General Officers who administer the affairs of the union between conventions, and in the Referendum, which may be invoked at any time. As a matter of established practice, the general will also finds expression in the General Membership Mass Meeting, and in the Joint Meeting of all Local Union Executive Boards of any given locality.

Next in authority to the industrial unit are the trade units of the various localities, which constitutionally are governed by the several Joint Boards or Councils—for instance, the Amalgamated New York Joint Board of Men's Clothing. Extra-legally, the trade unit is much influenced by meetings of the Shop Chairmen of the locality and trade. The Joint Boards are made up of delegates from Local Unions, whereas the Shop Chairmen represent the workers by shops, and are in constant touch with the rank and file at their places of work.

The smallest constitutional unit is the Local Union; this subdivision is merely for administrative purposes and as a rule wields virtually no authority in control of industrial action. Strikes, for instance, are usually called by Joint Boards rather than by Locals. Because of its purely administrative functions the composition of the local varies widely.

Extra-legally, the smallest unit is the shop, with its shop committee or price committee and shop chairman, elected by the members employed in a given manufacturing plant or subdivision of such plant. This is a most important functional division in the industrial activities of the union.

In order to give a clear idea of this administrative machinery, it is necessary to describe it in more detail, beginning with the smaller units and working up to the main one.

The local union consists as a rule of the workers at a single craft or operation, such as cutters, operators, pressers, basters, tailors, blockers, sizers, trimmers, finishers, muff-bed makers, hat frame makers, etc. Sometimes it consists of workers of different crafts but of the same nationality. Such, for instance, is Local 280 of the Amalgamated, consisting of Italian workers of all crafts in the pants trade, or Local 43, consisting of Jewish operators, finishers, and pressesrs living in Brooklyn. There is now a tendency, in distinct sections of a large city or in smaller towns where the membership is not too large, to make the local union coterminous with the locality irrespective of craft. A similar principle is applied to minority nationality groups such as Lithuanians, Italians, Slovenians, Russians, and Poles.

The nature of administrative functions differs among locals, even within the same organization. The special history of the craft, its position in the trade or industry, the extent of its organization, are responsible for these differences. There are, however, some functions that are common to all locals. The local is the unit of representation in the general convention, the number of delegates to which it is entitled depending on its size. Another common function is the election of delegates to the Joint Board. Practically all locals in the International Ladies' Garment Workers, and some in the other unions, collect the per capita tax from the members, see that they remain in good standing, serve as employment agencies for manufacturers and members, and give consideration to grievances of members which are later submitted to the Joint Board for action. The locals give preliminary consideration to trade problems with the purpose of bringing in recommendations to the Joint Board, and serve as voting units for all decisions of the Joint Board submitted to the membership for ratification. They discuss and decide any disputes among their members. Finally, perhaps the main function of the local is the cultivation of good will and good fellowship among the members. It is the social force of cohesion and propaganda in the union. This accounts in large measure for the varied forms which the locals take.

The government of the local is in the hands of the meeting, the local executive board, and the local officials. The meeting is the supreme authority, subject only to referendum of the membership. There are no fixed rules as to the use of the referendum, but it is usually ordered only by a vote of the meeting. Many locals elect their executive boards and officials by this means; no local will decide a question effecting vitally its whole membership—such as the raising of dues—without a referendum.

The local executive board, consisting of no less than five members, is the governing body of the local between meetings. It is usually elected for a term of from six to twelve months. The officials are subject to the supervision of the executive board. The number and kind of officials depends upon the size and nature of the local. The chairman of the executive board, sometimes called also the president of the local, is an unpaid officer but an influential one. The recording secretary is usually paid a nominal sum and his duty is to keep the minutes of local and board meetings; but he is also an influential officer. In the larger locals there is a paid secretary, devoting all his time to the work. The one paid officer in all locals is the financial secretary. He is charged with the collection of dues, initiation fees, and assessments, whenever this duty is left to the local, and with the paying of bills and guarding the funds unless, as in the case of some large locals, responsibility for the account is placed with a special unpaid treasurer. Some of the larger locals, including virtually all those in the Ladies' Garment Workers, also have paid managers. The duties of the manager are not clearly defined. He has a general supervision over the office staff, and serves as a link between the general office or the Joint Board and the membership of his local. He also exercises a sort of moral leadership and guidance. This office is now becoming obsolete.

The next larger unit, the local trade or sub-industry, is governed by the Joint Board, also known as the Joint Council or District Council. There are, however, cases where the functions of the trade unit are exercised by a local union. Such a case is Local 25 of the International Ladies' Garment Workers, which represents the whole New York dress and waist making trade, including all the crafts with the single exception of the cutters. Other cases are the industrial locals previously mentioned, such as Local 7 of the United Cloth Hat and Cap Makers, a Boston unit which embraces all the crafts, including the cutters. There are many such cases in the Ladies' Garment Workers, because this industry is divided into so many distinct trades, each with a comparatively small number of employees.

In New York City, the largest center of the women's clothing industry, the International Ladies' Garment Workers has nine trade units. The Cloakmakers Joint Board, which embraces ten locals, is the largest and oldest, having a total membership of over 40,000. The second is Local 25, with a membership of well over 25,000. The cause for the growth of such a large local without subdivisions lies in its dramatic history. The local began with a small nucleus, and when it called its first big strike in 1909, it did not expect that nearly the entire trade would join it. Since then its activity and prestige have

PHILOSOPHY, STRUCTURE, STRATEGY 179

tended to keep it together. Now, however, it has become so large as to be a little unwieldy, and subdivision by race and craft is beginning, though control of industrial action is left as usual in the hands of the trade unit. At the end of 1919 an Italian branch know as Local 89 of Ladies Waist and Dress Makers was created. There is also a movement to make subdivisions for drapers, finishers, tuckers, hemstitchers, and pressers. The introduction of new machinery bringing with it increased specialization strengthens this tendency. The other trade units are, respectively, Local 62, White Goods Workers, Local 6, Embroidery Workers on machine embroidery, Local 66, Bonnaz Embroidery Workers on fancy embroidery, Local 41, House Dress, Kimono and Bath Robe Workers, Local 45, Petticoat Workers, a newly organized trade, Local 50, Children's Dress Makers, and finally, Local 44, a nucleus for Corset Workers.[3]

The United Cloth Hat and Cap Makers have in New York two trade units, the Joint Council of the Cap Makers, with a membership of over 5,000, and the Joint Board of the Ladies' Straw Hat and Millinery Workers, with a membership of about 7,000.

The International Fur Workers Union has three trade units, the New York Fur Workers Joint Board, with 4 locals aggregating 8,000 members, the Fur Cap and Trimming Workers Board with 4 locals

[3] The corset workers have only recently been organized. The strongest locals are in Bridgeport, Conn., Local 33, consisting of all crafts except cutters, and 34, the cutters.

ing secretary. In the Amalgamated Clothing Workers, the Joint Board elects from its own number a Board of Directors consisting of fourteen members, as an executive committee with authority to act between meetings and with the duty of giving preliminary consideration to every important question and bringing in a report with recommendations to the Joint Board. The number and kind of paid officers vary with the size of the respective Boards and the business they have to attend to. In most cases the Joint Board has a General Manager, a Secretary-Treasurer, District Managers or Trade Managers, Assistant Managers, and as many Business Agents as may be necessary. The International Ladies' Garment Workers Joint Board also has a Recording Secretary.

The General Manager is elected either by the Joint Board (Ladies' Garment Workers, Furriers) or by a referendum vote of the membership (Amalgamated). Nominations in the latter case are made by the local unions, every local being entitled to nominate one candidate by majority vote. The District Managers of the Ladies' Garment Workers are appointed by the Joint Board from among the Business Agents. The Trade Managers exist only in the Amalgamated, on account of the special structure of the men's clothing industry. It is subdivided into three sections: the making of coats, pants, and vests, which are produced as a rule in separate shops. These divisions are highly specialized, and an operator or presser in one cannot easily be replaced

PHILOSOPHY, STRUCTURE, STRATEGY

by a worker of the same craft in another. Each of these three subtrades therefore has an advisory joint board, which has no authority, but gives special consideration to the needs of the trade and brings in reports and recommendations to the Joint Board of Men's Clothing. Each advisory board has it Trade Manager, elected by a referendum vote of the members concerned. The Trade Managers follow closely the development of their trades, and serve as links between the General Manager of the Joint Board and the respective subdivisions. The Italian locals also have an advisory joint board of their own, which has an Assistant Manager, but no Manager. The Assistant Managers in the other boards are appointed by the Manager with the approval of the Board of Directors.

The Business Agents perform many duties, but are chiefly used as emissaries of the Joint Board in dealing with individual manufacturers, in settling minor disputes, and in seeing that agreements are carried out. If trouble arises in any shop which cannot be settled without reference to the Joint Board, the Business Agent is at once called in. The system of selecting the Business Agents varies. In the Ladies' Garment Workers they used to be nominated by locals and elected by general ballot, each local being entitled to a quota of Business Agents depending on its size. This process depended too much on electioneering and resulted frequently in the choice of unqualified candidates, since the members as a whole had little knowledge of the long list of names submitted. Now, after the quotas of Business Agents for the several locals have been apportioned, an announcement is issued by the Joint Board that all who feel themselves qualified for the office shall make applications. A sort of civil service examination is then held, the examining board consisting of a committee from the Joint Board, with members invited from among prominent persons in the labor movement. Those receiving the highest marks are appointed, provided, however, that the quotas from the several locals are properly filled. The practice in the Amalgamated Clothing Workers is similar, but in this case all candidates who receive a passing mark are submitted to referendum vote of the locals in the respective trades, the trades voting separately. In the other unions, one or the other of these two systems, with slight modifications, is used.

The taxation systems of the unions are carefully planned. In the Amalgamated Clothing Workers the Joint Board collects all the dues through the central office. Out of the 35c. weekly per capita, the Board retains 17½c. pays 12½c. to the General Office, and 5c. to the local union. A similar procedure obtains in the Furriers Union. In the United Cloth Hat and Cap Makers, the local unions collect the dues—30c. per week—and pass on to the Joint Board 5c., to the Joint Council 8c., and to the General Office 12c. There is a movement here to substitute the method of the Amalgamated. The International Ladies' Garment Workers have an entirely different system. At

PHILOSOPHY, STRUCTURE, STRATEGY

the beginning of each six-months' period, the Joint Board makes up a budget of expenditures. A revolving fund is then created to cover the expenses of one month. Each local contributes its share to this fund in proportion to its membership. At the end of the month a statement of actual expenditures is made up and the total sum divided proportionally among the locals. Bills are sent to the locals for their respective shares. This revolving fund at present is $25,000; the per capita which the Joint Board thus receives amounts to about 11c. per week; besides this, the locals pay 6c. a week to the General Office, and retain the remainder of the dues themselves. The local unions, of course, do not need for current expenses all the money in their treasuries; the greater part of it goes toward building up reserve and defense funds to be used in case of a strike. In an emergency the locals supply the Joint Board with proportional contributions.

The extra-legal shop committees and shop chairmen are highly important factors in the trade units. The shop chairman is an unpaid official elected by all the workers of a shop out of their own number, irrespective of their crafts. In the very big shops, separate crafts may have chairmen of their own, but there is always a general chairman for the entire shop. The shop committee consists of several workers elected to act with the chairman. Where the crafts have chairmen of their own, these act as members of the committee. Whenever a dispute arises in a shop, it must be handled first by the shop chairman and committee. The collective agreements usually provide for this preliminary negotiation. If a settlement is arrived at with the employer on the spot, it is virtually final, though the members have the right of appeal to the executive board of their local and through it to the Joint Board, which may reopen the issue in the way prescribed in the agreement. In the few shops still under a piece-work system, the shop chairman and shop committee also negotiate about prices.

But the shop chairmen perform a far more important function as the direct channel between the organization and the rank and file. They are the immediate guardians of the spiritual and material assets of the organization. According to established practice, there are a thousand and one duties which they must perform. The shop chairman must see to it that every union member in the shop remains in good standing, and that the general provisions of the collective agreement are observed. He must see that the members pay their assessments. Whenever an appeal is made to the membership for contributions, either to assist another division of the same organization or another union during a strike, or to support some enterprise of the labor movement, such as the battle for civil liberties or the defense of the ousted Socialist Assemblymen at Albany, the shop chairman impresses on the workers the importance of the cause and makes the collection. He reports on all important developments in the trade. He secures the correct names and addresses for the mailing list of the official journal. Whenever an important movement is inaugurated by the union, the shop chairmen explain it, help create a sentiment for it, and smooth over the difficulties that may be in the way. Joint Boards seldom undertake a large project without launching it first at a meeting of shop chairmen, and securing their adherence to it. Whether it be a plan for change from piece to week work, a proposed increase in the per capita tax, preparations for a general strike, or an educational campaign, the shop chairmen will be consulted before a decision is arrived at.

The advantages of this extensive use of the shop unit in place of the local union are obvious, especially for a democratic and active organization. The shop chairmen are in contact with the members at their places of work; they see all the members every day. They do not have to rely on the minority who attend meetings. Their point of view is that of the worker at his job, the worker in production. They furnish a continuous means of communication which can be instantly invoked. The fact that their growing function has not entirely eliminated the necessity of the local is due partly to tradition, partly to the social and racial elements involved, and partly, in the strictly clothing trades, to the extreme impermanence of the small establishments and the fluidity of labor. The local union must be retained as a permanent nucleus. It is interesting to note, by the way, that the use of shop chairmen had already become established in the American clothing unions long before the shop steward movement arose in England during the war.

The General Officers of the unions are a General President and a General Secretary or Secretary-Treasurer, both full-time, salaried officials. Sometimes there is also a General Treasurer, but he is unpaid, his duties are small, and his position is not far different from that of any General Executive Board Member. The main duties of the General President are assisting in the adjustment of important disputes between workers and employers, adjusting differences between local unions, presiding over meetings of the General Executive Board, and directing all organizing work. The General Secretary conducts the correspondence of the organization, is the guardian of the seal, documents, papers, labels; he keeps account of all financial transactions and pays bills as authorized either by the constitution or the General Executive Board. Both officers are in practice entrusted with the main responsibility for guidance of the organization. They submit their reports to the Convention, and in the interim to the General Executive Board.

Between Conventions, the General Executive Board is the supreme authority. It consists of the General Officers and a number of other members elected by thé same process.[4] It decides all points

---

[4] The General Executive Board members of the International Ladies' Garment Workers, besides the President and Secretary, are called Vice Presidents: there are thirteen of these, of whom seven must be resident in New York City. The Hat and Cap Makers have fifteen members on the Board, of whom no less than eleven must be residents of New York. The Amalgamated Executive Board has eleven members, with no restrictions on residence.

of law or interpretation of the constitution, all claims, grievances and appeals. It has the power to authorize a general strike, to issue charters to newly organized local unions; it publishes the official journals; it elects trustees for any of the special funds, such as sick benefit and defense funds; and it has general supervision over the affairs of the organization. If a vacancy occurs between conventions, the board nominates candidates for it, who are then submitted to a referendum vote—in the Amalgamated, of the entire membership, and in the Cap and Hat Makers, of the membership of the local unions in the city which is entitled to the seat. No referendum is required in the Ladies' Garment Workers.

The Convention is the highest legislative authority. It consists of delegates elected by the local unions in proportion to the size of average membership for which a per capita tax was paid for a period ranging from six months to two years preceding the Convention. Each local is entitled to at least one delegate, and in the Ladies' Garment Workers, to two delegates; the number of members entitled to additional delegates progressively increases with the increase of the membership of the local. The Amalgamated is an exception to this rule, as it grants the local union an additional delegate for every 300 members above the first hundred. The constitution of the Amalgamated provides that a local of 1,000 members must send to the convention no less than three delegates. In all the other unions each delegate has a single vote regardless of the number of members he represents. In the Amalgamated each delegate is entitled to one vote for every 100 members. The regular conventions of these unions meet biennially in the month of May. At the request of five locals, no two of which shall be in the same state or province, the General Executive Board is obliged to take a referendum on the subject of calling a special convention. A favorable two-thirds or three-fourths vote is necessary for adoption of the proposition. The General Executive Board also has the right on its own initiative to submit such a referendum.

The referendum is required by all these organizations for the passage of any amendment to the constitution which may be adopted by the convention and, in the previously specified cases, for the election of General Officers. It has become the custom for conventions to submit vital questions to a referendum vote.

The joint meetings of all local executive boards is an extra-legal institution invoked in cases where a whole industry is involved, just as shop-chairmen meetings are used when a single trade is involved. On important occasions General Membership Mass Meetings are arranged simultaneously in as many halls as are necessary. They include all members of a certain locality independent of craft or trade, and are called usually at the initiative of a joint executive board meeting. A proposal to declare a general strike, or to impose a general assessment on the membership or to launch a campaign for a 44-hour week or for a week-work system, is the typical subject for such a meeting. Sometimes the entire industry of a certain city is stopped during the working hours and the union members, headed by their shop chairmen, march *en masse* to the previously assigned halls. In such cases, virtually the entire membership is reached. This method is employed in preference to a referendum, or parallel to a referendum, because it has the advantage of giving the worker a chance to deliberate on the question, and to exchange opinions before making up his mind to vote one way or the other.

The strategy employed by these organizations must be interpreted in the light of their philosophy and structure. Both old and new unions, to be sure, employ similar weapons, such as the strike and the collective bargain. Behind this superficial uniformity of method, however, there is a vast difference of emphasis and attitude. The question is not so much what weapons a union uses, as how it uses them, what relative importance it attaches to them, and what strategic positions it regards as secondary and what as primary.

An analysis of the strategy of the new unionism will discover in it two fundamental objectives to which all other policies are subordinated. The first is to organize *all* the workers in the industry; the second is to develop them, through their daily struggles, into a class-conscious labor army, able and ready to assume control of industry. These fundamentals may not always be clear even in the minds of the leaders, but a study of policies will reveal them.

The supreme importance attached to the organization of all the workers in the industry is revealed by the attitude of the new unionism to such questions of policy as the admission of new members, apprenticeship, immigration, the union label, jurisdiction, and formation of employers' associations.

As soon as a union gains control over a trade or any part of it, the selfish instinct of its members under present conditions is naturally to keep the gain to themselves, and to restrict as far as possible, the invasion of their sphere of influence by new workers. Most business unions have high initiation fees, complicated examinations, and other means of making admission difficult. There are cases of successful unions who close their membership books for ten years or more. The clothing unions, however, raise no obstacles against the entry of new members. The constitution of the Hat and Cap Makers definitely provides that no local union shall charge more than $25 for initiation, which shall include all payments to the various funds. The Ladies' Garment Workers cannot charge more than $15 for admission of men and $10 for women. The Amalgamated has had no constitutional limitations, except that the local must receive the approval of the General Executive Board for its initiation fee. A movement lately arose in the Amalgamated in New York to inaugurate high initiation fees, but it was checked at the very start, and the 1920 convention established a legal limit of $10.00. The practice of these unions is even more liberal than their constitution limitations. During general organization campaigns, which occur frequently, members are admitted at a nominal fee, in some cases as low as 50c.

The same difference in policy applies to apprenticeship. The restrictions and regulations which the new unionists enforce with regard to apprentices aim not to bar apprentices from the trade but to prevent their being used by the employer to weaken the organization through exploitation and underpayment. The clothing unions merely insist that no more apprentices shall be admitted than are actually needed by the industry, that they shall receive the same treatment as the organized workers of the trade, and that their work shall be paid for at the full amount of its value under established union standards. The period of apprenticeship must be no longer than necessary, and as soon as it is over, the apprentice must join the union. This agreement is not merely a business arrangement, but is a means of enlisting every new recruit as soon as possible into the real labor army.

The old unionism always combats immigration. The new unionism, however, thinks of capitalist industry as not limited by the boundaries of a nation, and believes that the prospective immigrant remaining in his own country affects the labor market as much in the long run as if he is admitted to our shores. The new unionism never opposes immigration; at several hearings before congressional committees its representatives have demanded that no new restrictions on immigration be imposed.

All the clothing unions have an official union label. In none of them except the United Garment Workers, which typifies the old unionism, is much significance attached to it. The label, distinguishing union-made from non-union goods, is meant as a premium for the unionized shop and a deterrent for the others, by regulating the patronage of union sympathisers. This device stresses indirect protection of the union shops rather than organization of the non-union. The benefits which the members receive from the use of the label sometimes lead to a tendency on the part of the business union actually to refrain from organizing the whole industry.

In disputes about jurisdiction the motives of the two types differ. The old type will look for extension of jurisdiction as a method of increasing the number of jobs for its members, or of adding to the "per-capita" in the treasury. The new unionism, on the other hand, will seek extended jurisdiction primarily as an opportunity of organizing all the workers in an industry, and so extending the economic power of the whole group. The controversy between the United Hatters and the Hat and Cap Makers is an example (see Chapter III). The International Ladies' Garment Workers has made repeated attempts to induce the American Federation of Labor to organize a department to serve all the needle-trades unions, while the United Garment Workers has always stubbornly fought this proposition.

The attitude towards the formation of an employers' association will, with the old unionism, depend primarily upon whether the association is for or against collective bargaining. The attitude of the new unionism in this matter will be determined largely by the question whether the existence of the association will create more or less favorable conditions for the organization of more workers in the industry. In the needle trades, as we have seen, the progress of the unions was hampered by the extreme divergence of conditions in the many shops. Employers' associations furnished a means of exerting a standardizing influence on the trade. In the early stages of the struggle, the unions concerned not merely looked with favor on the formation of such associations, but in some cases actively encouraged it. The association of hat and cap manufacturers was, for instance, brought into being partly through the influence of the young union.

The second of the fundamental strategic policies of the new unionism—the importance it attaches to cultivating the solidarity of the workers and making them ready to assume control of industry—is revealed by its attitude toward mutual insurance, strikes, collective bargaining and agreements, system of payment for work, productivity and sabotage, the general labor movement and independent political action.

Mutual insurance is relegated to the background. In the old unionism large insurance funds are likely to stand in the way of aggressive action, to prevent the enrollment of many new members, and to be a barrier against amalgamation. Only such benefits as are directly related to militant action have a prominent place in the new unionism. The clothing unions pay liberal strike benefits, more liberal than do many organizations of the old type. But the strike benefit is not rigidly fixed in their constitutions, and is not an insurance payment in the ordinary sense, since the entire resources of the union and often of its individual members as well are mobilized in support of strikers once a battle is on. Only one of the unions under consideration has provisions for the payment of sick benefit—the United Cloth Hat and Cap Makers. But here the payment is not made from an isolated fund, though of course a separate book account is maintained. Even with the Cap Makers, participation in this benefit is voluntary, and side by side with many beneficiary members there are many non-beneficiary, who prefer to pay a smaller per capita tax. Now that the bulk of the needle trades have been organized, and the vested interest tends to weaken the organizing zeal, there is a more favorable attitude toward mutual insurance.

There is more in common between the two types of unionism in their attitude toward the strike as a weapon of last resort than to any other practice of unions. Both consider the right to strike vital to

PHILOSOPHY, STRUCTURE, STRATEGY 197

their continued existence, and will zealously guard this right. The old unionism, however, regards the strike as a weapon of sections of the workers against unreasonable employers, and believes that strikes may be altogether avoided against those employers whose views "come in entire accord with the organization of the working people." The new unionism, on the other hand, thinks of the strike not as a weapon of particular employees against particular employers, but as an irrepressible manifestation of the class struggle, and it denies that durable harmonious relations between the employing class and the workers may be expected.

In the actual employment of the strike the old unionism is more ready than the new. The business union will use the strike wherever it may have a chance of bringing immediately desired results. It will permit strikes of one craft in an establishment without the others, thus tying up work for the benefit of a few. It will strike against one or more employers rather than against a whole trade. It will single out the unreasonable from the reasonable. The new unionism as far as possible reserves the strike for a last weapon in clashes over the degree of control of industry. It anxiously avoids guerilla warfare. It seeks decisive issues and movement in masses. It does not permit strikes of single crafts. Not ascribing too much value to immediate betterment, it will strike against the whole body of employers in a trade or industry rather than against individuals or sections. It almost never strikes for wages alone, but places the emphasis on the introduction of better systems of work, shorter hours or greater control. The tendency now is to conserve the strike almost entirely for this latter aim, letting other gains follow incidentally.

Collective bargaining and the collective agreement is to the old unionism an aim in itself—in many cases the highest aim. The new unionism, on the contrary, regards the entire necessity of bargaining as a result of economic oppression. Improved bargaining conditions therefore have the same significance to it as modified autocracy to the real democrat. It uses collective bargaining as a means of eliminating minor disputes so that its strength may be reserved for the main issues, as a means of defining those issues, and as a means of extending and strengthening the organization. The exercise of collective bargaining makes concerted action on the part of employees a habit, and serves to give expression to class solidarity within the frame of the existing order.

The collective agreement is merely the record of the balance of power between employers and employees at a given time. In the old unionism the agreement is often thought of as the end of the struggle, with the new it is an incident in it. The agreement is a sort of political constitution enforced upon autocratic rulers by the people; the real significance of such a constitution depends upon the independent spirit of the people and their readiness to defend their rights. The provisions of a collective agreement have an entirely different meaning in practice according to whether the strength of the union as compared with that of the employers increases or decreases during the life of the agreement.

The collective agreement—strange as it may seem—is more seldom broken by unions adhering to the new philosophy than by those who adopt the old. While the sanctity of contract as such between labor and capital means little to the new unionist, there is no inducement for him to break a contract for trivial reasons. It would be absurd, in his form of strategy, to incur for scattering advantages the danger and expense of the battle which breaking an agreement would involve. Expecting beforehand that changes in the balance of power and in the desires of the workers will take place, he either concludes peace for so short a term that no great development can occur before the contract terminates, or gives it a flexible nature, with machinery for making minor adjustments. The tendency now is to avoid written constitutions altogether. The employers in the clothing industries have themselves become infected with this conception of life as a fluid process which cannot be confined by rigid stipulations.

The old unionist thinks of the agreement as a fixed law whose observance becomes a matter of good faith only. The result is that, influenced as he is bound to be, more by the conditions of his existence than by abstract sanctity of contract, he is led to break it whenever conditions have materially changed or there is a tempting possibility of immediate betterment. The danger of breach of contract by the business union is still further increased because the agreement is more the result of bargaining shrewdness on the part of officials than the real expression of the existing balance of power. Negotiations are frequently carried on and concluded by national officers without the participation of the masses, who therefore do not feel that the contract expresses their own will, and are more inclined to discard it. An inquiry the results of which were published by the New York *World* October 19, 1919, although it revealed many breaches of contract in nearly all other industries, did not show a single agreement broken by the unions in the clothing industries. In justice to the old unionism, it should be stated that this inquiry shows an abnormal state of affairs. Rigid agreements concluded during the recent era of rising prices had far less chance of survival than usual.

The attitude of the business union toward method of payment revolves chiefly about the relation between compensation and effort. That system is favored which gives the greater compensation for the smaller effort. With the new unionism the question is what system will better preserve the vitality of the working class, and will promote common will and action. If payment by the week is preferred to payment by the piece, it is primarily because the former helps to develop solidarity among the workers and makes it necessary for those whose demands on life are highest to seek improvement for their entire group or class.[5]

Opposition to the practice of ca' canny or slacking on the job, as well as toward sabotage in all its forms, is in the old unionism due to the principle of "a fair day's work for a fair day's wage," while the new unionism regards it as an enemy of the class consciousness of the workers and of their readiness to assume control of industry. Inefficient work is an instinctive expression of dissatisfaction and lack of interest, and is in some measure unavoidable under the capitalist system; it can be mitigated only in so far as the worker feels a pride in his job. The new unionism, by laying emphasis on increasing control of the process, strikes at the roots of sabotage, whereas the old unionism, by emphasizing the bargaining process, creates a favorable atmosphere for it even while formally opposing it. Moreover, the new unionism has much stronger reasons to discourage it. Sabotage is a method that must be employed individually rather than by concerted action. It cannot be practised openly and therefore has a harmful influence on the dignity and personality of the worker—a factor of prime concern to the new unionism. It directs the struggle against the individual rather than against the employers as a whole, while the new unionism professes no enmity against the individual and battles merely with the system. Finally, sabotage may undermine the industry itself, and, what is more important, the psychological readiness of the workers to control it.

[5] See Appendix.

Similar motives prompt the new unionism to be far more receptive to improved machinery and management than the old. To the exclusive business union, a device for increasing productivity is merely a threat to replace skill with a mechanical process, and so to rob the craftsman of his monopoly. To the socialist, it may be a valuable contribution to industrial technique, which if put to the right uses will lighten the burden on all the workers. The concern of the new unionist is not so much to prevent the introduction of machinery or better management as to see that they do not become instruments of oppressing the worker, or of diverting to the employer an abnormally increased share in the rewards of his toil. The Amalgamated set a new precedent when at its 1920 convention it voted to establish standards of production.

The new unionism naturally takes a wider interest and a more active part in the life of the labor movement as a whole than does the old. Every battle of a union anywhere it regards as its own battle. During the street-car strike in New York City a few years ago the workers of the needle trades for long weeks faithfully walked to their jobs or used all kinds of unfamiliar conveyances, but until the last refused to have anything to do with cars run by strikebreakers. Hardly a struggle conducted by a union in the country which has needed financial assistance has failed to receive it in generous measure from the clothing workers. The recent strikes of textile workers and steel workers are noteworthy examples

—to the steel strike the needle trades pledged half a million dollars, and before its close had actually contributed as much as any other group of unions in the country, including those who officially called the strike. The same attitude is demonstrated in another way. Thinking of themselves as part of the general labor movement, the clothing unions have remained, as far as they could, within the existing Federation, regardless of their objections to policies of its leaders. This policy is not due chiefly to selfish motives, since the unions of the needle trades have received negligible support from the Federation. The contributions of all the A. F. of L. unions toward the great Cloakmakers' strike in 1910 was not above a few hundred dollars. The desire to remain affiliated with the Federation is purely a sign of loyalty to the working class, and of a belief in the ultimate justice of the cause of labor, no matter what fallacies its officials may temporarily profess.

The old unionism, having no quarrel with the present social order, has no compelling reason to undertake independent political action. In politics as in industry it seeks merely to trade for immediate concessions, which may be wrested by promises and threats from either of the two old parties. The new unionism, opposed as it is not merely to the minor evils of the social order but also to its fundamentals, naturally cannot rely on parties which are themselves expressions of that order and organs of the powers that support it. The new unionism may desire the same minor improvements which the old unionism seeks, but they are not intimately enough related with its cause to determine its politics. The preamble to the constitution of the International Ladies' Garment Workers Union provides for the support of a party whose aim is the abolition of the capitalist system. While the other constitutions do not all have definite provisions to that effect, the practice of the clothing unions is the same. They are always in favor of vigorous independent political action, and they cooperate with the Socialist Party.[6]

It would be impossible to enter into the minor details of strategy, since the interests and activities of the new unions extend to so many fields of human endeavor. It may be said that nothing humane is foreign to them.

[6] The founding of a national Labor Party is striking evidence of the drift of the old unionism toward the new. The natural tendency of the clothing unions, with their feeling for labor solidarity, would be to work for amalgamation between the two working class parties, but before doing so they must give the new movement time to establish itself and prove whether it can be permanent and sincere.

CHAPTER VIII

EDUCATION

THE educational work of the labor organizations in the needle trades, though but a few years old, has already reached a stage where its tendencies can be roughly defined. The extent of these educational efforts, and still more the broad vision which they have revealed, have attracted considerable attention, on the part both of the labor movement and the general public. The 1918 convention of the American Federation of Labor found the subject of sufficient interest to direct the Executive Council to appoint a special committee to investigate the educational system of the International Ladies' Garment Workers Union and other similar schools, with a view of reporting to the 1919 convention whether the methods employed could not be applied generally to the labor movement of the United States and Canada. The numerous articles in the press, and the formation of the Art, Labor and Science Conference with the express purpose of cooperating with these trade unions in education, are indications of the growing interest in this work.

It is generally recognized that, in a sense, every labor union is an educational institution in itself. The elementary principles of democracy, the conception of majority rule, the rudiments of representative government, the significance and practice of the ballot, the first inklings of taxation by the will of the people and the realization of the significance of self-discipline in a democracy, are perhaps nowhere learned in a more direct and immediate way than in a labor union. No amount of school training could ever cultivate that simple understanding of the basic principles and practices of self-government which is naturally acquired by every active member. In addition, the regular trade activities of a labor organization are educational in many other ways. The process of determining the demands which the organization is to present to the manufacturers, the struggle for these demands, the consideration and settlement of grievances and disputes, the practice of mediation, conciliation, and arbitration—all these activities touch upon the fundamentals of economics and sociology, and more directly upon questions concerning management and control of industry. This explains why many a labor man, with only very scant opportunities for a systematic education, has attained such a high degree of knowledge and culture. The educational value of the regular trade activities of labor unions varies, however, with the type and character of the unions.

The broader the principles upon which a labor organization is built, the wider its horizon, the greater the community with which it identifies itself—the greater is its educational value. The union which limits its philosophy to the immediate betterment of its own craft must necessarily provide fewer opportunities for education than the one that considers its work for the immediate betterment of the industry as a mere link in the social process leading towards full industrial and political democracy for the entire people. The member of a craft union can follow the work of his organization without giving much attention to the general economic, social, or political problems of the times. The trade unionist of the old type does not see any close connection between these general conditions and the immediate tasks of his own organization. The situation is entirely different in the needle trade unions. As shown in a previous chapter, the success and very existence of the organizations in these trades depended upon their active adherence to the philosophy of the new unionism. Scattered in trades of an inferior industrial structure, they could draw their organized strength only from the ties of conscious working-class solidarity. With the prospect of immediate betterment seemingly so remote, their appeal to the workers for organization had to be based on the greater promise of the full emancipation of the working class. This fundamental philosophy made it necessary for the unions in the needle trades from the very start to devote considerable attention to subjects with which the average union of the old type never concerned itself. It can be said that, in this sense, the educational work in the needle trades began with their first attempts at organization.

During the early 'eighties, when the first attempts at organization in the needle trades were made, the unions had an ephemeral character. Every year small and transient trade unions sprang up and disappeared before sending forth roots. During this time these unions were rather debating societies than real trade organizations. The members of such unions were often more interested in the theoretical battles between the different philosophical schools fighting for supremacy on the East Side than in their trade activities. The evident futility of their efforts to gain immediate improvements in sweatshop conditions gave abnormal impulse to their hopes of accomplishing this purpose, and more, by means of a general reconstruction of society on the basis of one or another of the philosophies propounded to them. Another contributing factor was the fact that all the early efforts at organization were directed by a comparatively small number of immigrant revolutionary intellectuals. The state of mind of these immigrant intellectuals is described best by one of them in an article written many years later.[2]

These men "suddenly found themselves under the influence of three main schools. The teachers who dominated the three schools were idolized by their followers. One of them was William Frey who taught Positivism and the 'religion of humanity;' another was Felix Adler who preached Ethical Culture; and a third was Johann Moste who taught

[2] Dr. H. Spivack quoted in The History of the Jewish Labor Movement by H. Burgin, 1915.

Anarchism. Eager audiences flocked to all three. But, at the beginning, the teachings of the three were confused in the minds of the youth into an Ethical-Anarchistic-Positivistic hash.''

Debates between the adherents of all these philosophical schools, and especially between socialists and anarchists, were a very frequent occurrence at the union meetings. Many a time the debates were transferred from the local union meetings to the central body, the United Hebrew Trades. A characteristic example of the interest which the workers in the needle trades took in these chiefly abstract discussions is supplied by a debate held in Cooper Union in 1889 on the interesting subject, Whether the workers ought or ought not participate in the movement for an eight-hour day. During all these years numerous societies and clubs for self-education were organized and were working hand in hand with the trade unions. They were, however, as ephemeral and transient as the unions themselves.

An early attempt to create a labor college for systematic education is recorded in 1899, when the so-called Workers' School was organized by Drs. Peskin, I. N. Stone, and A. Ingerman. Systematic courses in economics, natural science, socialism, and allied subjects, were given in this school, which existed for several years, and was reorganized into the Workers' Educational League. Another attempt at systematic education was made by John Deitsch, who in 1901 organized the Jewish Workers League for the purpose of studying industrial problems, economics, and so on. The constitution of this League contained a provision that it must remain entirely non-partisan. When the Rand School of Social Science was established in 1905 it met, to a great extent, the demand for systematic education which by this time was prevalent among the more alert element of the unions in the needle trades, especially those who had succeeded in gaining a satisfactory knowledge of the English language. The Rand School always drew a very considerable percentage of its students from the needle trades.

The first decade of the twentieth century was the time when all the present great organizations of the needle trades were built up; it was the time of rapid constructive trade union progress. But even during this period, when all these industries were raised from the sweatshop to civilized conditions, the interest of the membership in the wider social and economic problems rather increased than decreased. During this decade the unions made repeated attempts to organize educational work of their own. Many local unions appointed educational committees. Lectures at the regular meetings, musicales, etc., were arranged sporadically by many of the large locals. It is also worthy of mention that during this decade the branches of the Workmen's Circle [3] increased their educational activities

[3] The Workmen's Circle is a Jewish fraternal order established in 1900, paying to its members sick, death and consumption benefit, and providing for them many other forms of assistance in time of need or distress. At present it has a membership of 80,000, of which about 75% are workers of the needle trades. The Workmen's Circle does a great deal of educational work through its

which reached an ever growing number of Yiddish-speaking workers.

As soon as the unions in the needle trades were established on a firm foundation, the need for educational work not merely increased, but also changed in character. In the early stages of their history it was upon the necessity of solidarity and organization that their educational efforts were concentrated. The lectures in economics or sociology were an indirect agitation for organization. They were meant primarily to solidify the ranks by a common consciousness which would make possible control over industries which, owing to their inferior structure, presented almost insurpassable difficulties to organization. Even the debates among the different social and philosophic factions struggling for supremacy within these unions were more in the nature of general agitation, limited to first principles and scratching only the surface of the subjects, than a systematic analysis of social and economic phenomena. The main purpose, consciously or unconsciously, was to develop that state of mind which makes possible concerted action upon the part of tens of thousands of loosely organized workers, scattered in thousands of shops with endless variety of working conditions, with no firmly fixed demarcation line between employer and employee, and subject, in addition, to all the miseries of the sweatshop, tene-

---

branches, and since 1910 also through its General Office. Among others, the Workmen's Circle published a number of good popular books in Yiddish on different social and economic subjects, including a text-book on Trade Unionism by Dr. Louis Levine.

ment home-work and all kinds of sub-manufacturing and sub-contracting. By the end of the first decade of the century this task of creating a common consciousness had been fairly well accomplished. The unions in the needle trades succeeded in solidifying their ranks and making concerted action on their part the established rule and practice; they succeeded in gaining a substantial control over their industries. More than that, by virtue of the more highly developed common consciousness they were fairly on the way to catching up with the standards achieved by the general labor movement of this country. The need for primitive education, which was primarily agitation, had lost by this time its urgency and importance. Something more fundamental grew necessary.

The first record of this necessity for fundamental education on a large scale we find in the reports of the proceedings of the 1914 convention of the International Ladies' Garment Workers Union. That convention recognized the need "to dwell particularly upon the more solid and preparatory work of education and not to devote much time to the mere superficial forms of agitation and propaganda which have been the main features of our educational work in the past." The same motive we find in the report of the General Secretary, Max Zuckerman, to the convention of the United Cloth Hat and Cap Makers held in May, 1917. Speaking of the unsatisfactory results of the many educational efforts made by the various local unions at different times, he gives as one of the reasons for this failure "the mistake of merely advocating it as a general proposition instead of arranging a definite system to carry on the educational work." Perhaps the best analysis of the causes necessitating change in the character of the educational work is supplied by a recent editorial (August 22, 1919) in the *Fortschritt,* the official organ of the Amalgamated Clothing Workers of America, of which the General Secretary, Joseph Schlossberg, is the editor. Since the Amalgamated Clothing Workers came into existence later than the other unions of the needle trades, the passage from the primitive education to the more fundamental education arose with them at a later date. Says the editorial:

"Our main power always lay in the fact that we educated the membership on the questions which they had to solve through our organization. . . . This was education on the special tasks as they arose. These tasks have now been accomplished. Today a different education is demanded. We now need such educational work as will explain to our workers the world events, their social position, the true purpose of a labor organization and its task under the present world conditions.

"We have reached a point when education is no less important than the organization itself. We must have it or we cannot continue our work, unless we are satisfied that the Amalgamated shall sink to the level of a reactionary bureaucracy in which the members are mere duespayers and the officials are the organization.

"Our duties grow, and our responsibilities grow: the intelligence and the education of the members must grow together with them, or the Amalgamated will cease to be what it has been until now. . . .

"The burning question before us is: What are we to do in order that our organization may always remain young, fresh, militant and rich in spirit? The answer is, that we must immediately inaugurate efficient educational work among our members."

It took some time for the unions to settle on definite methods. The system is not yet completed. But at this writing it is sufficiently advanced to make fairly certain both its permanency and its form. An analysis of the educational work as at present conducted reveals the following principles underlying it. It is planned so as to be closely connected and interrelated with the usual trade activities of the organizations. Their aspiration is to make the educational and trade activities become two phases of the same movement, completing and helping one another. It aims on the one hand to increase the proportion of the membership which has a thorough understanding of the labor movement and its problems and can carry the burden of the work of the organization, and on the other hand to develop a stronger sentiment of fellowship among the membership at large, to raise the morale in the ranks of the organizations by imbuing them with a deeper devotion to the ideals of the labor movement and a greater readiness to fight for their achievement. It seeks to supply adequate mental food and facilities for a broad cultural life for that element which already craves it, but it still more endeavors to stimulate among the great masses of the rank and file the want for knowledge and culture. The direct connection between the educational and the trade activities is shown by the fact that the former contribute greatly to the raising of the general standard of living of the rank and file, thus increasing its material wants. At the same time the higher level of intelligence makes it possible for the organization to accomplish more easily the task of improving conditions and increasing wages so as to meet the higher standard of living.

The International Ladies' Garment Workers Union was the first organization in the needle trades to begin this systematic educational work. As far as is known, this union was the pioneer in education in the labor movement of America. In accordance with the decision of the convention of 1914 their General Executive Board appointed a special educational committee. This committee naturally first sought to take advantage of the educational institutions which were already existing and active in the needle trades. Arrangements were made with the Rand School for a number of regular courses to be conducted under the joint direction of the International educational committee and the School. History, Theory and Practice of the Labor Movement, Method of Organization, and English were included in this program. A number of systematic lectures and tours, both in English and Yiddish, were arranged by the same committee. A further impetus to this work was given by the Waist and

Dress Makers Union of the city of New York (Local 25), a local of the International, which independently inaugurated, under the direction of Miss Juliet Stuart Poyntz, a vigorous educational campaign among its membership. The 1916 convention of the International Ladies' Garment Workers Union accepted a plan for an extensive educational campaign and voted $5,000 for that purpose, and the last convention of the International, held in 1918, decided further to extend the work and appropriated a sum of $10,000 yearly for it.

At present the International Ladies' Garment Workers Union has in its national office in New York a special educational department consisting of a staff headed by Director Dr. Louis S. Friedland and Secretary Fannia Cohn, working under the supervision of the educational committee appointed by the president of the International. This department conducts classes directly in the city of New York and also advises and helps the local unions of the International, both in the city of New York and in other cities, in planning and carrying out their own educational work. In New York, the International has secured the cooperation of the municipal Board of Education for the use of the public school buildings and for the assignment of teachers for their English classes. Six public schools in the various residential sections of the city serve as "Unity Centers" where numerous classes in English, economics, literature, physical training, and other subjects are conducted for the ladies' garment workers. These schools also serve as centers for various recreational and social activities. This work is of a more elementary nature, calculated to reach a large portion of the membership. More advanced educational work is carried on in Washington Irving High School under the name of the Workers' University of the International Ladies' Garment Workers Union. Among the courses given there the following may be mentioned: Social interpretation of Literature, Evolution of the Labor Movement, Problems of Reconstruction, Sociology and Civilization, Labor Legislation, Social Problems, Trade Unionism, Cooperation. In both the Unity Centers and the Workers' University concerts are arranged from time to time. Lectures arranged by local unions are also frequently accompanied by a concert.

Since December, 1918, the Philadelphia organization of the I. L. G. W. U. has conducted educational projects among its membership similar to those in New York. Efforts are being made to extend this movement to Boston and other centers of the women's clothing industry.

The United Cloth Hat and Cap Makers convention in 1917 adopted a plan for systematic education on a large scale. As a result, an educational center known as the Headgear Workers Institute was organized in a public school. The activities were similar to those of the ladies' garment workers—classes in English, physical training, civics, history of the labor movement, public speaking and parliamentary law, and collective bargaining. A number of general lectures and excursions to the Metropolitan Museum of Art and several "family gatherings" were added. The program of the "family gathering" consisted of a concert, lecture and educational moving pictures; it was intended for the membership and their families and friends. The Hat and Cap Makers did not continue their educational work long, before they inaugurated a campaign for uniting the interested labor organizations in a general educational enterprise.

The Amalgamated Clothing Workers made their beginning at systematic education only at the end of 1917. The trade problems with which this organization was faced were up to that time so numerous, pressing, and in most cases, of such an emergency nature that they took up all the energies of the organization. At the end of 1917 the beginning was made simultaneously in Baltimore, Chicago, and New York. This initial effort met with considerable success in Chicago and Baltimore, but it proved rather abortive in New York. The 1918 convention of the Amalgamated Clothing Workers instructed the General Board to continue and extend their educational work. It was at that time that the United Labor Education Committee was launched and the Amalgamated Clothing Workers decided to join this common enterprise. Since the organization of the United Labor Education Committee, both the Amalgamated and the Hat and Cap Makers have continued their educational activities through this common committee.

Cooperation of these unions in education was initiated first in June, 1918, at an informal conference held between delegates to the A. F. of L. convention at St. Paul. The United Labor Education Committee was finally founded in November, 1918, by the following organizations: Amalgamated Clothing Workers, United Cloth Hat and Cap Makers, Furriers' Union, Fancy Leather Goods Workers Union, and the Workmen's Circle. An Executive Board, consisting of two representatives from each of these bodies established a joint office and took charge of all their educational work. While originally begun by needle trade organizations, the United Labor Education Committee later embraced a number of other unions and consists at present of about twenty labor organizations.

From the report submitted by the chairman of this Committee, J. M. Budish, to the Educational Conference of the United Labor Education Committee, held on February 7, 1920, the following summary of its first year's activities is derived:

An educational undertaking of this sort, serving so large a constituency, and with such limited resources—$17,450 was appropriated by the affiliated organizations—was faced by the necessity of an important choice of policy. Any classes which it could establish would include only a small proportion of the union members. Should the emphasis, then, be laid upon reaching the people in as large masses as possible, and inducing a mental attitude receptive to education, an aspiration which might in great part be satisfied by outside agencies? Or should all the effort be concentrated on supplying in detail the wants of a few? The former course was adopted in a memorandum approved by the committee at the start. "The fundamental necessity," said this memorandum, "is that the center of gravity of the educational work shall be transferred from supplying systematic knowledge to creating a steadily increasing demand for it, based upon the firm conviction that the Kingdom of Heaven is open to him who seriously looks for it." At the same time, "no efforts certainly must be spared to supply the elements who are craving regular systematic education with the necessary classes, courses, etc."

The pioneer work of the committee of course encountered difficulties. It was necessary to try experiments, to stir the rank and file to their own need for education, and to accustom them to forms of instruction quite different from the agitation to which they had been subjected in the past. Obstacles were set up by local public officials, particularly those in charge of the school buildings, many of whom, frightened by the prevailing anti-revolutionary hysteria, feared this might be some new form of Bolshevik propaganda. It was impossible, for instance, to hold classes or lectures in the school buildings in the Yiddish language, although this was the one chiefly spoken and understood by a large proportion of the membership.

One of the most successful activities of the committee was the holding of forty-seven forums in various parts of New York, which were attended by about 11,200 persons in all. At these forums, in addition to lectures by widely known speakers on various important subjects, there were recitals of good music by soloists and string quartets, educational moving pictures, lecture-recitals in which the musical compositions presented were explained by competent musicians, and dramatic recitals by Miss Edith Wynne Matthison and Charles Rann Kennedy. The music for the forums was provided by a Section on Music of which Josef Stransky, conductor of the Philharmonic Orchestra, was chairman.

In order to bring education directly to the rank and file, lecturers were sent to many regular meetings of the union locals. To arrange such lectures properly, it was necessary for each local to elect an educational committee, which should choose the most convenient time of meeting and select from the list of lecturers and subjects the ones preferred. Since most of these lectures were given at regular business meetings they had to be short; it was a difficult task for the speaker to gauge properly the temper of his audience, to develop his subject in twenty or thirty minutes without sacrificing the standards of accuracy, and at the same time to interest a group of active unionists many of whom had only the most rudimentary understanding of

English. If college instructors were submitted to discipline of this sort they might gain in color and directness. Naturally the lectures were not uniformly successful, but on the whole the experiment was judged satisfactory by the union members themselves, who in a democratic undertaking of this sort have the final authority over what shall be done. In all, 97 lectures were given at local meetings which had a total attendance of 13,715.

Excellent opportunities to make contact with the rank and file were furnished by the meetings called by the unions conducting strikes. Arrangements were made by the Committee to make use of the leisure of the strikers for educational and recreational purposes. During six strikes by affiliated unions, 59 meetings with a total attendance of over 45,000 were supplied with speakers and concerts of the highest standard. Union officials and other observers often remark on the fact that in a strike, when people are united in a common purpose and their emotions are unusually stimulated, their imaginations become active and they are in a peculiarly receptive mood for social and cultural values. Instruction of a more practical sort was furnished to girl strikers in the form of talks on sex hygiene, given in cooperation with the American Social Hygiene Association.

Perhaps the most ambitious undertaking of the Committee was the provision of three concerts in Carnegie Hall by the Philharmonic Orchestra, solely for the affiliated membership, at a price far below that which the general public has to pay. It was felt by the committee that something must be done to counteract the degrading effect on the personality of the worker which is produced by the amusements easily accessible, such as cheap moving pictures and musical shows. Most workers seldom patronize good concerts and theaters, first because the cost is too high, and second because these forms of recreation having been in effect monopolized by more fortunate members of society, the workers feel little interest in them. Nothing, however, could be more demoralizing, both to labor and to art, than the identification of fine and serious productions with a remote stratum of society with which the worker has nothing in common. On this account it was thought advisable to give concerts under the auspices of the unions, solely for their own membership. Few concessions to popular taste were made in the programs, on the theory that the way to learn to appreciate the best music is to hear it. The result, of course, was that the concerts were rather thinly attended and proved a heavy financial burden; but a steady and rapid rise in attendance from the first concert to the last gave hope that if the experiment were continued it might before long become self-supporting.

A similar experiment in drama was projected; it was planned to have a Workmen's Theater in English, giving serious productions of masterpieces seldom heard on Broadway, under the best possible direction. This plan did not mature, but the Committee did cooperate with the Jewish Art Theater, organized by Louis Schnitzer, Ben-Ami and Emmanuel Reicher and others, and performances of a high standard were furnished to union members at less than half price. Here enough support came from the membership to make the experiment self-sustaining. An English-language theater is still on the program and may be founded before long.

According to the policy adopted by the Committee in the beginning, classes offering continuous and systematic instruction in special subjects were the last to be developed. Several classes in English, Economics, Industrial History and History and Appreciation of Art were successfully carried on, but on the whole this side of the movement is still in the formative stage. In the meantime, a cooperative agreement was made with the Rand School, by which members of affiliated unions may join classes at the school without expense to themselves.

In order to symbolize the contact with artists and intellectual leaders which the labor movement must make in any broad attempt at education, an Art, Labor, and Science Conference was created by those interested; this conference constituted itself a permanent body and elected Sections to cooperate with the Committee in the various undertakings which it had in mind. Much valuable assistance was rendered by members of this conference—for instance, by Professor Charles A. Beard, by Josef Stransky and others of the Music Section, and by Richard Ordynski and others of the Drama Section. The con-

EDUCATION 225

ference has interesting possibilities of future development.

Friendly relations were established with other bodies carrying on labor education in America, and with the Workers' Educational Association of Great Britain. A national information bureau or central office may be formed to correlate and serve the various union educational activities in the United States.

In the eyes of the educator, perhaps the most interesting feature of all is the democratic nature of the enterprise. The report of the Chairman, from which the above account was extracted, was presented to a conference of delegates from the local unions which the Committee had been serving. It was as if the faculty of a university had to submit a report of its year's activities to the student body, who in turn had the right of unlimited criticism, and could grant or withhold the funds for the support of the institution. Criticism of all sorts was indeed freely voiced, but defenders of the work were also at hand, and after the Committee had had an opportunity to hear every ground of dissatisfaction, the report was unanimously accepted. Contact of this nature insures that as long as the Committee survives, it will be a vital institution. The conference itself was not the least educational of its undertakings.

The report of the committee appointed by the American Federation of Labor to investigate workers' educational enterprises is included in the report of the Executive Council to the thirty-ninth annual convention of the Federation held in June, 1919, at Atlantic City. It has for this study a special interest because it reveals a cleavage between the business type of unionism and the new unionism.

"Your committee recommends," says the report in the general summary of conclusions, "that central labor bodies through securing representation on boards of education and through the presentation of a popular demand for increased facilities for adult education make every effort to obtain from the public schools liberally conducted classes in English, public speaking, parliamentary law, economics, industrial legislation, history of industry and of the trade union movement, and any other subjects that may be requested by a sufficient number, such classes to be offered at times and places which would make them available to workers. If the public school system does not show willingness to cooperate in offering appropriate courses and type of instruction, the central labor body should organize such classes with as much cooperation from the public schools as may be obtained. Interested local unions should take the initative when necessary."

This report was unanimously endorsed by the convention with the addition that the Executive Council was instructed to appoint a committee to investigate the matter of selecting or preparing and publishing unbiassed text-books on different subjects concerning the labor movement.

The difference between this conception of labor education and the one of the new unionism may be compared with the difference between applied science and science. The function of education for the business unionism is merely to supply the members with a little more knowledge and information, from which they may derive immediate benefit, especially in connection with their direct trade activities. The new unonism thinks of educational work rather in the light of its vision of a coming commonwealth with a new culture. The business unionism would burden itself with this work only in case the public school system is so reactionary and so entirely uninfluenced by the labor movement that it refuses to supply the necessary classes in English, public speaking, economics, etc. The new unionism regards the creation of a labor culture, towards which educational work is a mere initial step, as its foremost aspiration, and as much a part of the task to be undertaken by the workers themselves as the struggle for political and industrial democracy. Says the report of the Executive Council, "But such classes (under union auspices) should be considered a stop-gap. The sound solution is a progressive board of education responsive to the public." As against this conception of labor education as a temporary stop-gap, the new unionism believes that labor must create its own educational agencies because they are a step towards a new and finer culture, towards the mental and spiritual emancipation of the people. For the new unionism the freedom from ready-made conceptions, the habit of independent thinking, the searching attitude of mind towards life, the creative imagination, the ready response to the delicate and noble impressions of nature and the treasures of human thought and intuition, the free and many-sided personality—and a society of equals built on this foundation—is that higher ideal which underlies, consciously or unconsciously, all phases of the labor struggle. Labor education is therefore to the new unionism not a mere passing activity made necessary by a temporary wave of reaction, but perhaps the most conscious expression of all its aspirations.

CHAPTER IX

LABOR PRESS AND COOPERATIVES

THE larger the community, the greater is the power of the press. It may be said that the power of the press increases as the power of the spoken word decreases. During the period in which the labor organizations of the needle trades developed, the press in America was gaining rapidly in influence. The city population grew enormously, social and industrial relations became steadily more complicated. The links connecting producer and consumer have now so multiplied that the appreciation of the connection has almost disappeared from the mind of the man in the street. With the development of large corporations the relation between the job holder and the power controlling the job has become more impersonal. The intricate development of the money and credit system has still further removed from the people any expert knowledge of their economic environment. With increased transportation facilities, the ties holding together small communities have weakened. The exchange of opinion between neighbors, local gossip and tradition, have declined and lost their effect. Ever increasing specialization narrows the range of personal experience of the wage-worker.

The isolation of man in the modern city is unique. It may be compared with the isolation of the tree-dweller among the ravaging elements. Our social and industrial environment are to the modern city dweller as fetichized, all-powerful and incomprehensible forces as were the powers of nature to the tree-dweller—and they have the same suppressive effect. And the average man must depend upon the press for almost all the information on which his interpretation of life is based. He must depend upon it for his imaginative connection with the world as a whole. The concepts suggested day by day, supported as they are by information supplied, and protected by the withholding of information, influence more and more profoundly the social viewpoint of the reader.

Industrial development not only made it possible for a single newspaper to reach hundreds of thousands of people, but it also brought about the concentration of control of the news. As a result, the selection and treatment of news becomes increasingly uniform. With a few exceptions, the people receive the same information in approximately the same form. A virtual uniformity may be observed also in opinions, both in the news and the editorial columns. For months the entire press suggested the idea that the Russian Soviet government was wicked and unstable. Then for weeks it prepared us, with equal thoroughness, for a recognition of the Soviet government. With the same information supplied in the same form, and with the same suggestions offered daily to the minds of the people, their views of life must to a great extent become stiff and ready-made. Consideration of the dangers in such artificial uniformity, making life colorless, leveling the people by machine-made ideas, replacing the conflict of thought with the conflict of brute selfishness, lies beyond the scope of this book, though it would make an interesting contribution to a study of the degeneracy of modern industrial society. We are directly concerned, however, with the influence of the capitalized press upon the labor movement.

For the press is now as much a part of business enterprise as is any other great industry. The metropolitan daily or the chain of newspapers and the popular magazine with a national circulation are, if they are making money, financially in exactly the same position as any industrial corporation. A newspaper or magazine publisher depends upon the same sources of credit as do other large proprietors. If the journal is one which is not profitable, it is likely to exist for no other purpose than to express the views of someone with enough money to support it. Frequently the holder of newspaper shares or bonds is also the holder of industrial shares and bonds. Often he is a landowner. He applies the same policies wherever his influence counts. The newspaper and magazine publisher, with almost negligible exceptions, by his social and economic position, by his education, belongs to the class against whose encroachment the labor movement struggles.

The character of the owners and managers of the

press would of itself, without any deliberate intention on their part, give to their publications a tone out of harmony with the inherent aspirations of the labor movement. In selecting from the enormous flow of events what deserves public notice and what does not, what is to be stressed and what minimized, the most candid publisher has little other guide than his own view of life and the prevailing opinions of the social group to which he belongs. Only in those few issues where there is involved the most immediate and obvious interest of the people who read his paper will their opinion be sufficiently crystallized to furnish a check to his normal inclination. By force of mere circumstance, the press gives prominence to such news and opinion as may justify the existing social order, as will suggest that its fundamentals are eternal. The press will naturally support the cause of the employers in most clashes with employees. On the other hand, the press usually avoids any news or opinions which might suggest that the present social order is but a passing and imperfect stage in the history of mankind, or which might exalt the cause of the workers as against that of their employers.

By virtue of the same disposition the press discriminates among different types of labor organization. While the labor movement was establishing itself it was in great measure ignored. Now that the movement as a whole has become an unavoidable evil the press seeks to play one part of it against another, to favor those forms of organization which are least inimical to the interests of private capital. It rarely favors them as against employers, but it frequently holds them up for the emulation of factions of the labor movement which it seems to consider more dangerous. When Mr. Gompers opposes a political party for labor, he is praised in the highest terms, but when he supports the striking steel workers or miners, the press sadly notes that he is losing his good judgment. The press gives preference to company-welfare unionism as against uplift or friendly unionism, to uplift as against business unionism, to business unionism as against the new or socialist unionism. The natural tendency of the press is to select such news, to couch it in such terms, to introduce it with such headlines, and to cap it with such editorials as to create in the working people an attitude most favorable to those parts of the labor movement towards which employers have least hostility.

These tendencies of the press have lately been much strengthened by a well considered and conscious policy on the part of many large corporations. The development of the newspaper has made it dependent for solvency upon its advertising columns. Selling at a price considerably below the cost of production, the newspaper derives its revenue from the advertisers. The prosperity of business enterprise thus becomes more directly than ever the concern of the publisher. He becomes the defender of advertisers as a class. The employers in any one industry might take a liberal position when there is a conflict between labor and capital in another industry. A similar division sometimes occurs between local sections of industry, or between different classes of employers in the same industry. As long as the press was guided merely by the personal inclinations of the publisher, it was able to favor the cause of the workers in any strike which did not touch it too closely. In a large number of minor industrial conflicts the press has in the past remained unbiased.

But with the dependence of the press on advertisers, and the rapidly growing mobilization of advertisers through chambers of commerce, manufacturers' associations, and their innumerable ramifications, any objective attitude towards the labor movement has a tendency to disappear. The advertising and publicity departments of business firms are now closely linked together, and few journals are strong enough to gain the patronage of advertisers if their news and editorials on so vital a subject as labor do not find favor with the "publicity" experts of big business. It would be a mistake to think that this influence often takes so crude a form as threats or bribes. It does not need to. It is good form for American editors to think what the managers of business think, just as in autocratic courts one does not contradict royalty. Moreover, few large corporations rely any longer upon the initiative of the newspaper in gathering industrial news; they interpose their own press agents between the reporter and the facts. From a mere unconscious coloring of news, from a mere natural bias, the press has come to the point of garbling, suppressing, and falsifying news as a result of calculated and aggressive propaganda, not only in favor of the existing social order, but of any condition which the employers of any great industry are bent on continuing.[1] This propaganda misleads not only the general public, but, what is more serious from the labor point of view, the workers themselves.

It was not, however, the anti-labor attitude of the general press so much as its total blindness to the labor movement which first impelled English-speaking unions to found journals for their immediate needs. As soon as the unions became national in scope, the spoken word became insufficient to supply the members with information concerning the activities of their own organization or with the ideas necessary to strengthen their cohesion. Such information was indispensable in time of industrial conflict. The national labor unions were therefore compelled to establish their own organs, for the most part monthlies and weeklies. Up to the early 'seventies over 100 such papers had come into existence. Since

[1] This growing hostility of the press to the labor movement is of course a process which in the end leads to the negation of its own purpose. When it goes far enough it becomes so apparent that it loses its effect. Many working people have now ceased to take news at its face value, and have begun to clamor for a press of their own. Thus the Central Labor Union of Seattle established during the war its own daily paper, the Seattle *Union Record*, which at last accounts had the largest circulation of any daily in the Northwest. Other similar projects are in formation. There is now a special cooperative press service for labor papers. The unreliability of the New York City press on labor matters explains the growing influence of the socialist New York *Call* among anti-socialist elements of labor.

then they have multiplied and have remained an institution of the American labor movement. The journals of the several unions originally could not, and later have not contemplated any competition with the general press. Their scope has remained limited to the immediate trade interests of the respective organizations. As a result, they have been unable to combat effectively the steadily increasing pressure of the general press upon the mind of the worker: upon his attitude toward economic and social conditions, the remedial measures for the most obvious evils from which he suffers, or his half-conscious dreams for the modification of the present structure of society. In this way a division of spheres of influence has come about between the general press and the labor journals, within the mind of the worker. The union member has become accustomed to taking his economics, his politics, his philosophy, his science and art, from the general publication, and his narrow trade interests, discussions concerning his hours and wages, and the politics of his organization, from his union journal.

Thus it happens that the American labor union press, though it is many times larger than the labor press of any other country, has remained until recently without any noticeable influence upon public opinion or upon the broader policies of the community. The general public in this country hardly knows of the existence of this press, while in European countries the comparatively few labor publications are frequently quoted by the general press and

LABOR PRESS AND COOPERATIVES 237

exert a noticeable influence upon the currents of public opinion.

This narrowness of the American union journal has no doubt had its share in the development of the social viewpoint of the old unionism. Man's mind is not after all divided as in water-tight compartments; the sources from which he derives his more fundamental conceptions will rule many of his minor interests. The dependence of the old unionism on the capitalist press can easily be traced in the bitter hostility of the adherents of business unionism towards socialism, in their lack of a conception of solidarity of the labor movement, and especially in the striking identity of the terms with which leaders of the conservative unions and the capitalist editors attack the more radical sections of the labor movement. The method of approach, the arguments used, and the very style are so remarkably similar that some statements of the representatives of business unionism can hardly be distinguished from statements by leaders of the financial world. The theory of a complete mutuality of interest between capital and labor, of round-the-table bargaining as the paramount cause of improvement, and the emphasis on "immediate betterments" as the dominant motive of the labor movement, carry all the earmarks of that interpretation of life which underlies the selection of news and opinion by our business editors. Traces of the same influence are also apparent in the bitter hostility which the old unionism has to all forms of independent political action by labor. Such identity, not only in basic principles but also in forms of language, would hardly have been possible without the uniform, steady, and powerful mental pressure exerted by the general press, uncorrected by any effective resistance from the union journals.

Many of the labor weeklies are even private enterprises which, though they are recognized as the official organs of city or state central bodies, are just as dependent on big advertisers as are the capitalist papers themselves. With the theories of business unionism firmly established, there was no good reason why labor publications should not seek the support and patronage of business proprietors. Such support, of course, could not remain without influence on the policy of the papers. A flagrant instance of this sort was a journal published in Pittsburgh, which until the late fall of 1919 still had the indorsement of the city central body. It was, nevertheless, attacking the current steel strike and its leaders in terms as virulent as any employed by the capitalist press, and was accepting advertisements from the big business interests of the district. The indorsement was of course withdrawn in this case.

The press serving the needle trades from the time when union organization was first attempted followed an entirely different course of development. The workers in these industries were nearly all immigrants. The general English-language press did not have the slightest influence on them for many years. Even if the workers could have read English,

LABOR PRESS AND COOPERATIVES

the mental attitudes and traditions of the immigrants were such that the general press was not adapted to their requirements. They had to depend for their daily stock of information and opinion upon journals of their own.

Catering to the immigrant masses who spoke their native languages and were mostly laborers or poor tradesmen, these papers never developed into substantial capitalist institutions. By their birth and environment, by their social position and economic status, the publishers of the foreign-language papers were little removed from the people they served. Advertising was almost negligible, and the little there was consisted largely of notices of labor meetings, and classified and personal columns. As a result the daily press, as far as the needle trades are concerned, has been for many years a labor press, and became so long before the unions found it either necessary or possible to develop journals of their own. Since the Jews are the prevailing element in the needle trades and it is with them that the labor organizations originated, it will be sufficient here to trace the development of the Jewish press.

In the early 'eighties, when the great flood of Jewish immigration began its flow to New York, there were two small general Jewish papers in the city, the weekly *Yiddishe Gazetten* and the *New Yorker Zeitung*. Both spoke for the orthodox religious elements, and were extremely hostile to all the currents of radical thought that were so stormily struggling for the adherence of the Jewish masses. Their antipathy to the workers was so primitive and crude that it soon deprived them of influence among the garment trades. As early as June, 1886, two worker-intellectuals, Ch. Rayefsky and Abraham Cahan, the present editor of the Jewish daily *Forward,* made an unsuccessful attempt to issue a paper representing the socialist and labor point of view, *Die Naye Zeit.* It existed only a few weeks and disappeared in July of the same year. An indication of the status of the Jewish press at this time is that the "financial" partner in this enterprise, Mr. Rayefsky, was employed in a soap factory at $6.00 a week.

A more substantial and successful enterprise was the New York *Yiddishe Volks Zeitung,* a weekly publication which began to appear at the end of June, 1886, and existed for three and a half years, until 1890. The publishers were two socialists who put several hundred dollars into the business. The paper attempted to maintain an impartial attitude with regard to the socialist factions of the East Side. At the same time, however, it definitely supported the socialist movement as a whole, and was loyal to the United Hebrew Trades. The paper devoted much space to popular articles on natural science, thus indicating the diversity of interest among the Jewish workers of that time. Occasionally serious works on economics were serialized, for example, Wages and Capital, by Karl Marx. Thus the pioneer general Yiddish newspaper included both the socialist and educational features which are characteristic of the labor organizations in the needle trades.

LABOR PRESS AND COOPERATIVES 241

In March, 1890, the organized socialists, after a split with the anarchists, founded a weekly, the *Arbeiter Zeitung,* which presently was recognized as the official organ of the United Hebrew Trades. In 1894 the same group began the publication also of an evening daily, the *Abendblatt.* Both these papers existed until the middle of 1902. After the division in the Socialist Labor Party in 1897, the *Abendblatt* remained the official organ of the parent body, while the Jewish members of the new Socialist Party established the Jewish daily *Forward,* which was destined to play a large part in the labor movement in the needle trades.

During the first few years of its existence the *Forward* had a precarious footing, its fortunes varying as the Socialist Labor Party or the Socialist Party temporarily gained the upper hand. Only since 1902 has the *Forward* become the universally recognized newspaper of the Yiddish-speaking workers. Its circulation in that year was 18,000 and has since then steadily increased. It reached 72,000 in 1908, and it is now about 200,000.

In a recent issue of the *Forward* (September 14, 1919) Max Pine, who was one of its founders, writes of the initial struggle of this publication:

"The writer remembers an evening when a meeting of the Publishing Society was called and it was explained that there was no money available to start the publication. Almost the entire night was spent on a discussion of funds. It was decided that notwithstanding the fact that there was no money, we proceed at once to issue the

Forward. However impossible it may sound now, that it was decided to publish a newspaper without money, it is nevertheless a fact. Nothing but boundless enthusiasm, wonderful optimism, the aspiration to accomplish a great and noble task, could have made this possible. When finally the decision was reached—it was almost dawn—it was decided to raise at least $500.00. Considering the impoverished state of the labor movement at that time this was a considerable sum. A motion was passed that everyone should contribute to this $500.00 fund. Those who had no money on hand hurried home, roused their neighbors, borrowed and returned with their share. The $500.00 was raised. Two offices were rented, one for the editorial office and the composing room and another for the business office. The editorial office was on Duane Street and the business office was in Debs' place where Seward Park is located at present, just opposite the present Forward Building. After the composing room was fitted up with old stands and cases for the type and other typographical materials, there were only a few dollars left with which the publication of a daily paper, the *Forward,* was begun—a paper which at present has a circulation of over 200,000. The first number of the *Forward* appeared on May 20, 1897, and it has since appeared regularly without interruption until the present day.''

No other daily in America has for so long a period been so closely knit with the labor movement as the *Forward.* Only recently, with the appearance of the Seattle *Union Record,* has there arisen an English-language daily that can be compared with it in circulation and influence among the unions. The *Forward* is issued by a private corporation, the Forward Association, to which only members of the Socialist Party approved by two-thirds majority of

LABOR PRESS AND COOPERATIVES 243

the members of the Association can be elected. While the Association controls the property and business of the *Forward,* its members make no investment and of course receive no dividends. After expenses are paid, the surplus income is used in the enterprise itself. The Forward Association also makes frequent contributions to various branches of the labor movement. Besides being a socialist journal, the *Forward* is also a labor paper in the narrower sense of the word. It devotes at least as much space to the trade-union movement, especially in the needle trades, as to the socialist movement. The columns dealing with the clothing unions are fully representative of the spirit and policy of these organizations.

The workers in the needle trades have thus not suffered from any such division between the general and the labor press as that which has so profoundly influenced the English-speaking labor movement. From the beginning their daily newspaper has also been their labor journal, and only after the unions were firmly established and their character definitely formed did separate union journals appear. These are, moreover, kindred in spirit to the daily press read by the members.

From time to time other socialist or radical publications have existed in competition with the *Forward.* In the early days the anarchist factions started a number of journals. The only one of these to survive is the *Freie Arbeiter Stimme*—but its express anarchist character has disappeared long since. At present a stronger influence is perhaps exerted by *Die Naye Welt,* a weekly publication of the Jewish Socialist Federation, and by *Der Yiddisher Kempfer,* the organ of the Poale Zion, a nationalist socialist society of workers favoring the establishment of a Jewish cooperative commonwealth in Palestine. Outside of their special interests, these publications devote their space to articles on questions of the day, as well as on the history, theory, and practice of the labor movement in this country and abroad.[2]

An English-language socialist press grew up as the English-speaking members of the needle-trades unions increased, through the gradual acclimatization of the immigrant worker and the entry of American-born men and women into the industry. The first English socialist daily which had much influence in the needle trades was the *Daily People* of the Socialist Labor Party, of which the late Daniel DeLeon was the editor. It appeared first on June 28, 1900, and went out of existence on February 21, 1914. Its influence, however, had long been waning by the time of its extinction, with the influence of the party it represented. Ever since 1902 members of the Socialist Party, with the cooperation of the clothing unions, had been making efforts to establish a paper of their own, and as a result the New York

[2] With the development of a substantial middle class among the Jewish population a general press somewhat similar in nature to the capitalist English-language papers has begun to appear, but the process has not yet gone far. The various bourgeois dailies now existing in New York, Philadelphia and Chicago must still depend for much of their circulation upon the working masses. To exist at all they must remain liberal and at least impartial in industrial disputes. Among their editorial staffs they include numerous socialists, and their policy is indefinite. Their influence among the workers is limited and they may be left out of consideration.

Call appeared on May 30, 1908. This paper has had a steady growth, in spite of many difficulties, especially those put in its way by the Postmaster General during the war. To a degree, it has before for the English-speaking members of the clothing unions—as well as for many others—what the *Forward* is for the Yiddish-speaking membership.

When the labor organizations in the clothing industry grew strong, the general press could no longer satisfy all their needs. Founded as they were on the democratic participation of their membership, it became necessary for them to bring the main problems of their organizations before all their members. The life of the unions became more rich and complicated as they grew, and no general press, even the most sympathetic, could find sufficient space for all their special problems.

The first union in the needle trades to issue its own paper was the United Cloth Hat and Cap Makers. The *Cap Makers Journal,* a monthly, first appeared in May, 1903, and lived for three years. It was published both in Yiddish and English. The chief reason for its existence was the controversy in which this international was involved with the I. W. W. To combat the influence and expose the methods of the latter, to make the membership understand the dangers which threatened the disruption of the young international, was its task. After the battle was won, the journal ceased to appear (1906). It was revived in September, 1916, primarily because of the jurisdictional controversy in which the organization became involved with the United Hatters, which again threatened disruption. The publication was needed, however, on other grounds as well, since the union had become much larger and its problems more numerous. At present the Cap Makers publish two bi-weekly papers, one in English and the other in Yiddish, both called *The Headgear Worker*.

The Cloakmakers made an attempt in August, 1905, to issue a weekly, *The Cloakmaker*. It lived only a few months. It was revived in September, 1910, under the name of *Die Naye Post*. After that it appeared continuously until in 1919 it was merged with all the other publications issued by the various subsidiary unions of the International Ladies' Garment Workers, in the weekly of the International, *Justice,* which has Yiddish and Italian edtions called *Gerechtigkeit* and *Giustizia,* respectively. The other needle-trades organizations have now numerous journals in the principal languages spoken by their members. Even so small an organization as the Neckwear Makers published a monthly journal for a time, as did the Fancy Leather Goods Workers. It is unnecessary to enter into the history of each of these publications. In most cases they are distributed free to the entire membership.

Among the more important publications not mentioned above are those of the Amalgamated Clothing Workers: *Advance,* English-language weekly, *Fortschritt,* weekly, *Industrial Democracy* in both Polish and Bohemian, bi-weeklies, *Darbas,* Lithuanian bi-weekly, and *Rabochy Golos,* Russian monthly. The International Fur Workers Union publishes the *Fur Worker,* a monthly with English and Yiddish editions, and regular departments in Italian, French and Russian.

Two characteristics distinguish most of these journals—the wide range of subjects treated and the effort to deal with these subjects from a broad social viewpoint. Their pages are never devoted to trade matters only. Half or more of their space is given over to events in the labor movement, both in this country and abroad, and to the social, industrial, and political life of America. Virtually every kind of material found in the general magazine, including the short story and literary and dramatic criticism is found at some time or other among their contents. This wide range of subjects results from a habit of thinking of life as an entirety, as a unit of which their particular trade is but a single phase. Of still greater significance is the method of treatment. It is easy to discern a painstaking endeavor to discuss each question on the basis of general principles. The vicissitudes of the several organizations, of the labor movement, and of the entire body politic are scanned, not so much in the light of some immediate interest or policy, as of the enduring interest and ultimate emancipation of the working class. Just as in industrial action the new unionism is inherently hostile to the policy of living only from hand to mouth, of being concerned entirely with immediate betterments as they may be secured, so in the mental and spiritual sphere the new unionism is hostile to the method of thinking from hand to mouth and disregarding basic principles in each new situation which arises. It rather emphasizes the development of an all-embracing philosophy of life.

Cooperative enterprises on the part of labor are closely akin to its ventures in journalism, since they too are efforts to supply substitutes for the insufficient and often harmful social services offered to the workers by a business civilization. The first cooperative undertakings by the needle-trades unions, however, were for immediate benefit rather than for any far-reaching purpose. The International Ladies' Garment Workers, having established the dental clinic and the sanitarium mentioned in Chapter V, went on to create a place of rest and recuperation for members who did not need medical attention. This project was initiated by Local 25 of New York, the women dress and waistmakers. A vacation resort near the Delaware Water Gap in Pennsylvania, named Forest Park, was provided at a cost of about $100,000. The park consists of 750 acres of woodland, and includes an 80-acre lake. In it there are twelve houses with capacity for 500 workers. Athletic recreational facilities such as swimming pools, tennis courts, and bowling alleys have been constructed. A pleasant walk leads to the beautiful Bushkill waterfall. Thus, when seeking relief from the noisy shops, the hot pavements, and the crowded tenements, the girls of this union no longer have to compete with women who can afford expensive resorts, most of which are after all not adapted to those seeking rest and intimacy with nature. The Philadelphia waistmakers, Local 15, have provided for themselves a summer home also, earning the $50,000 necessary by overtime work. This local has in the city a cooperative lunchroom, which serves good food at low prices.

In the establishment of consumers' cooperative stores the clothing unions have naturally been outdistanced by such unions as the miners, who, living in isolated communities as they do, have found cooperation a more obvious remedy for extortionate prices. In large cities private retail shops are so numerous and expenses like rent and taxes are so high that the cooperative is later of development and finds a less secure footing than in the smaller towns. Nevertheless the Italian local 48 of the Ladies' Garment Workers has established two cooperative groceries in New York, and their example has been followed by a few members of the waistmakers. This movement will develop more rapidly when the union has its own building and can devote space to a wholesale.

The most substantial and far-reaching cooperative plans are those formed at the Chicago conference in February, 1920, in which the Amalgamated Clothing Workers participated, together with railway and other large unions, and various organizations of farmers.[3] This is not the place to discuss all the

[3] In the absence of President Benjamin Schlesinger in Europe, the International Ladies' Garment Workers were not represented, but they will probably participate in the work.

projects of the conference, which include a wide extension of both consumers' and producers' cooperation and the direct interchange of commodities among the several groups. One of these plans, however, directly and immediately concerns the needle trades. That is the foundation by the clothing unions of a cooperative bank in New York. This bank will be a depository for the funds of the organizations, which taken together are no inconsiderable sum, and also for the savings of their members. The money thus made available will not be used, as it now is in ordinary banking institutions, for the encouragement of private business enterprise, but for building loans to the unions themselves, for loans to cooperatives, and for the financing of other projects, such as newspapers, in which labor has a special interest. Since these great and firmly established unions have at least as good credit as the average business concern, and the aggregate earning power of their members is enormous and can never as a whole be destroyed, the stability of such a bank is beyond question. It is intended, moreover, to be one of a chain scattered throughout the country and serving the unions in many industries. An industrial depression would probably affect it less than a bank dependent on the solvency of business concerns, since it is almost inconceivable to think of the earning power of so many thousand workers being cut off sufficiently to wipe out its resources. Technical legal obstructions may arise in its path, but if they do, this will merely be an additional argument for labor to mobilize and use more effectively its political power.

In the end such banks will give labor a positive economic leverage it has never before been able to exercise—a partial control of credit. It would be inaccurate to say that in society as at present constituted this power will seriously compete with capitalist credit, but it will be a considerable influence in the struggle to make the working majority, rather than the privileged few, the center of our culture. In the hands of the old narrow unionism such a power would be not only dangerous to society as a whole, but to the labor movement itself. If successfully exercised, it would hopelessly compromise the unions by making them dependent on profitable business enterprise, and so effectively enslave their members. In the hands of adherents of the new unionism, however, the control of credit will be a decided force for beneficent social reconstruction. The possibilities for service which they will derive from such control will be a strong influence in leading the whole labor movement towards the aspirations of the new unionism.

CHAPTER X

TEXTILES

The boundary between the clothing industry and that which produces fabrics is in some places shadowy—as in sweaters and knit goods, hosiery, cloth gloves, and lace. It is not chiefly on account of this kinship, however, that we shall make a brief excursion into the textile industry, but rather to illustrate a characteristic of the new unionism that is rapidly emerging—the fact that it is inter-industrial as well as industrial. Just as the concentration of capital and credit brings allied industries under a more nearly unified control, so the advances of aggressive labor organizations are forcing them to look for practical harmony, and consequently for a more centralized administration, among closely related industrial groups. Since the textile mills furnish the material out of which clothing is made, it would be an obvious advantage for the clothing unions if the textile workers were also strongly organized and ready to coöperate with them. For the same reason the garment unions have much power to help organization in the textile industry.

The value of the annual product of the textile group is exceeded only by the industries which the census places under the heading of "food and kin-

TEXTILES

dred products." Its total capitalization was in 1914 about two and a quarter billions,[1] representing a larger investment than any other industrial group except iron and steel and food products. In number of wage-earners it leads all others; in 1914 its 5,942 establishments gave employment to 950,880. A high percentage of the mills is owned by corporations—some of them enormous corporations of the sort popularly called "trusts." Most of the enterprises have been highly profitable; their shares have advanced rapidly, are much sought after and are not easily obtainable.

The characteristics of the industry are not the same as those of the ready-made clothing trades. Here large-scale production, in factories representing heavy investment in plant, machinery, and power, is the rule. Of the cotton mills the largest group, 768 in number, had each in 1914 an annual product valued from $100,000 to $1,000,000, and there were 187 establishments with an annual product of over $1,000,000 each. The woolen mills also were large, with 455 producing between $100,000 and $1,000,000, and 84 over $1,000,000. The silk establishments average somewhat smaller. In both woolen and cotton mills, 35 per cent of the wage-earners worked in factories employing over 1,000 persons each; in the silk establishments, nearly 50 per cent of the workers were in mills employing from 100 to 500 each.

While the forces of capital are strongly entrenched

[1] Abstract of United States Census of Manufactures, 1914.

in the textile plants, therefore, the unions are not faced with the same obstacles as in the clothing industry. Territory here may be difficult to conquer, but once it is won it can be more easily retained. Home work is rare. Sweatshop competition is not always waiting around the corner for the first relaxation of vigilance. New establishments cannot spring up easily where they are least expected. Old ones cannot die so suddenly. A shop successfully organized means a leap to immediate power.

Although some seasonal variation is apparent in the textile establishments, it is not so severe as in the clothing shops. The amount of work available for those employed is less at some times than at others, but the number wholly out of work is comparatively small. The cotton mills in 1914 employed in the dullest month 94 per cent of those working in the busiest month; the silk mills 88 per cent, and the woolen mills 87 per cent. Some of this variation must be attributed to the industrial depression consequent to the beginning of the war.

The labor force in textiles shows more similarity to that in the clothing industry. With the installation of modern machinery, the processes have become easy enough so that with a few exceptions no high degree of skill is required. Immigrants who have never worked in factories can learn their trade without difficulty in a few months. Women and children can be employed in large numbers. In the northern mills foreign-born workers predominate. In Lawrence, Mass., the greater part of the employees are

South-Italians and French Canadians.[2] Then follow, in order of numbers, Poles, Lithuanians, Americans, Syrians, Greeks, Armenians, Jews, Russians, and Ukrainians. In Passaic, New Jersey, the Poles predominate; there are also large groups of Italians, Hungarians, Rumanians, South Slavs, Americans and smaller groups. Paterson shows much the same mixture of races, with the addition of some skilled workers from France. In Philadelphia many of the workers are American-born; about one-fifth are Jewish. The cotton mills of the South employ a larger proportion of American born, including many children. The following table shows the percentages of men, women, and children under 16, as they were in 1914:

	Men	Women	Children
Cotton	53.4	38.2	8.4
Silk	38.5	54.3	7.2
Woolen	54.5	41.7	3.8

The industry as a whole has a higher percentage of child labor than any other in the United States, and employs many more children in all than any other.

For several years numbers of the foreign workers, especially the South Italians, were transients, saving all they could out of their wages and then returning to their native lands to profit by the lower price levels in Europe. This element naturally was not easy to organize, and did not exert effective pressure for higher wages or better conditions. The

[2] From statement of union officials.

tendency has recently decreased, and emigration fell to a low level during the four years of the war. It was never so great in the textile centers as in the iron and steel and mining regions. Now that prices abroad have risen to or above the level in the United States, the chief cause of impermanency is removed.

Wages in the textile mills long remained low, and have always dragged behind the trades in which labor was well organized. Hours were long and working conditions bad. Occupational diseases are prevalent, especially those due to dust and lint which many of the workers must constantly inhale. Housing in most of the textile centers has been unsightly, inadequate, and insanitary.

The oldest national union in the industry is the United Textile Workers of America, a conservative organization affiliated with the American Federation of Labor. Since it has jurisdiction over all textile operatives it is in a sense industrial, but its industrialism is incomplete, as it does not admit engineers, machinists, clerks and other incidental employees. As a matter of practice it has retained the methods of craft unionism, paying special attention to the more highly skilled English-speaking groups. It has been unable to bring about modern conditions or gain general recognition until recently, and the dues-paying membership which it reported to the American Federation of Labor in the spring of 1919, 55,800, is but a small fraction of those eligible.

Spontaneous general strikes, in the nature of unorganized rebellions against existing conditions, broke out soon after 1910 in Paterson, Lawrence, and other centers. They were fought with great bitterness and caused much public interest. Members of the I. W. W. went into the cities after the trouble had begun and led the strikes, but neither the I. W. W., on account of its loose methods of organization, nor the United Textile Workers, on account of its conservatism, was able to hold the strikers after the trouble was over. Both unions continued to maintain locals in Paterson, and the United Textile Workers retained a few members in Lawrence, but these locals were small and ineffective. The Workers' International Industrial Union also maintained in recent years small and unimportant locals in textile towns.

In the late winter of 1918 the United Textile Workers inaugurated a nation-wide campaign for the 48-hour week, hoping to extend the influence of the union and gain membership. The eight-hour day movement, formally begun in 1877 and already successfully consummated by the majority of organized labor, had received a great stimulus by the favorable attitude of the British and American governments during the war, based on investigations showing that workers usually produced at least as much in eight hours as they did in a longer workday. This favorable background was supplemented by the fact that after the armistice a depression was felt in textiles, and the mills were not eager to keep their people through long hours.

In Lawrence an understanding was soon reached

by some of the companies and the 200 or more members of the United Textile Workers. The mills consented to grant the 48-hour week, but only at the same hourly rate which they had formerly paid for 54. This involved an actual reduction in weekly wages, and meant no financial sacrifice for the employer. Unions almost invariably, when demanding shorter hours, specify that the same weekly rate shall be paid as before, since shorter hours would not be worth winning if the slender pay-envelope must be reduced in proportion. In this case, however, the union consented, doubtless because it felt that a strike in the dull period would be difficult to win. It probably intended to ask for higher wages later on, when business should revive and a strike would be more inconvenient to the manufacturers. This was a cautious policy, of the type characteristic of conservative unionism.

The unorganized workers, however, did not understand this policy, and resented bitterly its results. When early in February the mills put in the pay envelopes a slip stating that the workng week would be reduced, but that wages would be reduced correspondingly, they walked out and an unorganized strike involving at different times from 18,000 to 28,000 wage-earners was the result. During the slack period their pay had fallen so low that they were unable to accept still smaller remuneration, in the face of the enormous living costs. This consequence might have been foreseen by the union if it had been in closer touch with the mass of workers, or had taken the pains to consult them and gain their cooperation.

No sooner had the strike broken out than the officials of the union, seconded by the conservative central labor body of the city, antagonized the unorganized strikers by calling them "Bolsheviki" and refused to support their demands for the old wages. The charge was echoed by officials of the American Federation of Labor, and even by the Secretary of Labor of the United States. The press bitterly assailed the supposititious revolutionary aims of what it termed the "undesirable foreign element" and the whole city administration and police force was mobilized against them. The strikers were not without sympathizers, liberal members of the public coming in to help them organize, raise funds, and plead their case.

For a long time the unions in the clothing trades, especially the Amalgamated Clothing Workers, had been looking with concern at the weakness of the textile operatives, and hoping something could be done not only to improve their condition but to bring them within the ranks of aggressive labor. Here was an opportunity. A spontaneous strike, needing experienced guidance, had been repudiated by the very union which for long had been, for one reason or another, unable to make much progress in the industry. The Amalgamated therefore sent organizers and contributed funds to the strikers. Other radical unions and many members of the public also contributed.

The strike, like any mass movement giving vent to long suppressed sense of wrong, had many dramatic aspects. Three former clergymen of American birth, young men who had decided that they could best serve their ideals by assisting the labor movement, came to Lawrence almost as soon as the strike began and took a leading part in the work. They and the other speakers urged the strikers not only to commit no violent acts, but to meet any attacks of the police and mill guards with folded arms—to carry out literally the principle of non-resistance. As a result, in spite of great provocation, no outbreaks occurred. The police broke up peaceable meetings, clubbed unresisting pickets, arrested hundreds of strikers against whom no evidence could be brought, and picked out the leaders, including the young ministers, for special persecution and physical abuse. Over a hundred of the strikers were returned soldiers. One of these, a volunteer who had spent several months in the trenches, ventured to appear on the picket line in his uniform. He was clubbed by the police, arrested, clubbed again in the police station until he was insensible, called "dirty foreigner" and "Bolsheviki," and sentenced to jail.

Each of the eleven nationalities involved elected a relief committee, and the chairmen of the various committees formed the General Relief Committee. Family tickets were distributed to the most needy, four soup kitchens were maintained to care for those who did not receive family tickets, coffee stalls were opened for the morning picketers, and the "Strikers' Cross" was organized for medical relief. In the tenth week of the strike, when funds began to run low, the Italians, who had been without relief for a week, voted not to accept tickets for another three days. An instance of the sympathy which the strike aroused is that of an Italian in a neighboring city who, with a wife and six children to support, was injured by a fall. Friends collected thirty-three dollars for him, but he sent it to the Lawrence strike committee.

When at length starvation began to stare the strikers in the face, sympathizers in other cities offered to care for their children. The children were smuggled out of Lawrence in moving vans, strict secrecy being preserved through fear of police interference. Week after week this exodus went on.

An offer of arbitration was made, the arbitrator suggested being one of the best known manufacturers in the state, but the mill managers would neither consent to arbitration nor meet representatives of the strikers. At length it seemed as if the end had come, and the workers were on the point of surrendering. The police were parading machine guns about the streets, and the city marshal announced that he had withdrawn public protection from the strikers. Immediately thereafter one of the organizers was taken at night from his hotel room by a band of masked men, carried out into the country in an automobile, beaten severely with clubs, and threatened with hanging. Whether or not the threat was in earnest, the ruffians were frightened away by the sound of an approaching car; their victim escaped and, half clad and injured as he was, wandered about until he found a farmhouse and was taken to a hospital. The news of this brutality so enraged the strikers that they resolved never to compromise, and a few who had actually entered the mills came out again.

By this time orders had begun to increase, and the mills, wishing to end the trouble, announced a 15 per cent. rise in wages, 2½ per cent. more than the workers had asked. Some of the largest establishments also consented to deal with the new union's shop committees. The strikers, after their sixteen weeks' struggle, voted to stay out one day more as a proof of their solidarity, and went back to work in a body with the consciousness of victory and faith in their new organization.

In the meantime, spontaneous strikes, most of them under the auspices of independent unions, had broken out in Passaic, New Jersey, and other textile centers. Paterson workers sent a delegation to the Amalgamated Clothing Workers' office and applied for a charter. The Amalgamated, however, decided that they did not wish to burden their existing offices with this immense new task, and so encouraged the organization of an international textile union with which they could cooperate. The result was a convention held in New York on April 12th, which founded the **Amalgamated Textile Workers of America.**

On account of their experience with the class struggle, the delegates did not have to be convinced of its existence. They adopted a constitution the preamble of which was borrowed because of its aptness from the constitution of the Amalgamated Clothing Workers.

This preamble is, perhaps, revolutionary doctrine, but it is not the sort of violent revolution which the press and administration of Lawrence thought they were fighting. Efficient organization and education are the main themes; there is nothing about revolt or coup d' état, but simply the expression of a purpose to make the working class ready, in the fullest sense, to assume control of production.

In its first six months the new union won strikes, not only in Lawrence, but in Passaic, Hudson County, and Paterson, New Jersey, and in New York City. At the end of them it had a total membership of 50,000, and a paid-up membership of 40,000. Although a number of locals formerly belonging to the United Textile Workers have come over to it, the larger part of its membership has come from formerly uncultivated territory, or from small independent locals.

A recent event of some significance is a simultaneous strike of textile workers and clothing workers in Utica, New York, under the auspices of the two Amalgamated unions. This event is merely symbolic, since there are few centers where the two industries exist together.

The aim to educate the working class and

strengthen the union as an instrument of service has already found expression in various ways. Three journals are published—a bi-weekly in English, and monthlies in Italian and Polish. A Young People's League with study groups in English and economics has been formed. In Lawrence the union has founded a cooperative bakery and a retail store, and others are planned.

The structure of the union is of course completely industrial. In places where an entirely new organization was effected, the basis is the shop committee, rather than the craft local, as in most older unions. Where the shop contains workers of only one craft, its committee naturally takes care of the craft interests; where it is composed of several crafts, a representative of each is elected to the committee. The chairmen of the shop committees form the executive board for the plant or the city, as the case may be. The workers of each city are organized into one local. In some places meetings of workers in the same craft throughout the city are held, but they are unofficial, thus reversing the old order in which the craft group was officially recognized and the shop committee had no legal place in the union machinery.

The structure itself insures a maximum of democratic control, but further safeguards exist in the constitution. Care is taken that representation in the conventions shall be proportionate to the size of the locals, and a referendum of the general membership is obligatory for election of the officers nominated by the convention, for amendments to the constitution, and for choice of a city for the convention. The initiative is allowed for a proposition to change the meeting place or to amend the constitution. The General Executive Board may invoke a referendum on any subject.

The struggle in Lawrence was merely an example on a large scale of the sort of opposition the union has met everywhere. In Paterson it has had difficulty in getting permits for meetings and in keeping its papers and headquarters out of the hands of the police. A hall which it finally leased for a term of years was bought by a prominent member of the Chamber of Commerce, who caused the fire exits to be boarded up so that meetings there would be illegal. Such obstacles, however, are usually overcome in the long run.

In the meantime the United Textile Workers have been progressing with their organizing campaign, especially in the cotton mills of the South. It is interesting to see that wherever the Amalgamated becomes strong, the employers urge their workpeople to leave it for the conservative union, but that where the Amalgamated has not penetrated, as in the South, the United encounters just as bitter opposition and finds as great difficulty as the radical union in establishing its right to free speech and freedom of assembly.

The competition between the Amalgamated and the United Textile Workers will furnish a valuable test of the effectiveness of the new unionism, as developed in the clothing trades, to accomplish the difficult task of organizing a great industry where large-scale production rules and capital is strongly in control. So far the old unionism has failed to make much headway in it, but the conditions are now more favorable than before, and it is certain that the employers, if they fear the growing strength of the radical union, will hasten to come to terms with the conservative one. Whether the vigor and democratic efficiency of the new union will suffice to overcome these obstacles remains to be seen.

The occasion of the Lawrence strike is an illustration of the comparatively weak points of the old unionism. A preoccupied concern with immediate policy, a lack of democratic connection with the mass of the workers, and an extreme readiness to assume hostility towards them in order to preserve the good will of the employer and the public official were there evident. Another illustration, perhaps a better one, is the subsequent strike in Paterson. There the workers strongly desired the 44-hour week, and voted to demand it—among them the members in good standing of the United Textile Workers. The demand was made in due order. The United officials, pursuing their usual policy of conciliation, agreed with the employers to submit the question to the National War Labor Board.

In the proceedings before the Board the officials assumed, as is their custom, that they represented all the workers, although as a matter of fact only a small number were members of the United Textile

Workers. The War Labor Board handed down a decision, early in the summer, granting the 44-hour week, but postponing its adoption until October. With this decision the workers were not satisfied, and a large number, members of the Amalgamated, voted not to accept it, but to strike for an immediate 44-hour week on August 4th. Since the Amalgamated had not consented to arbitration and had not been represented in the negotiations, this action involved no conceivable breach of faith.

As soon as news of this decision reached the United members, extreme dissatisfaction at once arose: it was apparent that the conciliatory action of their officials, adopted without the active assent of the members, had left them behind the rival union. Their officials saw the danger, and tried to reopen the case by begging the manufacturers, on the ground of the action of the Amalgamated, to grant the 44-hour week at once. The employers, however, as usual underestimating the danger of a successful strike, refused to do so. The United officials then appealed to the War Labor Board for a revision, but the Board naturally replied that the officials of the United in submitting the case had assumed responsibility for carrying out the decision, and that there was no sufficient ground now for changing the award. The United officials then adopted a threatening attitude toward their members, telling them that every means of discipline would be used to see that the award should be executed and that no strike should occur.

The Amalgamated members struck as they had voted to do, and it soon became apparent that they had the power to win. The United members, feeling that they had been led into a compromise which they did not sanction, struck also. The United officials thereupon expelled the members in question, thus vindicating their good faith with the employers and the War Labor Board by sacrificing the union. The strike was won, and of course most of the expelled members joined the Amalgamated.

Here was a case where the old union, relying on conciliation and governmental support rather than upon the strength of its own membership, was led into a compromise which the new union, by its aggressiveness and closeness to the rank and file, proved to have been unnecessary. The case is peculiarly interesting because all the parties acted in good faith throughout, according to their understanding of the situation. It may perhaps be said, on the one hand, that the officials of the United should have secured the sanction of their members for arbitration, or, on the other, that the members should have felt themselves bound by the action of their officials. But the significant fact is that such conflicts between the rank and file and the officials frequently arise in the old unions, and are almost a necessary consequence of their failure to provide for a fuller measure of democratic control. In any case if the United members had not struck, the prestige of their union among the other workers would have received a heavy blow which in the long run might have injured it as much as their own defection.

If we can draw any inference from the Paterson strike, it is that when the economic situation of the workers is favorable, the structure and tactics of the old unionism are likely to give way in active competition with the new unionism. It is possible that when the situation is less favorable, the reverse would be true. The Lawrence strike, however, illustrates the danger of underestimating the power of the workers in conditions that seem highly unfavorable. A prediction as to the eventual success of either type of union would, if this analysis is sound, rest chiefly upon one's estimate of the ability of labor, in the long run, to rely chiefly upon its own economic power.

A powerful aid to the growth of the Amalgamated Textile Workers will be its amalgamation with the Amalgamated Clothing Workers, decided upon at the 1920 convention of the latter organization. The young union has shown its vitality, and the older one is now ready to join with it formally.

CHAPTER XI

THE FUTURE

In speculating about the future, it is important to remember our analysis of the events of the past. What happened was not so much the consequence of intention on the part of any few persons or groups as it was the resultant of a number of deep human desires working themselves out in various sets of circumstances. The immigrants were driven out of Europe, they came to find one sort of liberty and were forced to adopt another; several kinds of unions and social philosophies competed for their allegiance, and one type prevailed because it proved more valuable to them. The Protocol of Peace was adopted to eliminate the necessity of strikes; it had valuable results but did not operate as people expected at the time of its adoption. In spite of anyone's deliberate intention, unforeseen factors intervened to destroy it.

So it would be useless to attempt to predict what will happen on the basis of any plans which responsible leaders or influential groups may now have. The authors wish particularly to avoid the inference that in this chapter they are speaking for any of the unions or their officials, or are expounding any existing intentions. It is possible of course to understand the conscious tendencies of the unions, to read in the preambles to their constitutions, and in the reports of their annual conventions, passages showing that they look forward to a time when labor will control production and the laborer will receive the full value of all he produces. But as an expression of intention, these passages will have little effect on what actually is to happen. Any validity they may have will lie rather in their accuracy in analyzing social tendencies which would exist if they had never been written, and so, by helping the workers to understand these tendencies, in adding to the morale and effectiveness of the unions.

As labor leaders have good cause to know, the ordinary reader of newspaper editorials greatly overestimates the power of the "agitator." People write and talk as if a man saying something were a sort of first cause, as if an orator could single-handed bring about a revolution. If one is thinking of small groups acting over short periods of time, there may be some truth in this attitude, but as the group in question becomes larger and the time lengthens out, the effectiveness of the agitator *per se* decreases to the vanishing point. There are many agitators saying different things; and the vast inarticulate masses, slow to move and acting practically in relation to their circumstances, pay little attention to any theory that does not in the long run find a basis in their experience. The agitator is powerless unless he becomes in fact the voice of the crowd, unless he understands the deep currents of desire that run through it so that in him the people hear themselves speaking. Such an agitator is of course dangerous to any vested interests which the people may oppose, because he arouses their consciousness and fires their will; but he is not the cause of what they may do, and if he is silenced there are sure to be others to take his place.

For the purpose of our speculation, therefore, let us get rid at once of this superstition by assuming for the moment that the unions in the clothing industry have no conscious social philosophy, that in all eventualities they will act, not according to any predetermined plan, but to safeguard the interests of the workers and their own continuity as organizations. This assumption is not far from the truth, since if the unions sacrificed the permanent interest of the members or the organization to follow a preconceived plan, they would not endure long or accomplish much.

In comparison with the conditions which existed before the unions became powerful, those which they have been able to bring about are highly satisfactory. In comparison with conditions which might be achieved, however, and those for which the workers long, the present status is by no means desirable. Although sweatshops and home work have been practically abolished, the old, overcrowded tenements still stand, and the congestion of the city increases the difficulty and discomfort of living day by day. Inhumanly packed transit lines constantly wear down the nerves and physical resistance to disease. Money wages have been greatly increased, but real wages have risen but little. To say this is not to belittle the achievements of the unions in raising wages; prices, rising as a result of many causes, go up without any communal effort, but the power of the unions is necessary to see that wages even keep pace with them. Seasonal variations, with their resulting hardship, have not ceased, and the activities of the unions have succeeded in doing no more than mitigating their effect. The industry is still susceptible to the calamitous alternation of general prosperity and depression: the "prosperous" periods sending prices so high that they soon empty purses, and the depressions causing unemployment, misery, and a weakening of the workers' economic power.

Especially we must take into account the more spiritual factors; the sense of human dignity which makes the worker wish to share on even terms the benefits of the more fortunate members of the community, not only for himself but for his children, and the more specific desire not to be a tool or an underling in the shop for someone else who owns, profits, and directs, but to be the master of his own work, subject only to the needs of the community as a whole.

Nothing is more certain than that the emotional pressures resulting from existing dissatisfaction will not permit the unions now to rest on their oars, merely to retain their present relative advantages.

What escape is there? Let us first investigate what further concessions the unions may gain from the employers, and what the employers and the unions may accomplish through cooperation.

In the matter of wages, a practical limit will before long be reached. If prices continue to rise, wages may rise correspondingly, but real wages must remain almost stationary. The classical "iron law of wages" has been discredited, but there is a sound iron law: wages are limited by the productivity of industry. Given a maximum productivity, real wages can rise only by diverting a larger share of the earnings to the workers; but under the present economic régime this process cannot go beyond a certain point without driving the employers out of business by making it impossible for them to secure further capital. Rising wages in a given industry may be covered by rises in the prices of its products, but such a process cannot continue far above the general price level. This expedient cannot in any case succeed in raising real wages for long in a world where the labor in practically all industries is organized. It is probably true that the unions in the clothing industry will soon have been able to increase real wages almost to the point where any further gains in the form of concessions from the employers will prove illusory. This conclusion of course applies to all forms of bonuses and profit-sharing as well as to wages in the ordinary sense.

What can be done, then, to increase productivity? As far as productivity is dependent on labor, the clothing unions have adopted a more constructive attitude towards it than most of the old craft unions. They have not seriously attempted to limit the labor supply. They have not interposed vigorous objection to the adoption of labor-saving machinery—in some cases, as in the introduction of electric power, they have actually insisted on more efficient methods. They have, it is true, opposed the old-fashioned kind of "speeding up," but it is an open question whether that did increase productivity in the long run. They have gradually substituted week work for piece prices, in order to bring about a standardization of wages, but they are ready to welcome any method of increasing production from which the workers will be guaranteed their full share of the benefits. It is probable that here as in other industries something can be done to increase the productivity of the labor force, but it will necessarily be accompanied by granting labor an increased share of control over the productive process, thus creating a heightened sense of pride and ownership in the job itself.

The shortening of weekly hours by the unions has been directed, not toward a net decrease in production but toward a more even distribution of production throughout the year. In so far as the unions have succeeded in forcing the shops to do their work in a shorter day during the busy seasons, and to operate for longer hours during the dull seasons, the limit on hours has actually increased production.

The chief limit to productivity arises, however, not from labor but from the characteristics of the industry under the existing régime.[1] The excessive competition for public favor, creating such an immense variety of styles that they are burdensome to the public as they are to the industry; the reaction of these ephemeral styles in intensifying the seasonal fluctuations of business; the existence of many small and inefficient concerns which, while they do not make a profit and soon fail, lower the efficiency of the industry as a whole; the unnecessary duplication of selling organizations; the money wasted in competitive advertising—these and other enormous bills must be charged against the industry on the employers' side. Any expert in large-scale production and merchandizing can see at a glance that a great saving might be made by intelligent regulation, under one management, of such a chaotic industrial region. But capital has been unable so far to bring about any approach to concentration. In the men's clothing industry a few large establishments have grown up, but they are as far as ever from anything like control of the industry.

If no Sherman law or Clayton law were in the way, it is possible to imagine an alliance between the unions and the more powerful manufacturers to bring about something like unified management. Large combinations of capital and powerful labor unions have so many divergent interests, however, that it is difficult to imagine any such alliance working smoothly and effectively. Even if it did succeed, many of the possible reforms would not be made,

[1] Cf. Chapter I.

and we might be in as much danger of limitation of production as ever, as is shown by our experience of the great industrial corporations now in existence.

For, in the current flood of advice to labor to increase production, the most important factor of all is usually overlooked. That is the tendency of capital to limit production, because it produces, not in relation to the existing need, but in relation to the demand for goods at prices such that the highest return on the investment can be secured. There has not been a time in the memory of men now living when the human need for goods of all sorts was greater than in the months immediately following the signing of the armistice between the Allies and Germany. Unemployment, too, was widespread; labor was clamoring for a chance to produce. Yet capital for months allowed its enterprises to lie idle or to run on part time. It had incurred certain obligations to the holders of shares, bonds, mortgages, and loans, and if it had to produce under conditions such that it could not satisfy those obligations, and satisfy them well, it could not produce at all. The uncertainty of prices and credit under the capitalist régime limited production. Unwillingness to buy materials at existing high prices with the possibility of having to sell the products on a falling market, unwillingness to borrow money at high rates when it might shortly be borrowed at lower rates, paralyzed the necessary industries of the country. In normal times also a similar process goes on. We frequently hear of good foodstuffs being wantonly destroyed, of subterranean agreements to limit production, because more profit can be made at the high prices which will ensue if the supply remains a little short of the demand. Even where limitation is not the result of deliberate control, the factor of private profit causes a practical limitation, as in the clothing industry at present. Such limitation of production can be avoided only by an entire remodeling of the system of production and credit, by a control governed not by the primary interest of private profit, but by the real need for goods.

Under the existing system of money and credit, it is idle to expect advantage to the workers in any one industry from a great increase in the productivity of that industry alone, even if it were possible. If all the present clothing workers should in the same weekly hours produce twice the number of garments they now turn out, the purchasers could not afford to spend any more for clothes than they now allot for that purpose. What would happen, if business could stand the strain, would be simply that clothing prices would go down at least to a point where everybody could afford two garments for every one he now possesses. The real wages of the clothing workers would increase only to the extent of the extra clothing which would be available for their personal use. A similar increase in productivity would be necessary in all industries before they could double their real wages. But of course no such general increase can take place as long as production is dependent on interest-bearing credit and profitable prices.

Let us analyze in the same way the pressure for alleviating seasonal unemployment. What can be done to assist those workers whose wages are reduced or cut off altogether during the dull seasons? There are, in the first place, the expedients already adopted by the unions—a reduction of maximum weekly hours coupled with a high rate for overtime above normal hours, and the stipulation of a minimum average weekly wage for the year. The result of both these expedients is to put financial pressure on the manufacturers, making it more expensive for them to do extra work in the busy seasons and to let their plants run at a low ebb during the slack seasons. Up to a certain point these measures are effective; in some cases the manufacturer can introduce staples which can be made in the dull seasons as well as in the busy ones. But the most profitable part of his business still remains the making of goods cut according to the latest styles, and subject to rush orders while the busy season is on. The increased expenses of making such goods, caused by the stipulations of the unions, is merely added to the price, and the resulting prices are not high enough to decrease materially the effective demand. Furthermore, the manufacturer in his effort to avoid overtime is as likely, instead of pushing back busy-season work into the dull season, and so taking the risk of having large stocks of an unsalable line, simply to employ extra people during the busy season as long as there is any surplus in the labor supply. This way round his difficulty actually tends to increase seasonal unemployment, since it brings more people into the industry who cannot work in the dull seasons.

There is another method which remains to be tried —unemployment insurance. The manufacturers have a certain interest in keeping their labor force in the industry, and at a degree of health such that they will remain efficient workers. This interest is not sufficient to lead the manufacturers to keep a full force employed throughout the year, except in rare cases, but it might be sufficient to make them club together to pay unemployment benefits at a rate somewhat below the minimum wage. The attitude of the unions would have a large influence in the adoption of any such plan. Unions are justly suspicious of all "welfare work" initiated by the employer, since in most such schemes they detect a subtle intention to undermine the power of the union and bind the individual workman more closely to the individual employer. It is possible, however, that the unions and employers' associations might come to some agreement in this matter: they might decide that relief of those out of work through seasonal variation is a legitimate burden on the industry as a whole, and devise some machinery of joint administration which would protect the union.

While unemployment insurance would afford welcome relief to individual workers, it would not in the end solve the problem of seasonal variations. The worker does not want a long period of idleness, mitigated by a pittance paid at public expense; he wants a job at which he can earn a good living. Unemployment benefits, furthermore, would not increase by a cent the real wages of the whole labor force; they would simply spread out thinner and more equally the amount available for wages. If the profit of capital had not already shrunk to a minimum this might be a means of diverting a larger share of the earnings to labor, but sooner or later the limit would be reached.

Again we are forced back to the question of productive control. There is no solution of seasonal unemployment short of eliminating the dull seasons, and that cannot be accomplished under a competitive régime. It is possible to conceive a powerful combination of employers agreeing to a standardization of styles which would permit larger production in the dull season, but such a combination is most unlikely in most parts of the clothing industry without active discipline exercised by a strong union over individual manufacturers. There would always be a tendency for the aggressive manufacturer to violate his agreement and enlarge his business by adding new styles; and the only check on such a procedure would be a strike. Since effective discipline of this sort would create as much friction as it would remove, we come to the conclusion that a fundamental solution of the seasonal problem is highly improbable as long as the control of production remains with the manufacturer.

We have not touched at all upon other sources of dissatisfaction—those for instance arising from congestion in the great cities; inadequate housing and disease, high rents due to high land values, overcrowded traction lines, and so on. One can dream of model factories and settlements in the country; but the same forces that have caused the clothing manufacturers to cling to the city are likely to continue in operation. There is the large and fluid supply of labor; isolated factories are more at the mercy of their employees. And there is, too, the powerful factor of the attraction exercised by a city like New York upon the out-of-town buyer. Under competition the manufacturer, particularly the small one who attends to his own selling, cannot remain far from Broadway.

Even if there were no direct reasons for the unions to assume more control of the productive process, the vitality of organization itself would exert a tendency in that direction. Any great social organism develops a sort of inertia which keeps it moving in the direction in which it has been going. The people composing it have formed habits of associating in it; their wills and hopes are to large extent tied to it. They expect persistence from it, and put in power those able to satisfy that expectation. Mere momentum would cause the unions to move for a long time in the direction of greater control, even if they had no new motives for doing so. The converse is true of the manufacturers' associations. There is always latent the danger of a general engagement, whch is likely to be all the more severe and determined the larger and more powerful the respective associations become. The fear of aggression on the part of both is likely to lead to a flaring up in each of a desire to vanquish and perhaps exterminate the other. An analogy is furnished by international war. Ordinarily it is far more advantageous for nations to settle their differences and live at peace, but if a situation arises where two nations having opposite ideals and circumstances find themselves continually in conflict at a certain point in their relations, so that each lives in fear of an attack by the other, a large element in each will believe that the point at issue can reach a final settlement only by a complete victory of one country or the other, and war is always a possibility. It is worth noting that aggression is as likely to initiate with the manufacturers as with the unions.

If our analysis is correct, moreover, the momentum of the unions will be serving a real function. It is possible that the employers can find some way of raising real wages, decreasing unemployment, and relinquishing control in the shop, to such a degree that the workers will at length be satisfied and their pressure will cease. But the preceding analysis seems to show that the employers are powerless to grant concessions of any value beyond a certain point, that that point is not far off, and that the workers will by no means be satisfied when it is reached. In arriving at this conclusion we have taken no account of the more general burdens which the present economic régime places upon the community, such as its diversion of credit and labor from the production of necessities for the many to the production of luxuries for the few, its waste in inefficient methods of distribution and in competitive armament and war, its restrictive control of land and natural resources, its oscillation between booms and depressions. One need not admit that capitalism is responsible for these evils in order to see that sooner or later the clothing workers are likely to demand that the control of the employer and the primary interest of private capital be eliminated from their industry. The pressure of their normal wants having led them to this decision, it will be fortified by their desire to be their own masters, by the momentum of their organizations, and by their conscious social philosophy.

If this demand becomes insistent, how will it be satisfied? Nothing is more unlikely than that the employers will voluntarily satisfy it, and even if they did graciously step aside, something else would have to take their place. There is no way out but for the unions themselves to assume the productive control, to develop into a syndicate or guild. But to say this is by no means to solve the problem. If the statement is to mean anything concrete, the process by which effective control may be achieved must be investigated more carefully.

As we have seen in Chapter I, nothing is easier than to open a small establishment for the manufacture of ready-made clothing. Many an experi-

THE FUTURE

enced wage-earner has done so, and many of those who have done so have succeeded and are now themselves employers. There are cases on record of former union officials becoming manufacturers and being selected by their fellow-employers to negotiate with union committees. There is without question enough expert knowledge of production and enough managerial ability of the right sort in the unions so that they would be capable of operating clothing shops.

A method of gaining a hold on production that might present itself would therefore be for the union to set up a few shops of its own in competition with the established manufacturers, and from the profits to enlarge the field of control until enough collectively owned plants were in operation so that the union could dictate the management of the industry at large and in the end form a monopoly. Let us assume for the moment that for any such attempt the unions would receive as fair treatment as the private employer—that the selling concerns and the retailers would handle their goods, that the banks would give them credit, and the manufacturers of machinery and materials would deal with them on the usual terms. Still the unions would be in the most of the larger matters at the same disadvantage as the private employer. They could not make any radical changes in the productive régime until they had acquired complete control. Acquiring complete control would be a long and hazardous process. In the meantime they would have to oppose and deny many of the normal demands of the workers in their own shops; it is not only conceivable but probable that before long the workers in the union-owned shops would be striking against their officials, and the attempt at gradual permeation would end in disaster. Our primary assumption, moreover, is itself an absurd one. Adherents of the present economic régime may boast of its opportunity for anyone who wishes to enter the competitive struggle for wealth and power, but even they cannot imagine that the banks and commercial organizations would refrain from boycotting a movement aimed at the ending of private enterprise in a great industry.

These objections do not of course operate so powerfully against a single clothing shop operated by the union, such as is now projected by the New York Cutter's local of the Amalgamated Clothing Workers, provided it is regarded as an experimental station rather than as the first step in a deliberate invasion of production. With a standardized product which could be sold to members of the union itself, the shop could easily be profitable enough to keep the workers well satisfied and still sell the garments considerably below the prevailing market price. At the same time valuable data about management, proper accounting, and the relation of labor cost to production cost could be accumulated.

The development of consumers' cooperation, coöperative banks, and direct exchange of products between farmers' associations and unions may lead to a sound growth of clothing manufacture by the unions, yet it is easy to over-estimate the possibilities of such a movement. Clothing may be exchanged for raw produce or perhaps even for flour and manufactured foods, but when it comes to exchanging clothing for products of other lines of industry, the chances are not great, since it will be by no means as easy for unions engaged in trades having more substantial investment in property and plant to enter the productive field by permeation. The consumers' cooperative movement is indeed growing rapidly, but not rapidly enough to promise for many years a market for the bulk of ready-made clothing. At the best we may see the establishment of a number of union plants making certain standardized garments for farmers and cooperatives, whose main service in building an ultimate cooperative commonwealth will be the training of working-class technicians and the development of a body of knowledge useful in cooperative production.

Another possibility is that the unions might make an attempt to set up their control at a single stroke. Imagine a nation-wide strike in the industry, caused by natural and justifiable demands which the employers were incapable of granting, or a nation-wide lockout, arising perhaps out of a minor dispute, but maintained by the employers through a desire to destroy the unions. Suppose, in such an event, the unions should decide the time was ripe for them to produce for themselves. The essential investment in plant, material and power is far less than in most other industries, and it would not be as necessary for the unions to acquire the property of the existing employers, as it would, for instance, if a similar plan should be adopted in the case of mines or railroads. Still, the project would be a gigantic one, impossible of execution in a short period. It would, moreover, require the assistance, or at least the absence of hostility, of those in control of credit, distribution, and the manufacture of machinery and material. The consequence is that such an undertaking would be hopeless unless the control of credit had already been taken from private capital, workers' control of production existed in the manufacture of machinery and textiles, and distribution were in the hands of a democratic state, a distributive guild, or consumers' cooperatives.

We must therefore admit that, while it is unlikely that the clothing workers will long consent to a continued control of private capital in their industry, it is just as unlikely that they could gain control for themselves without powerful assistance from outside. How could the ground be prepared for that assistance?

There is, of course, the traditional plan put forward by revolutionary syndicalists—that of a general strike of all labor with the aim of assuming simultaneous control in all industries. This plan, however, could never be adopted by hard-headed union officials, except in desperation. The hardships and dislocation of sudden revolution are too certain, and its ultimate success too problematical, for it ever to form a part of the calculations of any but theoreticians with no responsibilities in the daily struggle of the trade unions. To say this is not to say that such an event is impossible. A severe crisis might bring such suffering and dissatisfaction to the people that anything would seem better than their misery, and they might in such a case force drastic action. The same is true of a coup d'état through force of arms. But we must regard the possibility of violent revolution much as we regard the possibility of an earthquake or a volcanic eruption. It may come; indeed it is sure to come if there is no other escape for vast natural forces; but we cannot bring it about by the power of will, and to attempt to do so would be madness as long as all other methods of giving vent to social pressures remain untried.

Gradual permeation is impossible for one industry considered by itself, but it may be possible, if methodically undertaken, one by one, for industries as a whole. If it is to be achieved, it must begin with the basic industries. Suppose a political party, controlled by labor and its sympathisers, powerful enough to be the deciding voice in the state. Suppose, then, that the basic industries, one after another, come under a new control in the form of a partnership between the democratic state and the workers in the several industries. The gaining of such control would probably be the work of political and economic action combined. It might begin with the railways. The state, governed by a labor party, would vote to acquire the railroad property by some such moderate expedient as that proposed by the railway unions. Against the opposition with which capital would attempt to render such legislation ineffective the economic power of the unions would be a safeguard.

With this corner-stone safely laid, the public ownership of the mines and their operation by the miners might follow. The more radical farmers, allied with the employees in packing houses and other food industries, would insure public, democratic control of the food supply. Then would come the iron and steel plants, and the subsidiary metal products. The distributive system, at least in vital points, would be in the hands of consumers' co-operative societies, which even now are growing rapidly, and which would grow still more rapidly the moment labor attained the power and self-consciousness to bring about these fundamental changes. Once the railways, mines, food products, machinery plants, and textile mills were controlled by labor or by a partnership between labor and a democratic state, the clothing workers could set up their own control without much difficulty. Whether the state would buy the existing plants or furnish credit to start new ones would be a minor question to be determined by expediency when the time arrived. It is probable that a combination of the two methods would prove advisable. New model factories might be erected in better locations, while the best of the old machinery might be bought from the manufacturers. If the manufacturers refused to sell, they would have no other market, and the certainty that the state could furnish new machinery might bring them to terms.

The matter of credit is a highly complicated one and deserves special consideration. Our short sketch of the method of establishing workers' control can be at best merely suggestive of a difficult process concerning which no one can predict with any certainty. Adequate treatment of the credit problem alone would require a large volume, but a few hints concerning it can be thrown out. The borrowing power of the state under the capitalist régime seems at times indefinitely extensible, but there is nevertheless a limit somewhere, and our government is probably near that limit at the present moment. How would it be possible, then, to raise the money necessary for the vast purchases which, under the plan just outlined, it would be necessary to make? Would the people devote their savings and the business men their surplus capital and the banks their credit to the purchase of bonds issued for the purpose of buying out private owners and abolishing the profit system?

It is just possible that, seeing the ruin of the old system ahead of them and fearing a crash in which they would lose all, the owners of surplus capital would choose this comfortable way out of their difficulty, even at some loss. With a labor government in power and labor unrest prevalent everywhere, the prosperity of private enterprise might be so uncertain that capital would seek large issues of government bonds as the safest haven in the storm. But it is more probable that the credit of the government itself would be injured by the uncertain prospect, and people would prefer to run their chances with the old system or hoard their money instead of entrusting it to the government. Doubts of the most serious nature would be drilled into their minds. Where would the government get the money to pay the interest on its bonds, once its taxing power on private enterprise had vanished? Would the efficiency of the new régime be such that any surplus from the railroads or the industries would be available for interest? The ruling bankers would see that if they could prevent the government from getting credit, the whole project would fail, and a decisive victory might be won for the old order. To be sure, such a victory might provoke a resort to force; but when it comes to force, the powers that be always feel at home. They might even prefer to have the unrest take this form, thinking that they could crush it the more easily.

Along the road of attempting to float popular bond issues, with certain partial exceptions which we shall mention later, lies danger and defeat. But let us consider for the moment what the government would really have in mind. It would not be borrowing money to make tanks and explosives and aeroplanes—destructive objects which produce nothing and in turn demand more money for their upkeep and accessories. It would not even be borrowing to construct buildings, roads or parks—useful things which, nevertheless, do not as a rule bring in any income. It would simply be acquiring title to productive enterprises. What more natural than that it should hand over to the present owners of these enterprises its note for their value, and pay the interest out of future profits? As long as surplus earnings existed, no resort to taxation for this purpose would be necessary. The procedure would not involve any addition to the public debt, as that debt is ordinarily understood.

Of course, the present owners might and probably would object to the sale, and would have to be coerced by the superior power of the majority. They would raise legal obstructions of every sort. But in the end, if the political power of labor were secure and its economic power were well directed, they could be defeated, even if revision of the Constitution were necessary. However difficult the path of the government might be, peaceable and orderly changes would be possible, provided the minority did not resort to arms.

We assume, of course, that the new management would be efficient, and would produce a surplus value. The task of demonstrating it we must leave to others, but if the case of the clothing industry is any indication, the assumption is not a hazardous one. The necessity of paying interest on the debt would be a burden, but it would not be so great a burden as the successive additions to capitalization which occur under private ownership. Furthermore, the government would recover a large part of the interest by income and inheritance taxes. The bonds would be simply an expedient for socializing industry with the least hardship to those who benefit from the present régime.

The attempt of the government to secure the credit so that it could acquire property without expropriation would be most difficult at first, and would decrease with every successive step. By the time it had acquired the railways and mines, the superior efficiency of the new management would have provided a surplus. Before it reached the end of the cycle, government credit would be practically self-contained. Indeed, credit would assume its fundamental form of advances of labor and materials in expectation of future return in kind. Even now consumers' cooperatives often grant credit, without interest, to striking unions whose members are also members of the cooperative. This means merely that they advance goods to their members without immediate payment. There are also cooperative banks in existence, and more may easily arise, which could be expected to invest largely in government or labor enterprises. Eventually, the guilds of workers in railroads, mines, metal establishments and so on could, either directly or through the state, contribute the surplus of their labor to the task of founding new guilds, in the knowledge that they, as consumers, would benefit in the end. And when the entire process was completed, interest-bearing credit in the ordinary sense would exist no longer. The task of the government—or of the guilds—would simply be to direct surplus production in the channels where public welfare demanded it. Production at last could be adjusted to need rather than to profit.

Speculation on the methods of the new industrial revolution is really beyond the province of this book; we have indulged in it merely to indicate the broad lines which the future interest of the clothing unions and the consuming public is likely to take. For the workers, the inference is that every democratic and broadening characteristic of their movement is again justified. All exclusive and narrow tendencies, all inner friction inherited from the old conception of unionism, will prove an increased source of weakness as time goes on. Not only must the unions be well knit within themselves, and ready to share all the benefits equally among their members, but unity must be sought in the whole labor movement, unity both economic and political. It is probably unnecessary to stress the need of economic solidarity, since it is such a well-established principle already, but political solidarity is no less essential. There does not seem to be any way to bring about effective workers' control of industry without political control of the state. This is true even if a catastrophic revolution should occur, but it is doubly true in an attempt to bring about a revolution without disorder.

It is also obvious that the change will come the more easily the better the workers fit themselves to undertake production on their own account. They have nothing to lose, but everything to gain, from all improvements in technique and in shop management calculated to increase production without imposing hardship upon them. They may rest assured that any marked increase in productivity can be secured only by granting the workers increased control. The propaganda for higher productivity will, in the long run, react in their favor.

Since the clothing workers need unity among themselves, unity with labor in more fundamental industries, and, in fact, unity with other elements not ordinarily classed with organized labor, the cultural side of their movement is of the highest importance. The bond of a common culture is the strongest bond that can exist outside of the purely economic one; indeed, in the case of people not fully conscious of their economic position it is often stronger than the economic. Conscious propaganda is a puny instrument beside a culture naturally and unconsciously permeated with the ideals of its creators. There is no more effective barrier to the progress of the labor movement today, in so far as it is a broad movement for human liberation and a finer life, than the popular culture of the daily press, the cheap moving picture, the sensational magazine, shallow music, and a poor-spirited education. The kind of culture which the workers have begun to provide for themselves is infinitely stronger and better fitted to survive than that with which the sensibility of the public is now dulled, because it does not depend on the commercialism which has determined the character of the prevailing substitutes for art, literature, music, drama, journalism, and education. No effort should be spared, therefore, to strengthen the cultural activities of the labor movement and to extend their influence.

In sum, the labor movement will prosper in so far as it remains true to its nature. It is essentially a generous movement, devoted to enriching the life of the great masses of humanity. It is necessarily equalitarian and democratic, it is necessarily associated with ideas and ideals. The moment any section of labor departs from its true genius, becomes exclusive, and refuses to see beyond immediate material gains, it courts defeat, because that is a realm which property knows better than labor. Exclusive motives developed capitalism, and they tend to maintain it. In so far as they remain in the ascendency, the labor movement will be unable to profit much from any victory which it may win.

Members of the public who regard themselves as not directly concerned in the struggle between owner and labor, except as consumers and citizens affected by the welfare of the community, will find it increasingly necessary to side with one party or the other as times goes on. It is therefore to their interest to examine the issue carefully in order to see which side they ought to espouse. If they take the conventional view of the labor movement—that it is simply a means of protecting the interest of manual workers against grasping employers—they are likely to misinterpret what is almost sure to happen. The time will come—indeed in some fields it is here already—when labor will demand more remuneration and control than the employer is able to grant. If the public takes the position that labor's demands can be justified only by their reasonableness from the employer's point of view, it will decide that these demands are unjust and will take the part of capital against labor. But such a position will not make the demands unjust from labor's point of view, for they will be based not so much on the power of the employer to grant them as on the necessities of a decent standard of life and a full measure of human dignity. The fact that the demands are refused will not prevent their being repeated with increasing insistence. And the turmoil of the industrial conflict, so costly and inconvenient to the public, will merely be intensified.

It cannot be intensified indefinitely, however, without an explosion. Such a catastrophe, incalculable as its results are, is the last thing desired by those who take the old-fashioned view of the labor movement. Yet the only escape from it seems to be the development of some way of satisfying the just demands of labor after the present industrial régime becomes incapable of doing so. This is the function of the labor movement itself, considered in the light of the new unionism. The associations of labor characterized by the new unionism, with its aspiration towards industrial control, its constructive attitude towards production, its democracy and idealism, are the only social organisms now powerful, out of which a beneficent new order might flow. The truly far-sighted policy is to encourage them and to strengthen their hands.

A logical ground upon which a member of the public might out of self-interest oppose the more self-conscious wing of the labor movement is the chance that a crisis may be precipitated in which the forces of labor will be decisively defeated and scattered and a final victory won for capitalism. A study of the history of the labor movement makes this chance seem slight indeed. Labor is used to defeat, and thrives on it. It has been defeated many times in what at the moment looked like a decisive way, but it has always arisen from its own ashes. Even if a final defeat were possible, the industrial serfdom which would result is a thing which no liberal-minded man should wish to contemplate.

It is ordinarily assumed that "conservative" unions, because they have no conscious social philosophy, are a bulwark against violence, while the "radical" unions are dangerous disturbers of the peace. Something very like the contrary, however, is the fact. The conservative unions make as many demands for material improvement as the radical ones, and they are no more likely to stop when the limit of the employer is reached. They therefore actually do as much, if not more, to intensify the industrial conflict and hasten the day of reckoning. On the other hand, their absence of constructive policy will tend to make that day of reckoning a blind plunge into chaos rather than a reasoned attempt to find a civilized way out of the difficulty. Here, as elsewhere, obscurantism is no protection against upheaval.

If labor cannot be either decisively defeated or satisfied under the present régime, the only way out of the existing turmoil is a radical change in the system of production and distribution. Why should any member of the public, whose livelihood is dependent on his daily work, hesitate to welcome such a change? It promises a closer unity between man as producer and man as consumer, through the assumption by both of the function of the private profit maker, who, by his intervention, causes enormous wastes and maladjustments. It would tend to make effective the mutual interest of producer and consumer in high productivity of necessities, in production regulated according to public need. It would not be a dividing up of existing wealth by plunder of rich men, at which the anti-socialist scoffs, but the installation of new and better social machinery for increasing the total sum of wealth and for distributing it more rationally. And, even more important than its material benefits, it would release immense potential forces of democracy, goodwill and culture now imprisoned by the bitter limitations of an unnecessarily competitive world.

For an attempt to regulate this change we have both the motive of fear and the motive of hope. The dissolution of the present economic system, brought nearer by relentless social forces, will not wait. The crisis may come either in the clumsy and dangerous way of a violent explosion, or in the orderly way of a planned reconstruction carried out at the behest of an enlightened majority. In a sense we are spectators of a race between the approach of the crisis and the effort of intelligence to prepare for it. At present the majority is not enlightened, and we are far from the ability to carry through an orderly and radical reconstruction. If the power of intelligence is to be increased, it is necessary for the public to renounce all superstitious repression, to hear and consider all proposals for change, however unfamiliar they may be, to give active support to political measures by which basic change may be introduced. As long as men are put in prison for expressing their opinions, or journals are suppressed, or force is used in any way to stifle thought and discussion, we are robbing ourselves of collective power to act intelligently.

Strong and justified as the motive of fear is, however, the motive of courage is stronger. For a long time apologists for the existing order have been ridiculing proposals for change by scoffing at Utopian perfection and saying that no new plan would "work." Such arguments are rapidly failing to arouse timidity. Not many people after a moment's reflection can believe either that the present system "works" or that it is necessary to conceive a heaven on earth in order to imagine a more efficient one. Many of us are in a mood to take a risk of something worse in the hope of something better. Experiment and discovery, in spite of all doubts and dangers, remain a habit of the human race.

BIBLIOGRAPHY

Amalgamated Clothing Workers of America, Documentary History of. Vol. I, 1914-16; Vol. II, 1916-20. N. Y., Amalgamated Clothing Workers.
American Labor Yearbook, 1918-19, 1919-20; ed. by Alexander Trachtenberg. N. Y., Rand School of Social Science.
BERNHEIMER, CHARLES S.: The Shirt Waist Strike. N. Y., University Settlement, 1910.
BRISSENDEN, P. F.: The I. W. W. N. Y., Longman's Green & Co.
BRUÈRE, ROBERT W.: On the trail of the I. W. W. N. Y., Evening Post, 1918.
COHEN, JULIUS HENRY: Law and Order in Industry. N. Y., Macmillan Co., 1916.
COLE, G. D. H.: Introduction to Trade Unionism. London, Labor Research Dept., 1918.
COLE, G. D. H.: Labour in the Commonwealth. New York Huebsch, 1919.
COLE, G. D. H.: Self-Government in Industry. N. Y., Macmillan Co., 1918.
COMMONS, JOHN R. and Others: History of Labor in the United States. N. Y., Macmillan Co., 1918.
EATON, ISABEL: Receipts and Expenditures of Certain Wage Earners in the Garment Trades. American Statistical Association, 1894-1895.
Factors Affecting the Health of Garment Makers. Philadelphia, Henry Phipps Institute, 1915.
FOERSTER, ROBERT F.: The Italian Immigration of Our Times. Cambridge, Harvard University Press, 1919.
HILLQUIT, MORRIS: History of Socialism in the United States. N. Y., Funk and Wagnalls Co., 1910.
HILLQUIT, MORRIS: Not Guilty (Opening Address of Counsel for Defendants in trial of 8 Cloakmakers in 1915). N. Y., International Ladies' Garment Workers Union, 1915.
HOURWICH, ISAAC A.: Immigration and Labor. N. Y., G. P. Putnam's Sons, 1912.
HOXIE, ROBERT F.: Trade Unionism in the United States. N. Y., D. Appleton & Co., 1917.
IZOLD, HENRIETTA: Elements of the Jewish Population in the United States. (In the Russian Jew in the United States, by Charles S. Bernheimer.)
JOINT BOARD OF SANITARY CONTROL. Annual Reports, 1911-1919. N. Y.
JOSEPH, SAMUEL: Jewish Immigration to the United States. N. Y., Columbia University, 1914.
Jubilee-Journal 10th Anniversary. United Neckwear Makers Union. N. Y., 1916.
LORD, ELIOT, and Others: The Italian in America. N. Y., B. F. Buck & Co., 1905.

BIBLIOGRAPHY

MAROT, HELEN: American Labor Unions. N. Y., D. Appleton & Co., 1917.
MASSACHUSETTS, COMMONWEALTH OF:
  Bureau of Statistics of Labor, Sixth Annual Report. Employment of Women at Sewing Machine Labor. 1875.
  Bureau of Statistics of Labor, Fifteenth Annual Report. The Working Girls of Boston. 1884.
  Bureau of Statistics. Industrial Home Work in Massachusetts. 1914.
  Minimum Wage Commission, Bulletin No. 9. Wages of Women in Women's Clothing Factories in Massachusetts. 1915.
NEW YORK, STATE OF:
  Bureau of Labor, Third Annual Report. Part I. Working Women; Their Trades, Wages, Homes and Social Conditions. 1885.
  Bureau of Labor, Twentieth Annual Report. Wages in the Clothing Trade, pp. 1-28. Earnings in Home Industries, pp. 37-289, 1902.
  Department of Labor. Report on the Growth of Industry in New York. 1902.
  Factory Investigating Commission Report. Wages in the Millinery Trade. 1914.
  Department of Labor. Special Bulletin No. 92. Weekly Earnings of Women in Five Industries. 1919.
ODENCRANTZ, LOUISE C.: Italian Women in Industry. N. Y., Russell Sage Foundation, 1919.
POPE, JESSE: The Clothing Industry in New York. University of Missouri. 1905.
SLICHTER, SUMNER H.: The Turnover of Factory Labor. N. Y., D. Appleton & Co., 1919.
SMELSER, D. P.: Unemployment and American Trade Unions. Baltimore, Johns Hopkins, 1919.
UNITED STATES GOVERNMENT REPORTS:
  United States Census, 1860, Manufactures, lxii. 1900, Manufactures, Pt. III, pp 261-302.
  Abstract of the Census of Manufactures, 1914.
  Sen. Doc. 645. Report on Condition of Women and Child Wage-Earners in the United States. Vol. II. Men's Ready-Made Clothing. 1911.
  Department of Commerce, Bureau of Foreign and Domestic Commerce. The Men's Factory-Made Clothing Industry. 1914.
  Public Health Service, Bulletin 71. The Health of Garment Workers. 1915.
  Department of Labor, Bureau of Labor Statistics. Bulletins No.
    146. Wages and Regularity of Employment and Standardization of Piece Rates in the Dress and Waist Industry. N. Y. City. 1914.
    147. Wages and Regularity of Employment in the Cloak, Suit and Skirt Industry. 1914.
    183. Regularity of Employment in the Women's Ready-to-Wear Garment Industries. 1915.
    145. Conciliation, Arbitration and Sanitation in the Dress and Waist Industry of N. Y. City. 1914.

144. Industrial Court of the Cloak, Suit and Skirt Industry of N. Y. City. 1914.
198. Collective Agreements in the Men's Clothing Industry. 1916.
175. Summary of the Report on Condition of Women and Child Wage-Earners in the United States. 1915.
193. Dressmaking as a Trade for Women in Massachusetts. 1916
215. Industrial Experience of Trade School Girls in Massachusetts. 1917.

Immigration Commission. Reports. Vol. 11, Part 6. Clothing Manufacturing. Part 7. Collar, Cuff and Shirt Manufacturing. Vols. 26 and 27. Immigrants in Cities. 1915.
Industrial Relations Commission. Final Report. 1915.
WEBB, SIDNEY, and BEATRICE: Industrial Democracy. N. Y., Longmans, Green & Co. 1914. History of Trade Unionism. N. Y., Longmans, Green & Co. 1920.
WHITNEY, NATHANIEL RUGGLES: Jurisdiction in American Trade Unions. Baltimore, Johns Hopkins, 1919.
WILLETT, MABEL HURD: Employment of Women in the Clothing Trade. N. Y. Columbia University Studies, 1902.

MISCELLANEOUS SOURCES

Occasional articles and comment in the *Survey*, *Journal of Political Economy*, *American Labor Legislation Review*, *Proceedings of American Academy of Political Science*.
Pamphlets issued by the National Consumers' League.
Constitutions and Reports of Conventions of the unions under discussion.
The following union journals:
Advance—Amalgamated Clothing Workers of America.
Fur Worker—International Furriers' Union.
Garment Worker—United Garment Workers.
Headgear Worker—United Cloth Hat and Cap Makers.
Justice—International Ladies' Garment Workers Union.
New Textile Worker—Amalgamated Textile Workers of America.
Tailor—Journeyman Tailors' Union.

APPENDIX I

CONSTITUTION OF AMALGAMATED CLOTHING WORKERS OF AMERICA

PREAMBLE

The economic organization of Labor has been called into existence by the capitalist system of production, under which the division between the ruling class and the ruled class is based upon the ownership of the means of production. The class owning those means is the one that is ruling, the class that possesses nothing but its labor power, which is always on the market as a commodity, is the one that is being ruled.

A constant and unceasing struggle is being waged between these two classes.

In this struggle the economic organization of Labor, the union, is a natural weapon of offense and defense in the hands of the working class.

But in order to be efficient, and effectively serve its purpose, the union must in its structure correspond to the prevailing system of the organization of industry.

Modern industrial methods are very rapidly wiping out the old craft demarcations, and the resultant conditions dictate the organization of Labor along industrial lines.

The history of the Class Struggle in this country for the past two decades amply testifies to the ineffectiveness of the form, methods, and spirit of craft unionism. It also shows how dearly the working class has paid for its failure to keep apace with industrial development.

The working class must accept the principles of Industrial Unionism or it is doomed to impotence.

The same forces that have been making for Industrial Unionism are likewise making for a closer inter-industrial alliance of the working class.

The industrial and inter-industrial organization, built upon the solid rock of clear knowledge and class consciousness, will put the organized working class in actual control of the system of production, and the working class will then be ready to take possession of it.

ARTICLE I

Name and Jurisdiction

Section 1. This body shall be known as the AMALGAMATED CLOTHING WORKERS OF AMERICA. In it alone is vested the power to establish subordinate Local Unions, and to it is reserved the right to finally determine and adjust all matters of general

APPENDIX

importance to the welfare of the various Local Unions or any members thereof, while to the subordinate Unions is conceded the right of making all necessary laws for local self-government, which do not conflict with the laws of the Amalgamated Clothing Workers of America.

Sec. 2. All legislative powers shall be reserved to the Amalgamated Clothing Workers of America duly convened in session; except as hereinafter provided for, its executive and judicial powers, when not in session, shall be vested in the General Executive Board.

ARTICLE II

Headquarters

Section 1. The headquarters of the Amalgamated Clothing Workers of America shall be in the city of New York, N. Y.

ARTICLE III

General Convention

Section 1. The Amalgamated Clothing Workers of America shall meet biennially in General Convention on the second Monday in May at ten (10) A.M., at such place as may have been chosen by the last convention and ratified by referendum vote.

Sec. 2. On motion of five (5) Local Unions, no two of which shall be of the same State or province, the place for holding the convention may be changed by a general vote, a two-thirds majority to decide. A special convention can be called in the same manner.

Sec. 3. Local Unions shall be entitled to representation in conventions according to the average membership on which they pay per capita tax for the twenty-four (24) months ending January 30th immediately preceding the convention on the following basis: One (1) delegate for each Local Union of one hundred (100) members or less and one (1) additional delegate for every additional three hundred (300) members. Local Unions having over one thousand (1000) members shall send no less than three (3.) delegates and one additional delegate for every additional one thousand (1000) members or majority fraction thereof. Each delegate shall be entitled to one (1) vote for every one hundred (100) members he represents.

Sec. 4. All Local Unions shall be notified by the General Secretary, sixty (60) days before the biennial convention takes place, to elect the number of delegates thev are entitled to on the basis of representation.

Sec. 5. Delegates shall be elected at a special meeting of their Local Union, by ballot, not later than March 31st preceding the convention, and a plurality vote shall constitute an election. No person shall be eligible to election as a delegate unless a member of the Amalgamated Clothing Workers of America, who shall have been a member in good standing of the Local Union he represents at least one year immediately preceding the date on which said election is held. At the same time and in the same manner that delegates are elected, there shall be elected an equal number of alternates. In case of death, resignation, inability or other disqualification of a delegate, the alternate having the highest number of votes at the election shall succeed to vacancy and become the delegate, with all the rights and privileges thereof.

Sec. 6. Delegates shall establish their right to a seat in the convention by credentials signed by the presiding officer and the secretary of the Local Union with the seal of the Local Union.

Sec. 7. Credentials shall be forwarded to the General Secretary by the Secretary of the Local Union immediately after the election of the delegate or delegates.

Sec. 8. Expenses of delegates to the convention shall be paid by the Local Union they represent.

Sec. 9. No Local Union shall be entitled to representation at the biennial convention unless the per capita tax and assessments are paid up to the first day of March preceding the convention, nor unless the Local Union has been organized at least three months prior to the convention.

Sec. 10. In order to provide for the presence of the General President and General Secretary at the next succeeding convention to render their reports, in case they should not be elected as delegates, the expense of their presence shall be taken out of the General Fund of the Amalgamated Clothing Workers of America.

Sec. 11. A quorum for the transaction of business shall consist of two-thirds of the delegates attending the convention. Delegates absent at roll call shall be fined one dollar ($1.00), unless they are sick or on business for the convention, which fine shall be paid forthwith. The hours of session shall be governed by the respective conventions.

Sec. 12. The convention shall be governed by the following order of business, unless suspended by a two-thirds majority.

Order of Business

1. Call to order by General President.

Immediately upon his calling the convention to order, and before addresses of welcome are made, the General President shall call for the nomination and election of a Credential Committee of five.

That Committee, as soon as elected, shall withdraw to pass upon the credentials presented, and shall submit a report before the first session adjourns.

2. Report of Credential Committee.
3. Roll Call.
4. Report of Officers.
5. Reading of Minutes.
6. Appointment of the following committees: Press, Resolution, Law, Reports of Officers, Appeals and Grievances, Organization, Label and Miscellaneous.
7. Reports of Local Unions.
8. Reports of Committees.
9. Unfinished Business.
10. New Business.
11. Nomination of Officers.
12. Selection of place for next convention.

APPENDIX

13. Good and Welfare.
14. Adjournment.

Sec. 13. Secretaries of Local Unions shall send a report of the conditions of the Local Unions to the General Secretary thirty days before the convention, to be printed in the convention number of the Official Journal. The seal of the respective Local Unions, together with the signatures of the President and the Secretary, must be attached to all reports.

Article IV

Referendum Vote—How Taken

Section 1. Any and all additions and amendments to this constitution adopted at any session of the convention shall not become a law until approved by a majority vote of the general membership. The General Secretary shall submit any and all changes made by the convention to a referendum vote within thirty (30) days after the close of the convention.

Sec. 2. During the interim between conventions any Local Union may propose amendments or additions to the constitution and if five (5) other Local Unions, no two of which shall be of the same State or Province, second the same, the General Secretary shall submit the proposition to a vote of the general membership, and if approved by a majority of the members voting the same shall become a law.

Sec. 3. When the General Executive Board considers a question of sufficient importance, a referendum vote must be ordered, and a two-thirds majority vote shall decide.

Sec. 4. When a referendum vote is ordered each Local Union shall call a special meeting and take action seriatim on all questions submitted for a vote, only members present to be counted.

Sec. 5. The President and Recording Secretary shall carefully record the vote and send the same, under their signatures and the seal of the Local Union, to the General Secretary.

Sec. 6. The General Secretary must issue a referendum ballot, when ordered, within two (2) weeks, and vote of Local Unions to be counted must be received within thirty (30) days from date of issue of any referendum ballot. The result of the referendum shall be published in the official publications of the Amalgamated Clothing Workers of America, in tabulated form.

Article V

General Officers and How Chosen

Section 1. The General Officers of the Amalgamated Clothing Workers of America shall consist of a General President, a General Secretary, and a General Treasurer. The General Executive Board shall consist of eleven members including the three General Officers.

Sec. 2. The General Executive Board shall meet to attend quarterly sessions during the months of March, June, September and December. Their expenses to be defrayed by the Amalgamated Clothing Workers of America.

Sec. 3. All officers shall be nominated by convention and elected by referendum.

Sec. 4. The convention shall elect a committee of five (5) to act as tellers on balloting for officers.

Sec. 5. No members shall be eligible to election as a General Officer unless at least one year a member of the Amalgamated Clothing Workers of America, in good standing.

ARTICLE VI

General President

Section 1. The General President shall preside over all meetings of the International Convention; attend to disputes between employers and employees; adjust differences between local unions; perform necessary organizing and other work usual to the office of General President. He shall keep a record of the work performed by him and make a detailed report of the same to the convention. All actions of the General President shall be under the direction of the General Executive Board. He shall sign all official documents when satisfied that they are correct. He shall at the end of each week submit to the General Secretary an itemized statement of all moneys expended by him in the interests of the International Union during the said week.

Sec. 2. He shall give bonds to the amount of ten thousand dollars ($10,000) in a first class surety company. The cost of the bond to be paid from the funds of the Amalgamated Clothing Workers of America.

Sec. 3. The General President shall devote his entire time to services of the Amalgamated Clothing Workers of America, and shall receive as compensation the sum of four thousand dollars ($4,000) per annum.

General Secretary

Section 4. The General Secretary shall keep a correct record of the proceedings of the Convention and publish the same in pamphlet or small book form, preserve all important documents, papers, books, etc., all letters received by him and copies of letters sent on business of the A. C. W. of A. He shall be custodian of the seal of the A. C. W. of A. He shall conduct all correspondence of the A. C. W. of A., and lay the same regularly before the Executive Board and be subject to their direction. He shall receive all moneys due the A. C. W. of A., giving his receipt therefor. He shall keep a correct account of all financial business of the A. C. W. of A., and pay over to the General Treasurer, taking his receipt therefor, all funds in his hands at the end of each month, after paying all claims approved by the General Executive Board. The General Secretary shall have charge of the distribution of the label.

Sec. 5. The General Secretary shall act as Secretary of the General Executive Board. He shall receive all applications for charters, and shall issue the same when approved by the General Executive Board. He shall have power to hire such clerical help as shall be necessary to carry on the business of the A. C. W. of A.

Sec. 6. The General Secretary shall submit a biennial report, with any recommendations he may consider necessary, to the convention, and shall perform all duties devolving upon him under the Constitution or required of him by the General Executive Board.

Sec. 7. The General Secretary shall devote his entire time to the services of the A. C. W. of A., and shall receive as compensation the sum of four thousand dollars ($4,000) per annum. He shall give bonds to the amount of fifteen thousand dollars ($15,000), in some first class surety company, the cost of the bond to be paid from the funds of the A. C. W. of A.

Sec. 8. The General Secretary shall keep separate and itemized accounts of postage, telegram, printers' and office expenses. All bills of organizers and general officers must be fully itemized.

Sec. 9. The General Secretary shall issue an itemized monthly financial report to each Local Union. He shall also issue monthly report blanks to the Local Unions with instructions for filling out and returning same.

Sec. 10. The General Secretary shall promptly notify Local Unions when two months in arrears.

General Treasurer

Sec. 11. The General Treasurer shall, as provided for in Section 4, take charge of funds of the A. C. W. of A. He shall pay all warrants regularly drawn on him by a majority vote of the General Executive Board, and signed by the General Secretary and Chairman of the General Executive Board. He shall not hold in his possession more than two hundred dollars ($200), and all over that amount he shall deposit within twenty-four (24) hours in some savings or interest paying bank approved by the General Executive Board. He shall give bonds to the amount of twenty thousand dollars ($20,000) in some first class surety company, the cost of the bond to be paid from the funds of the A. C. W. of A. Should the amount in the bank be in excess of said amount, the said bond shall be increased accordingly. He shall, through the General Secretary, send to the convention a full report of all moneys received and paid out by him, together with any other information of importance to the A. C. W. of A. He shall receive for his service the sum of fifteen dollars ($15.00) per year.

General Executive Board

Sec. 12. The General Executive Board shall decide all points of law arising under the jurisdiction of the A. C. W. of A., also claims, grievances and appeals. Such decision shall stand until the next general or special convention of the A. C. W. of A., when, if not reversed, it shall be final.

Sec. 13. They shall have the power to authorize strikes in accordance with this constitution, shall have the general supervision of the affairs of the A. C. W. of A., and fill all vacancies which may occur. The General Executive Board shall present a report to the biennial international Convention, and shall include therein such recommendations as they may deem to be in the interests of the A. C. W. of A.

Sec. 14. Vacancies on the General Executive Board shall be filled in the following manner: The General Executive Board shall nominate not less than two (2) candidates for each vacancy and submit their names to a referendum vote. The one receiving the highest number of votes shall be elected to fill existing vacancy.

ARTICLE VII

Finance

Section 1. All Local Unions shall pay to the General Secretary a per capita tax of twenty-five (25) cents per month for each member.

Sec. 2. A monthly due stamp shall be issued by the General Secretary, the price of which shall be twenty-five (25) cents each, payable in advance. This stamp must be placed in the official due book of the A. C. W. of A. as a receipt for the per capita tax of each member. Members not having such stamps in their book must be declared in arrears.

Sec. 3. The Financial Secretary of the Local Union shall immediately after the first meeting in each month fill out the monthly report blanks issued by the General Secretary, sign the same, in conjunction with the President and Recording Secretary, and forward it, together with the amount due, to the General Secretary, keeping a duplicate copy on file. All money shall be sent by P. O. money order, express order or check.

Sec. 4. Any Local Union three (3) months in arrears shall be allowed until the seventh day of the fourth month to pay up its arrears; if not then paid the Local Union shall be suspended. The General Secretary shall notify the Local Union when two months in arrears.

Sec. 5. All assessments shall take precedence over per capita tax.

Sec. 6. No bills for expenses incurred in any city shall be paid unless authorized by the General Executive Board.

Sec. 7. All orders for due stamps and supplies, other than labels, must be accompanied by certified check, express or post office money order. Checks not certified will not be accepted.

Sec. 8. Every member of the Amalgamated Clothing Workers of America should be a subscriber to one of the official journals of the Organization, the subscription to be paid with the monthly or weekly per capita. (Resolution No. 88 of Baltimore Convention.)

ARTICLE VIII

Trials and Appeals

Section 1. Any member of the A. C. W. of A. may prefer charges against any member or officer of the A. C. W. of A. Such a charge must be submitted in writing to the Recording Secretary.

Sec. 2. Upon receipt of such charge the Secretary of the Local Union shall refer same to the Executive Board of the Local Union who shall investigate such charge and said Board shall have power

APPENDIX

to call for any books or papers, and demand the presence of any witnesses.

Sec. 3. The accused shall have the right in person or attorney (said attorney to be a member in good standing of the A. C. W. of A.) to question all witnesses and to present such evidence bearing on the charges, as to him seems advisable.

Sec. 4. Upon receiving all the evidence from both the accuser and the accused, the Board shall consult in executive session on the same and shall determine the guilt or innocence of the accused upon each charge and report its findings to the Local Union.

Sec. 5. Should any member be dissatisfied with the decision of the Local Union, he may appeal to the District Council or Joint Board within thirty (30) days. If still dissatisfied, he may appeal to the General Executive Board within thirty (30) days.

Sec. 6. Any appeal from the decision of the General Executive Board may be brought before the next general convention, provided appeal is filed with the General Secretary within thirty (30) days after ruling is made.

ARTICLE IX

Property

Section 1. All general and local union officers shall deliver to their successors all properties and moneys of the Local Union or A. C. W. of A., and shall not be released from their bonds until they have done so. Any officer or member who appropriates any funds of the A. C. W. of A. for his own use shall be legally prosecuted.

Sec. 2. Any officer or member of the A. C. W. of A. who knowingly supplies or issues, or aids in illegally supplying or issuing, the union label shall, upon conviction thereof, be legally prosecuted by the General Executive Board, and shall be debarred from membership in the A. C. W. of A.

ARTICLE X

Rules Governing Use of Union Label

Section 1. The label shall be granted to any firm entering into an agreement with a Central Body of the A. C. W. of A., subject to the approval of the General Executive Board.

Sec. 2. The General Secretary of the A. C. W. of A. shall be custodian of the label.

ARTICLE XI

Strikes and Lockouts

Section 1. When any difficulties arise between the members of any Local Union of the A. C. W. of A. and their employers, the officers of the Local Union or Joint Board shall immediately investigate the trouble and try to adjust the differences. If they fail in their effort to settle the trouble, the matter shall at once be

APPENDIX 315

submitted to the Central Body of the A. C. W. of A., whether the members shall be called on strike or not.

Sec. 2. Where there is no Central Body of the A. C. W. of A. the local union shall act as such.

Sec. 3. The result of their deliberation shall be submitted to the General Executive Board immediately for endorsement.

ARTICLE XII

Admission of Local Unions

Section 1. A local union may be organized by seven or more persons employed in the making of clothing.

Sec. 2. They shall apply to the General Secretary for a charter, and shall send sixteen dollars ($16.00) for charter fee and supplies. On receipt of the charter fee, the General Secretary shall forward the same to the new local union when approved by the General Executive Board.

Sec. 3. Each Local Union shall have its own by-laws as they may consider necessary, provided, however, that they shall not conflict with this Constitution or the by-laws of the Central Body of this organization.

ARTICLE XIII

Duties of Local Unions and District Councils

Section 1. Any Local Union which fails to hold regular meetings for two consecutive months shall forfeit its charter. Seven members shall constitute a quorum.

Sec. 2. Each Local Union shall maintain labor bureaus, join central labor unions and state federations, maintain friendly relations with other labor organizations, and do all in their power to strengthen and promote the Labor Movement.

Sec. 3. Where there are three or more local unions of the A. C. W. of A. in any city or locality they shall form a District Council; said Council shall transact business pertaining to the welfare of the various unions, such as organizing label agitation, and prevent one union from striking without the consent of the said District Council; adjust all local differences, if possible, before the same are referred to the General Executive Board. Such body shall be known as the AMALGAMATED CLOTHING WORKERS' DISTRICT COUNCIL, and shall be entitled to send one (1) delegate to represent it as a central body, with voice and vote at the general convention of the A. C. W. of A. The officers shall be elected for a term of one (1) year.

Sec. 4. District Councils shall be authorized to investigate at all times the financial condition of affiliated Local Unions and shall forward the results of the investigations to the General Executive Board.

Sec. 5. The proper officers of each Local Union shall promptly and properly fill all report blanks furnished them by the General Secretary. Failing to do so for two consecutive months, they shall be liable to a fine of not more than five dollars ($5.00) for the first offense.

Sec. 6. They shall produce the books of the Local Union when demanded by a General Officer. Failing to do so within forty-eight (48) hours, the local officers or Union shall be liable to suspension by the General Officer for insubordination.

Sec. 7. The General Secretary shall prepare a local Financial Secretary and Treasurers account book for the use of all Local Unions and all Local Unions shall purchase them and keep their accounts in accord therewith.

Sec. 8. All printing for the General Office and Local Unions to be done in strictly union shops, and shall bear the union label.

Sec. 9. Local Unions desiring financial assistance from the other Local Unions shall send their appeal to the General Secretary. In no case shall one Local Union appeal direct to the other locals attached to the A. C. W. of A., and all moneys contributed by locals shall be through the General Office. Donations to be published in the official paper.

Article XIV

Section 1. The officers of a Local Union shall consist of a President, Vice-President, Recording Secretary, Financial Secretary, Treasurer, Sergeant-at-Arms, three Trustees, Guide, three members of Finance Committee, an Executive Board of at least seven members and a correspondent for the Official Paper. They shall be elected semi-annually or annually. Those receiving the highest number of votes shall be declared elected.

Sec. 2. It shall be the duty of the President to preside at all meetings of the organization, preserve order during its deliberations, sign all orders on the Treasurer authorized by the body, appoint all officers not otherwise provided for, enforce the rules and usages as laid down in this Constitution, and transact such other business usual to the office of President.

Sec. 3. It shall be the duty of the Vice-President to perform all duties of the President in the event of his absence. Upon the death, removal or resignation of a President, the Vice-President becomes President until the next regular election. In that event the Vice-President shall be chosen at each meeting.

Sec. 4. It shall be the duty of the Recording Secretary to keep a correct account of the proceedings of the organization, which shall include a report of the Treasurer, the receipts and disbursements of the evening, as well as the number of each voucher issued. The amount of money in the treasury as reported by the Secretary must correspond with the Treasurer's report. He shall keep a special book, in which shall be recorded the names of all persons rejected, suspended or expelled, specifying for what offense each action was taken; conduct the correspondence of the organization and keep on file a copy of the same; have charge of the property not otherwise provided for; be held responsible for their safe keeping and prompt delivery to the successor in office, and perform such other duties as the organization may direct. He shall read all documents and correspondence for the organization and keep the same on file for future

APPENDIX 317

reference. He shall have charge of the seal of the organization and attach the same to all documents requiring authentication, and perform such other duties as are usual to the office.

Sec. 5. It shall be the duty of the Financial Secretary of each Local Union to keep a record of all finances and collect all the money due the Local Union and pay the same to the Treasurer, taking receipt therefor. He shall fill out the monthly report blanks issued by the General Secretary, sign the same in conjunction with the President and Recording Secretary and Treasurer, and forward it, with the necessary finances, to the General Secretary, keeping a duplicate copy on file. He shall prepare and send to the General Secretary a list of the members of the Local Union, also the date of each member's admittance, and the branch of the trade in which each member is engaged. He shall draw all orders for money on the Treasurer, attesting the same by signature, draw up quarterly financial reports and submit the same to the Local Union. He shall, on demand of the Auditor of the General Executive Board, produce his books for examination. At the close of his term of office he shall turn over to his successor all books and other property belonging to the organization which he may have in his possession.

Sec. 6. The Treasurer shall receive all moneys from the Financial Secretary, giving the receipt therefor, and deposit the same in the bank in the name and number of the Local Union. The moneys received must be deposited not later than forty-eight (48) hours thereafter in such bank as the organization may direct, reserving one hundred dollars ($100) for current expenses; keep a correct account of all moneys received, and pay all bills when properly attested.

Sec. 7. The Treasurer shall be bonded in some reliable surety company to the amount of not less than one thousand dollars ($1,000), the amount of the bond to be raised when necessary. Cost of the bond to be paid for by the Local Union.

Sec. 8. The Treasurer shall report in writing, at each regular meeting of the Local Union, the money received, paid out, and the amount still on deposit; and deliver to the successor in office all moneys and other property of the organization which he may have in his possession.

Sec. 9. It shall be the duty of the Sergeant-at-Arms to guard the door, inspect membership books, and perform such other duties as are usual to the office.

Sec. 10. It shall be the duty of the Guide to receive and inspect due books of members before opening of the meeting, obtain the names of all candidates in writing, report the same to the meeting, and perform such other duties as are usual to the office.

Sec. 11. It shall be the duty of the Board of Trustees to supervise the funds and property of the organization, and, together with the Treasurer, assume charge of all surplus money, and at least two members of the Board shall countersign all checks drawn on account of the organization from the bank by the Treasurer.

Sec. 12. It shall be the duty of the Finance Committee to examine all bills presented to the organization, and report any irregularity, at the end of each quarter, examine the accounts of the organization, and make the financial report in conjunction with the Financial Secretary.

Sec. 13. No member shall be eligible to any office in the union unless being at least six months a member in good standing.

Sec. 14. The Executive Board shall be composed of at least seven members. They shall transact all business of the organization when it is not in session, faithfully execute the orders of the organization and enforce the same, adopt measures either aggressive or defensive, in the interests of the organization or trade, and recommend such action to the organization as they may deem necessary for its interests. All acts of the Executive Board shall be subject to the ratification of the organization. In cases where a boycott is considered necessary by the local Executive Board, the matter shall be submitted to the General Executive Board or the General Convention, for approval and action.

Sec. 15. It shall be the duty of the correspondent to send semi-weekly reports to the editor of the official paper, all news and items concerning the Local Union, its members and the trade, giving the conditions thereof, and such other items as will be of interest to our members.

Article XV

Membership

Section 1. A candidate, male or female, to be admitted to membership of a Local Union of the A. C. W. of A., must be not less than sixteen (16) years of age, and employed in the manufacture of clothing.

Sec. 2. The initiation fee charge for members shall be optional with the Local Unions subject to the approval of the General Executive Board.

Sec. 3. Dues for all Local Unions shall not be less than fifty cents per month.

Sec. 4. No person who has been expelled, suspended or stricken from the roll or rejected by any Local Union shall be eligible for membership until all matters are settled to the satisfaction of the Local Union having the grievance against the person.

Sec. 5. No member of the A. C. W. of A. can be a member of more than one Local Union at the same time, or of any other organization of the trade, under a penalty of fine or expulsion by the Local Union of which he was first a member.

Sec. 6. Persons working at the trade in towns where there are not enough to form a Local Union, or where a Local Union has lapsed, shall be allowed to join the nearest Local Union.

Sec. 7. Local Unions shall not charge the difference of initiation fees to members traveling from one locality to another.

Sec. 8. It shall be optional with all Local Unions as to the acceptance of foremen or forewomen to membership.

Sec. 9. No member of the Amalgamated Clothing Workers of America who leaves the organization in order to accept a position as foreman or contractor or in any other capacity as representative of the employers shall be eligible for office, of whatever description, local or otherwise, for five years following the date of his rejoining the organization. (Resolution No. 86, passed by Third Biennial

APPENDIX 319

Convention, May, 1918, Baltimore, Md., and ratified by referendum vote of the membership as an amendment to the Constitution.)

ARTICLE XVI

Duties of Members

Section 1. No member of the A. C. W. of A. shall be allowed to injure the interests of other members by undermining them in wages or in any other willful manner.

Sec. 2. All business of the Local Union shall be kept strictly private from employers, except otherwise ordered by a vote of the Local Union. Any member violating sections 1 or 2 of this article may be punished by fine or expulsion, as the Local Union may decide.

Sec. 3. Members shall keep the Financial Secretary notified of their addresses, and shall attend all meetings of the Local Union, or shop, subject to such penalties as the Local Union may prescribe.

ARTICLE XVII

Members in Arrears—Reinstatement

Section 1. Members who are employed all or part of the time must pay dues monthly, and no member should be permitted to work on the first day of the month unless dues are paid for previous month. Working members are not in good standing who owe one month's dues.

Sec. 2. Members three months in arrears shall stand suspended from all rights and privileges of membership unless his or her dues are remitted by vote of the Local Union. If after three months more the member fails to meet his or her obligation, the name will be dropped from the roll.

Sec. 3. Any member who has been dropped from the roll can be reinstated only by paying the regular initiation fee, together with all the money due the organization at the time his name was dropped from the roll. His application for reinstatement shall be read and laid over until the next meeting, when a majority vote shall be sufficient to accept or reject the applicant.

ARTICLE XVIII

Withdrawal of Member

Section 1. Any member desiring to leave the country or quit the trade shall be allowed to withdraw from membership by paying all debts to date of withdrawal, surrender of his membership book or card and written notice of his withdrawal to the Local Union. The surrendered book or card shall be sent to the General Secretary.

ARTICLE XIX

Clearance Card

Section 1. Any member desiring to travel or transfer his membership shall apply to the Financial Secretary for a clearance card for a stated time, which time shall not exceed three months. This card shall be null and void, and the member shall be stricken from all rights and privileges and benefits, unless deposited in some Local Union or renewed before expiration.

Sec. 2. No Local Union shall have the right to collect per capita tax of the A. C. W. of A. again for the months paid for on the clearance card. The Local Union issuing the clearance card shall pay to the General Secretary the per capita tax for the member for the time the card holds good, and the member drawing a clearance card shall be considered a traveling member of the Local Union that issued the clearance card until the card is deposited with some other Local Union, when he shall become a member of the Local Union where the clearance card is deposited, and shall pay the Local Union dues from the time the card is deposited. The Recording Secretary of the Local Union receiving the Clearance Card shall immediately notify the Recording Secretary of the Local Union issuing the same.

Sec. 3. Any member depositing a clearance card shall be entitled to attend a meeting of any Local Union.

Sec. 4. Section 3 shall not entitle the member depositing a clearance card to any special sick or other benefits provided by the Local Union without payments of such amounts as the Local Union charges for participation therein, and subject to all special laws governing said benefits.

Sec. 5. Any member not depositing his clearance card within two weeks after arrival in any city or town, if there is a local union in said city or town, shall forfeit the clearance card and all rights and benefits as a member.

Sec. 6. Any member with a clearance card, working in a non-union city, can return the card before its expiration to the Local Union, where it was issued, and draw a new card for another period of time.

Sec. 7. No clearance card shall be granted to any member unless he or she has been a member of the A. C. W. of A. for at least six months.

Resolution No. 88, passed by the Third Biennial Convention, May, 1918, Baltimore, Md., and ratified by referendum vote of the membership as an amendment to the Constitution:

WHEREAS, The official organs of the Amalgamated Clothing Workers of America are published by the General Office in five different languages, English, Polish, Bohemian, Italian and Jewish, and we also expect that a Lithuanian paper will be published soon, therefore be it

RESOLVED, That every member of the Amalgamated Clothing Workers of America become a subscriber to one of the above mentioned papers, and that he or she pay for the subscription while paying the monthly or weekly dues.

APPENDIX II

BASIS OF AGREEMENT

Between Amalgamated Clothing Workers of America and the American Men's and Boys' Clothing Manufacturers' Association of New York.

(NOTE: There is no formal agreement, but the relations rest upon the three following reports of the Advisory Board.)

I

The undersigned, having been designated as an Advisory Board to consider the controversies existing between the Amalgamated Clothing Workers of America and the American Men's and Boys' Clothing Manufacturers Association, which have led to a cessation of the activities of both during the past three months, have met with Messrs. Sidney Hillman, representing the employees, and Max H. Friedman, representing the employers, with a view of arriving at an understanding which would terminate the existing deplorable conditions. They have presented the grievances of their respective organizations. The employees have asked for a curtailment of the hours of work, and a wage increase. The employers are not in accord with the contentions of the employees with respect to these points, and at the same time, have urged the necessity of establishing relations which will bring about better discipline and increased efficiency, and a proper standard of production in the industry.

In the short time that has elapsed since the creation of this Board, it has been impossible to obtain the data and information necessary to the making of satisfactory recommendations with respect to the many important propositions involved, and at the same time to enable an immediate return of the workmen to their employment and the resumption by the employers of their business activities, which is of primary importance. Impressed by the importance of an immediate resumption of the industry, the Board unanimously recommends:

1. The adoption of the 44-hour week to begin from the date when work shall be resumed. In this connection the hope is earnestly entertained that this precedent be recognized throughout the industry, in view of the desirability of bringing about its proper standardization. It would be regarded as unfortunate if the hours of labor should vary in this industry in the several important centers where it is extensively conducted.

2. In view of the absence of any reliable data indicating the existing basis of compensation to the employees, and the cost of living to which they are now subjected, it is impossible to reach any satisfactory conclusion without first obtaining the result of an inquiry and collation of facts by a skilled investigator. It is, therefore, recommended that such an investigator be designated by this Board, at the expense of both parties to this controversy, to

proceed forthwith to make the necessary inquiry and to report the facts as ascertained to the Board for further action.

3. The Board recognizes the importance, to employer and employed alike, of the formulation of principles and the establishment of machinery calculated to carry them into effect, which will result in its improvement as far as efficiency, discipline and production are concerned. To deal adequately with these problems will likewise require careful study by this Board, the assistance and opinions of those who have had experience in dealing with these phases of the problem, and an investigation of the bearings of the various propositions involved upon the industry in general.

Obviously a reasonable time will be required in which to take up this branch of the subject. In the meantime, the only conclusion that the Board has reached is that it will be of essential importance for the parties to agree upon the selection of an Impartial Chairman or Advisor to adjudicate upon the various questions that are certain to arise from time to time in the industry. Whatever plan may be ultimately determined upon will necessarily revolve around such a central figure.

This preliminary report, the Board is unanimously of the opinion that the employees should at once return to their post, and that the employers shall proceed to open their shops for regular operation.

WILLIAM Z. RIPLEY
LOUIS MARSHALL
FELIX FRANKFURTER

January 22, 1919.

II

The undersigned who constitute the Advisory Board designated by the Amalgamated Clothing Workers of America, hereinafter referred to as the Union, and the American Men's and Boys' Clothing Manufacturers' Association, hereinafter referred to as the Manufacturers, have, pursuant to the terms of their Preliminary Report dated January 22, 1919, given further consideration to the various matters in difference between these organizations and especially to those which relate to the formulation of principles and the establishment of machinery calculated to carry them into effect which will tend to improvement, as far as efficiency, discipline and production are concerned. The Board has had the benefit of expert advice and of the arguments of the representatives of the parties affected. Although there are a number of subjects which at the request of the parties are still held under advisement, the Board now makes this Intermediate Report as follows:

Contractors.

While the Board appreciates that the machinery and procedure applicable to the adjustment of problems arising between the Union and the Manufacturers are not in all respects suitable to the determination of the controversies that are likely to arise between the workers and the contractors, it nevertheless deems it desirable to adapt the machinery created for the adjustment of differences between the Manufacturers to the differences that may from time to time exist between the workers and the contractors so far as practicable. To this end the Board recommends the following procedure for the settlement of conflicts between the latter:

a) In the event that the workers in the shop of any contractor and the employer shall be unable to adjust any difference that may arise between them, it shall, in the first instance, be submitted for decision to the executive officers of the Union.

b) Should the decision rendered by such officers be unsatisfactory to the contractor, an official to be employed jointly by the several Contractors' Association or by such of them as shall seek to avail themselves of the procedure now contemplated, who is to be known as the Contractors' Appeal Agent, shall, with the approval of such officers of the Union, be entitled to appeal on behalf of the contractor, from the decision so rendered to the Impartial Chairman.

c) Should the matter in controversy involve a stoppage of operations in the shop of the contractor which shall have continued for a longer period than three days, the Contractors' Appeal Agent may appeal to the Impartial Chairman on behalf of the contractors, from the decision of the executive officers of the Union without their consent; provided, however, if this procedure shall operate prejudicially to the industry or shall result in multiplying appeals unduly or unreasonably the Impartial Chairman shall have the power to suspend or modify this clause.

d) Upon any appeal taken on behalf of a contractor to the Impartial Chairman, the Manufacturers shall be notified thereof and shall have the right to be heard thereon.

The Contractors' Appeal Agent shall be charged with the duty of promoting harmony between the Contractors and the Workers and so far as possible, shall seek to discourage the taking of a multiplicity of appeals to the Impartial Chairman and shall strive to confine such appeals to cases involving matters of substantial importance.

Discipline and Discharge.

It is recommended that the power of discipline and discharge shall remain with the employers and their agents, subject to the limitations and conditions hereinafter specified and with the understanding that it shall be exercised justly, with extreme care, and for good cause only. In regulation of this power the Manufacturers, with the concurrence of the Advisory Board and subject at all times to the approval of the Impartial Chairman, shall designate a man of high character and standing, to be known as the Employment Agent, whose compensation shall be paid by the Manufacturers and who, among other duties, shall deal with matters relating to the discharge in accordance with the following procedure:

a) The employer shall in each shop maintain a complaint book in which shall be entered all complaints against employees, who shall severally be informed of all entries made therein against them and shall have an opportunity to be heard with respect thereto before the Employment Agent whenever he shall be thereunto requested.

b) No worker shall be suspended by the employer during working hours except in aggravated instances and then only upon agreement to that effect between one of the Executive officers of the Union and the Employment Agent.

c) In all other cases, an employer desiring to discharge an employee shall first give to the latter notice in writing of his intention so to do, with a brief statement of the reason therefor.

d) A duplicate of such notice and statement shall be immediately lodged with the Employment Agent, who shall within twenty-four hours thereafter give a hearing to the parties concerned, and who shall, in the meantime, seek to conciliate the parties.

e) If the Employment Agent shall be of the opinion that the facts presented on such hearing constitute probable cause for discipline, he may, cases of sufficient gravity, and with the sanction of the Impartial Chairman, suspend the worker from employment.

f) In any case either party may appeal to the Impartial Chairman from the decision of the Employment Agent.

g) In the event of a suspension of an employee in the manner aforesaid the Impartial Chairman may, if after hearing the appeal he shall decide that the suspension was unwarranted, direct that the employee shall be reinstated with full pay for the time lost by him in consequence of such suspension.

Miscellaneous.

With reference to other subjects submitted to the Advisory Board it recommends that all questions that may from time to time arise with respect to the operation of the hiring system, to the employment of apprentices, to the functions and activities of shop chairmen and their procedure, and to the recognition of a temporary working force in any shop, shall be acted upon in conference between the executive officers of the Union and the Employment Agent.

Reserved Matters.

The questions relating to the introduction of new machinery, the distribution of work, and the fixing of the rates of wages, including compensation for overtime, are by consent of the parties reserved for further consideration and are to be made the subject of the final report of the Board.

The recommendations herein contained represent the unanimous action of the Board.

Respectfully submitted,
February 14, 1919.

III

The Advisory Board designated by the Amalgamated Clothing Workers of America (hereinafter referred to as the Union) and the American Men's and Boys' Clothing Manufacturers' Association (hereinafter referred to as the Manufacturers) rendered a preliminary report dated January 14, 1919, with respect to a portion of the questions submitted for consideration to it.

Mr. Frankfurter having resigned from the Board owing to his departure for Europe, the undersigned Samuel J. Rosensohn has been duly designated to fill the vacancy.

This Board having given further consideration to the matters reserved by the term of its previous report, now makes this final report as follows:

The Rate of Wages.

The Board recognizes the difficulties surrounding this subject, due to the uncertainties of business conditions in the immediate future, which may call for an early reconstruction in all industries. It is, however, persuaded that, owing to the continuing high cost of living, coupled with the fact that the clothing industry is at present seasonal in character, under existing conditions a moderate increase in the rate of wages should be allowed to the workers.

Carefully weighing all of the elements which enter into the problem, including the recent reduction of the length of the working day to forty-four hours, and the reduction in output consequent thereon without a corresponding reduction in wages, and for the purpose of establishing a fair and equitable rate, the Board recommends an increase of the present rates of compensation to all day-workers of two dollars weekly, and an increase to piece-workers engaged in pants shops of ten per cent upon the present piece rates, and an increase to piece-workers in knee-pants shops of twelve and one-half per cent on the present piece rates. The foregoing increases shall go into effect on April 1, 1919. This date is fixed because of the fact that the manufacturers have heretofore entered into contracts for the sale of merchandise largely based on the present wage scale.

The Board further recommends that an investigation shall be made under the supervision of the Impartial Chairman on or before October 1, 1919, into the cost of living of the workers and their families, and in the event that such investigation shall disclose the fact that there has occurred a substantial reduction in such cost, such fact shall be deemed to constitute in itself a sufficient ground for a revision of the then existing rates.

As to compensation for overtime and the distribution of work, the Board recommends that these subjects be investigated by the Impartial Chairman, and that after the completion of his inquiry they be made the subject of negotiation between the Union and the Manufacturers.

The Board deems it its duty to give emphatic expression to its conviction that the workers are under the obligation of co-operating with the Manufacturers, to the end that there be assured efficiency in production and adequacy of output. There have unfortunately in the past occurred some serious violations of this principle, the repetition of which threaten the success of the industry, thereby operating to the inquiry of employer and employee alike. A spirit of helpful co-operation and pride of workmanship should be fostered. Its development is essential to the mutual advantage of both interests. The establishment of the various agencies recommended in the previous reports of the Board, it is believed, affords an opportunity to both the Union and the Manufacturers for the stimulation of the free play of those constructive forces in industry which have unfortunately in the past not received due appreciation. The voluntary or deliberate interference with efficiency or reduction of output is a matter of such seriousness as to be regarded as justifying the immediate suspension by the Employment Agent, with the sanction of the Impartial Chairman, and the dismissal by the **Impartial Chairman** of any worker committing such an act.

Introducing of New Machinery.

It was conceded by the Union and the Manufacturers on the hearing before the Board that a proper development of the industry as well as the public interest require the introduction of new and improved machinery from time to time. Due regard for the welfare of the workers, however, makes it important that they shall not alone be made to bear the burden incident to changes in mechanism. To this end, it is recommended that in all cases where such machinery is introduced, employees displaced thereby shall receive an equivalent in employment or otherwise in such manner as shall be determined by the Impartial Chairman.

All questions relating to the introduction of machinery in contractors' shops shall be determined in the manner provided in the Intermediate Report with respect to controversies arising in such shops.

The recommendations herein contained, as well as all recommendations made in previous reports of the Advisory Board, represent its unanimous action.

Respectfully submitted,

Dated, March 4, 1919.

APPENDIX III

AGREEMENT

Cloak, Suit and Skirt Manufacturers' Protective Association with International Ladies' Garments Makers' Union and Joint Board of Cloak Makers' Unions of the City of New York.

THIS AGREEMENT, made and entered into this 29th day of May, 1919, by and between THE CLOAK, SUIT & SKIRT MANUFACTURERS' PROTECTIVE ASSOCIATION, hereinafter styled the "ASSOCIATION," and THE INTERNATIONAL LADIES' GARMENT WORKERS' UNION, and the JOINT BOARD OF CLOAK MAKERS' UNION OF THE CITY OF NEW YORK, composed of and representing Locals Nos. 1, 3, 9, 10, 11, 17, 21, 23, 35, 64, and 82, all collectively designated as the "UNION," contracting herein for and in behalf of the said Unions and for and in behalf of the members thereof, now employed and hereafter to be employed by the members of the Association.

WITNESSETH:

WHEREAS, the Association is composed of a large number of manufacturers engaged in the Cloak, Suit and Skirt Industry in the City of New York, and the Union represents the workers in the said trade, and

WHEREAS, the parties hereto desire to establish terms and conditions upon which members of the Union shall work for members of the Association:

Now THEREFORE, The parties hereto agree as follows:

Mutual Obligations

1. The Association obligates itself for its members that they will live up in good faith to all the provisions of this agreement. The Union, believing in the principle of "A fair day's labor for a fair day's pay," obligates itself in good faith for all of its members, that they will perform their work conscientiously, faithfully and efficiently.

2. Each member of the Association shall maintain a preferential union shop. A preferential union shop is hereby defined to be a shop in which members of the union in good standing shall be preferred in the hiring and retention of help. The Association agrees that its members will not discriminate in any manner against their workers for Union membership or activity. A Union worker within the meaning of this provision, shall be a worker who proves his union membership to the satisfaction of the employer or his representative, and the shop Chairman.

3. A week's work shall consist of forty-four (44) hours in (6) week days divided as follows: On the first five (5) working

days of the week, work shall begin at 8 A.M. and continue until 5 P.M., with one hour interval for lunch. On Saturdays, work shall be done from 8 A.M. until 12 M. Workers observing Saturday as the day of the Sabbath may work on Sunday instead from 8 A.M. to 12 M.

4. No overtime work shall be exacted or permitted in the manufacture of cloaks and suits between November 15th and December 31st, nor between May 1st and July 15th. Manufacturers engaged in special lines, such as the manufacture of skirts, pile fabrics, linens and summer goods, shall have the right to establish periods different from those above stated, according to the demands of their business, provided that such periods, in all cases, do not exceed eight (8) months in the year.

In the seasons in which overtime is permitted, such overtime shall not exceed ten (10) hours in any week, nor two and one-half (2½) hours in any day, and shall be restricted to the first five working days of the week. Additional overtime shall not be permitted except in cases of emergency, and then only with the consent of the Union.

5. All workers except buttonhole makers shall work by the week. The minimum wage[1] scale shall be as follows:

Cloak and Dress Cutters	$39.00
Skirt Cutters	34.50
Sample Makers	32.00
Jacket, Coat, Reefer and Dress Operators	44.00
Skirt Operators	42.00
Piece Tailors	38.00
Reefer, Jacket and Coat Finishers	35.50
Jacket, Coat and Reefer Finishers' Helpers	28.00
Jacket, Coat, Reefer and Dress Upper Pressers	36.50
Jacket, Coat, Reefer and Dress Under Pressers	32.00
Skirt Upper Pressers	32.50
Skirt Under Pressers	25.50
Skirt Basters	22.00
Skirt Finishers	18.00
Drapers	24.00
Begraders on Skirts	28.00
Girl Begraders	24.00
Cloak Bushelers	22.00
Bushelmen who also do Pinning, Marking and General Work on Garments	30.00

Buttonhole makers shall be paid one dollar and ten cents ($1.10) per hundred buttonholes, employer to furnish machine, silk and finishing: If silk is supplied by the buttonhole maker, the employer shall pay ten cents (10c.) additional, per one hundred buttonholes.

No workers shall receive less than the above scale except those who are deficient in their production by reason of their age or physical condition.

[1] An increase in wages was secured without a strike in January, 1920.

The wages for such workers shall be agreed upon between the employer and the worker, subject to the approval of the Union.

All operators, finishers and piece tailors shall be paid at the rate of time and one-half for overtime. All other classes of workers for whom the last agreement provided that double time shall be paid for overtime, shall receive that rate under this agreement.

All wages shall be paid weekly on a fixed day and in cash.

6. All workers shall be paid for the following legal holidays, to-wit: Washington's Birthday, Memorial Day, Independence Day, Labor Day, Thanksgiving Day, Christmas, and for one-half day of Election Day. And such holidays shall be observed.

Workers may also refrain from work on the first day of May, but without pay.

Italian workers may also refrain from working on Columbus Day, but without pay.

During the week in which a legal holiday occurs, employees working less than a full week shall be paid for the holidays pro rata for the hours worked.

Should any legal holiday fall on a Saturday, the workers who observe Saturday as the Sabbath, shall be allowed to celebrate the Sunday following and be paid for the same.

7. No contracting or sub-contracting within the shop shall be permitted.

No work shall be given to workers to be made at home.

8. There shall be no time contracts between the members of the Association and their workers, either individually or in groups.

9. The employer shall furnish all workers with sewing machines, driven by electric power, and with all material and the requisites of work.

10. All members of the Association shall register with the Association and the Association shall register with the Union, the names and addresses of all contractors whom they employ, or who do work for them.

The Association assumes the following guaranties for the contractors thus to be registered:

That such contractors will operate ten (10) machines and will maintain in their shops proper sanitary conditions to the satisfaction of the Joint Board of Sanitary Control.

That such contractors will maintain the standards of wages, hours, holidays, and other shop standards provided for in this agreement.

That they will pay for work done on garments of members of the Association, and if the contractors should default in the payment of such wages, the Association members will pay to the extent of work done on their garments, provided that notice of default is given to such Association members within one week after such default.

A contractor within the meaning of the above provisions is:

a. One who makes up garments from material delivered to him by a member of the Association in cut form.

b. One who makes up garments from uncut material and who works exclusively for one manufacturer who is a member of this Association.

11. The Joint Board of Sanitary Control existing in the industry shall be continued at joint expense.

12. Should there be a shortage of labor in the industry, and the Union unable to supply the employers with workers, the employers may engage apprentices to make up the deficiency. The wages to be paid to such apprentices as well as the conditions and regulations under which they shall work, shall be determined between the Union and the Association when such emergency arises.

13. The employer may discharge his workers for causes such as:
Incompetency.
Misconduct.
Insubordination in the performance of his work.
Breach of reasonable rules to be jointly established.
Soldiering on the job.

14. There shall be no lock-out or strike in the shops of the members of the Association during the period of this agreement, nor shall there be any individual shop lock-out, stoppage or shop strike pending the determination of any complaint or grievance. Should there be a stoppage of work or shop strike in any factory, immediate notice thereof shall be given by the Association to the Union. The Union agrees to return the striking workers to their work within twenty-four hours after the receipt by the Union of such notice, and until the expiration of such time it shall not be deemed that the striking workers have abandoned their employment. The consideration of stoppage cases shall have precedence over all other complaints and grievances arising hereunder.

15. In times when the employer shall be unable to supply his workers with work full time, the available work in the shop shall be divided as equally as possible among all the workers who are competent to do the work, and they shall be paid for the actual time consumed.

Workers may be divided into shifts and alternated.

As to cutters:—When there is insufficient work, the work shall be divided equally by the week. As to pressers:—The managing presser shall be entitled to no more work than the other pressers in the factory.

16. The Association and the Union are in accord that the interests of the industry will be best served by large factory units and to that end fix as a minimum fourteen (14) working machines to a factory organization.

Since the Union has provided in its contract with independent manufacturers for the employment of a minimum of fourteen (14) working machines, the Association will use its best efforts with its members that they increase their plants to the capacity herein stated.

17. The Association will urge its members to make in their inside factories the skirts required for the suit jackets produced in their inside factories; and when suit skirts are made in outside shops, they be sent to as few contractors as possible.

18. Each member of the Association shall have the right in good faith to reorganize his factory. A reorganization in good faith shall mean a bona fide reorganization of the employer's business, necessitated by a permanent curtailment of his business or a fundamental change in the character of his business.

19. No member of the Association shall do work for an independent employer whose workers are on a strike because of the

APPENDIX 331

violation of any of the prescribed standards of this agreement. Nor shall any member of the Association make or cause any work to be made directly or indirectly, in any shop where the Union has declared a strike for violating the standards provided for in this agreement.

20. All complaints, disputes or grievances arising between the parties hereto during the life of this agreement shall be submitted in writing, and the manager of the Association and the manager of the Union, or their deputies, shall in the first instance jointly investigate such complaints, grievances or disputes and attempt an adjustment. Decisions reached by the managers or their deputies shall be binding on the parties hereto.

Should the managers fail to agree, the case in question shall be referred to a Trial Board consisting of one member from each organization and an impartial person who shall be selected from a list of names previously agreed upon between the Union and the Association. The case shall be reviewed upon its merits and the collective agreement shall constitute the basis upon which the decision shall be rendered. No decision shall be used as a precedent for any subsequent case. Discharge cases shall have precedence over all other cases and a decision shall be rendered within forty-eight (48) hours after the complaint in writing has been made, unless the time is extended by mutual consent. A decision of a majority of this Board shall be final and binding upon both sides. If the case involves a discharged worker and the decision of the majority of said Board is in favor of the discharged worker, he shall be reinstated with pay for the time lost by reason of the discharge.

Expenses connected with the said Board shall be borne equally by the parties hereto.

21. Should any member of the Association or the Union fail to comply with any decision of the Chief Clerks, or Trial Board within seventy-two (72) hours after a decision is rendered, said member shall forfeit all benefits and rights of this agreement.

22. Before accepting a new member, the Association shall inform the Union, in writing, of the application. If a strike or dispute is pending between the applicant and the Union at the time, the Union shall give the Association, in writing, full particulars of the nature 'of the dispute. The Association may undertake to adjust the dispute on the basis of the provisions of this contract. The adjustment, however, shall not conflict with the provisions of the agreement existing between the applicant and the Union.

This agreement shall enter into force on the day of the execution hereof and shall continue to and including the first day of June, 1922.

IN WITNESS WHEREOF the parties hereto have hereunto set their hands and seals the day and year first above written.

This agreement is signed subject to Ratification by the Respective Association and Union.

In the Presence of:
WM. KLEIN

INTERNATIONAL LADIES'
GARMENT WORKERS'
UNION.

APPENDIX

By BENJAMIN SCHLESINGER
President.
And M. SIGMAN,
Manager Joint Board.

SKIRT MANUFACTURERS'
THE CLOAK, SUIT &
PROTECTIVE ASSOCIATION.

By SAUL SINGER,
Chairman.

APPENDIX IV

EXAMINATION OF CANDIDATES FOR BUSINESS AGENT

New York Joint Board, Amalgamated Clothing Workers of America

February 18, 1920

INSTRUCTIONS: Put name, address, and length of service (if any) in the organization on top of your answer paper.
Where question requires a "yes" or "no" answer, answer by "yes" or "no."
Be brief in your answers.
Examination begins at 3 P.M. sharp and ends at 5 P.M.

First Paper

I

There has been some talk in our trade recently about a so-called "blockade." Are you in favor or opposed to this method? Give reasons for your opinion.

II

Are you in favor of combining the children's clothing and men's clothing workers into one Joint Board? Give 2 reasons for your answer.

III

Give one argument in favor of collective bargaining and one against.

IV

In a shop of 50 workers, 3 workers in a section got together and placed certain demands before the boss. The boss rejected their demands, and they left their jobs. Has the organization a moral right to interfere with their action. Why?

V

Some members of the Amalgamated are beginning to consider seriously the advisability of our organization entering into cooperative enterprises. Do you believe this will benefit our organization? Give reasons for your answer.

Second Paper

I

There is a tendency on the part of some of our members to shift from one shop to another. Has the organization a right to restrict this tendency? Answer *yes* or *no*. State briefly the principle upon which your opinion is based.

II

One of Wilson's 14 points was "self-determination of smaller nations." In the light of this principle, is the New York Joint Board justified in trying to amalgamate the custom tailors' local with the other locals? Give reasons for your answer.

III

The New York Joint Board has contributed several thousands of dollars to the United Labor Education Committee this year. This money comes from the pockets of all the members. Some members are not interested in educational work. What moral right has the organization to tax these members?

IV

At the last meeting of the Joint Board, a suggestion was made that the organization should refuse to recognize any representative of the employers who is an ex-officer of our union. Do you agree with this proposition? Give reasons for your answer.

V

What should be the attitude of our organization toward the introduction of new machinery in our industry?

APPENDIX V

ATTITUDE TOWARDS LABOR PARTY AND SOCIALIST PARTY

(From report presented to Convention of United Cloth Hat and Cap Makers in 1919.)

The Committee considers the coming into existence of a National Labor Party as a welcome sign of the awakening of even the most conservative elements of Labor to the great problems of the time. The Committee heartily welcomes the organization of labor parties in various cities, as well as the movement for the organization of a National Labor Party. The Committee sees in the coming National Labor Party another great labor power which will, and shall in co-operation with all the other organized elements of the labor movement, presently bring about the full political and industrial democracy to which we all aspire.

The Committee recommends that this Convention express its unanimous sentiments, calling upon all the organized elements of labor to co-ordinate their efforts and work in co-operation. We especially wish to impress upon the labor parties, as well as upon the Socialist Party, the necessity of their finding some way by which the division of labor against itself should be avoided. Labor must be united, and it therefore behooves the Socialist Party and the labor parties, as well as all the other organized groups of the labor movement, to arrange for fraternal and friendly co-operation. Whatever differences with regard to the ultimate issue of the labor struggle that the Labor and Socialist Parties may have, or whatever differences may be between them with regard to the conception of the philosophy of the labor movement, the programs of action, as formulated by both parties, are so much alike that we feel that the Socialist Party and the Labor Party, while conserving their separate identity, could and should co-ordinate their activities, so that there should be no strife among brothers within the ranks of the labor movement.

We further recommend that this Convention call upon all organizations to co-operate with both the Socialist and Labor Parties to the effect that these parties co-ordinate their efforts directly towards the liberation of the working class and towards the establishment of full political and industrial democracy.

APPENDIX VI

ATTITUDE TOWARD PIECE WORK

(Report submitted to Convention of United Cloth Hat and Cap Makers of North America in 1919.)

The Committee on Resolutions has given careful consideration to the question of changing the system of work in our industry from piece to week work.

The evils of piece work have been repeatedly demonstrated in the history of the labor movement and could be summarized to consist in the main of the following:

Piece Work Tends to Lengthen the Hours of Labor. The piece worker frequently gets the mistaken conception that by working an hour longer he may increase his earnings. Working by piece, the average worker has difficulty to see the importance of shortening the hours of labor, since it seems to him that by working less hours he merely diminishes his opportunity to increase his earnings. On the other hand, the employer under a system of piece work is not interested in saving the time of his employees from being wasted in waiting for work or because of the failure to keep the machines in good condition and repair. The loss of time of the employee is not a loss of time to the employer. The misconception with regard to long hours, created in the minds of the workers by the system of piece work, and the lack of consideration under the system on the part of the employers to provide against loss of time by the workers, both of these conditions in the long run lengthen the hours of labor, and, in any case, create great difficulties in the way of shortening the working hours.

Piece Work Tends to Shorten the Busy Seasons and Lengthen the Dull Seasons. Because of the tendency to lengthen the hours of labor, because of the total absence of special overtime rates for piece workers, and because of the almost unavoidable false impression of the piece worker that abnormal speeding up and abnormal hours are in his own interests, the work of the season is sped up and is finished in an abnormally short time. Besides, the easy possibility of getting the work done at the shortest notice without any greater expense involved, makes the manufacturer leave his orders for the very last moment and this tends further to decrease the length of the busy season. Needless to say that the worker does not benefit in the slightest by this speeding up. The volume of work to be done is determined by the conditions of the market and the more is done in the busy season the less is left for the dull season. Moreover, the shortening of the season usually tends to diminish the volume of work in the trade. When the bulk of the work is done during the very short busy season, the tendency is to do very little during the rest of the year and the trade adapts itself to that condition in such a way that business which could easily have been picked up and for which there may be a real need in the market is neglected and is irreparably lost. Week work, on the contrary, tends to lengthen the busy season and to shorten the dull season. Under a system of week work overtime is connected with greater expenses to the manufacturer, the hours are therefore shorter and the orders must be placed at the earliest possible dates so as to give the manufacturers more time to fill them, which tends to lengthen the busy seasons.

Piece Work Tends to Increase the Instability of the Condition of the Worker. Under the system of piece work the earnings of the worker fluctuate a great deal more than under a system of week work. Actual investigations show that the earnings of piece workers fluctuate, even in the busy time, by about twenty-five per cent and in seasonal trades, especially of such an extreme nature as our millinery trade, the fluctuation is much greater. This creates an unstable condition for the worker. The worker cannot possibly arrange his expenses on a scientific basis of average earnings for the entire year, because even during the best weeks the worker earns so little that the earnings are spent as they come in, and in the weeks when the earnings are less it simply means that the worker has to live on so much less and reduce his expenses accordingly. A condition of instability is always prejudicial to the well-being of the workers. It increases the feeling of insecurity and hazard in the workingman's life, it diminishes his vitality and power to fight for better conditions.

Piece Work Tends to Lower the Standard of Living. The great fluctuation in the earnings caused by the system of piece work results in lowering the standard of living of the workingman. The standard of living of the workingman is determined not by the weeks of the larger earnings but by those weeks in which the worker is compelled to live on the smallest amount. Under present social conditions of capitalist society there is only one irreducible minimum below which the wages of organized labor cannot fall, and that is the irreducible minimum necessary for the subsistence of the workers under the standard of living of the given trade. When the workingmen in the weeks of the smallest income are compelled to reduce their necessities to the minimum, this minimum becomes the irreducible minimum of the standard of living and the wages have a tendency to be reduced to the level of that minimum. This process may not be so self-evident, but statistics and numerous investigations have proven beyond any reasonable doubt that the fluctuation of earnings in the long run reduce the standard of living to that of the weeks in which the worker gets the smallest earnings.

Piece Work Tends to Reduce Wages. By reducing the standard of living piece work reduces the wages. In the present capitalist society the standard of living is one of the main economic factors determining the wages of the workingman. The lower the standard of living the lower the wages, and vice versa. The effects of the reduction of the standard of living are especially dangerous because they increase in a geometric progression. When wages have been reduced as a result of the lowering of the standard of living, the reduced wages bring about a further lowering of the standard of living. This results in a further reduction of wages, which brings about a further lowering of the standard of living, and so on, ad infinitum.

Piece Work Interferes with the Exercise of the Collective Will of the Organization. Under a system of piece work, especially in the trades where the styles are so numerous and where it would be nearly impossible to prepare standardized piece prices for the entire trade, the settlement of piece prices must necessarily be left to shop committees. Instead, therefore, of the organization acting as a unit, with a single collective will, it is practically broken up into as many smaller organizations as there are shops, every one of which acts more or less independently. The actions of the shop committees vary greatly and depend to a great extent upon the accidental composition of the shop committee, upon the intelligence of the members in those committees, upon their devotion to the principles of the organization, upon their experience, firmness and so on. This condition prevents the standardization of the trade and hinders the working out of a common psychology and common will in the entire membership.

Piece Work Is Prejudicial to the Highest Degree of Solidarity Among the Workers. The earnings of piece workers vary too much, depending not merely upon their greater or lesser skill, but much more upon accidental conditions, favoritism of foremen, ability of speeding up, and so on. The piece workers, therefore, are quite frequently inclined to overestimate the value of individual effort as against collective effort. Under a system of week work the worker whose demands on life are highest, in order to improve his condition, must ask for the improvement of the condition of the entire group or class of the same workers. That is not necessarily the case under a system of piece work, where single individuals can raise their condition considerably above the general level and therefore do not feel as strongly as the week workers the immediate necessity of devoting all their efforts to the collective struggle for the general improvement of the conditions of the workers. The highest degree of solidarity is therefore best promoted by a system of week work only.

Piece Work Tends to Interfere with the Concentration of the Efforts of the Organization on the Really Important Issues. Under a system of piece work the price settlements, with all the squabbles and disputes connected with them, tend to take all the attention of the workers and the organization, gaining an importance which they really have not. Because these little disputes consume the best energies of the most active workers in the trade, the really important issues are removed to the background and frequently lost sight of. In the little daily struggles in connection with the price settlements, the energies and militancy of the workers of the trade are gradually spent, so that the organization meets with greater difficulties when there is a necessity to concentrate upon the battle general. Instead of concentrating all efforts at the moment of the renewal of the collective agreement to gain important concessions from the employers, the organization is compelled, under a system of piece work, to concentrate all efforts to make effective whatever little concessions could be gained at the renewal of the agreements. Under a system of piece work the organized workers are mostly compelled to spend their efforts in an incessant guerrilla warfare during the

APPENDIX 339

existence of the collective agreement instead of concentrating their energies upon a real offensive at the conclusion or renewal of agreements. Under the present social conditions guerrilla warfare in industry injures mainly the workers themselves, while the weakening of the organization for the general offensive is an irreparable loss to the workers. Under a system of week work, the guerrilla warfare during the existence of the agreement is reduced to the minimum and workers can concentrate all their energies and efforts for the preparation for the general offensive at the conclusion or renewal of the agreement, thus assuring substantial gains which, under week work, are safeguarded with a minimum of guerrilla warfare.

Piece Work Is Prejudicial to the Health of the Workers. Perhaps the greatest danger of piece work for the people is the undermining influence which it has upon the health of the workers. There is hardly anything more prejudicial to the health than the periodic succession of exhausting work by total idleness. Piece workers, especially in seasonal trades, are incessantly passing from a state of inhuman exertion to a state of almost total inactivity. While this irregularity in the physical effort demanded by the industry from the workers, under present capitalist conditions, is more or less of a general nature, it is not so prevalent and not so dangerous under week work as it is under piece work.

The Committee on Resolutions came to the conclusion that the enumerated evils of the system of piece work prevail both in the cap making and millinery branches of our industry, and perhaps to an even greater degree in the latter than in the former, since the millinery trade is of a more seasonal nature than the cap making. The conditions, however, in these trades, with regard to the changing of the piece work system to the week work system are not the same. While the cap making trade is almost entirely organized and has been so for a considerable number of years, the organization of the millinery trade has been in existence for a shorter period of time. The Committee on Resolutions therefore came to the conclusion that while a change from piece work to week work is an imperative necessity for both branches of our trade, it could and should be introduced at once only in the cap-making trade, leaving the introduction of the week work system in the millinery trade for the time when the propaganda, which is to be started at once, will in the opinion of the General Executive Board have made conditions ripe for this change.

With the above in mind, the Committee recommends the following resolution to be adopted as a substitute for all the resolutions introduced on this subject.

INDEX

Abendblatt, 241
Addams, Jane, 120
Adler, Felix, 208
Administrator for Army Clothing, 152
Advance, 246
Advisory Board, 152
Agitators, 67, 271
Agreement, Collective. See Collective Agreements
Amalgamated Clothing Workers of America, 88, 89, 170, 269
Amalgamated Textile Workers of America, 262, 269
American Federation of Labor, 71, 89, 166, 203, 205, 225
Anarchists, 71
Apprenticeship, 193
Arbeiter Zeitung, 167, 241
Art, Labor and Science Conference, 224

Baroff, Abraham, 2
Beard, Charles A., 224
Berger, D., 2
Biggs, Dr. Hermann M., 103
Black Bag, 106
Brandeis, Louis D., 115, 151
Board of Arbitration, 129
Board of Directors, of Joint Board, 182
Bohemian Immigrants, 65
Boston Labor Bureau, 25
Brotherhood of Tailors, 73
Budish, J. M., 219
Bund, The, 57
Business Agents, of Union, 183

Ca' Canny, 201
Cahan, Abraham, 66, 70, 240
Cap Makers Journal, 245
Chicago Federation of Labor, 120
Child Labor, in Textile Industry, 255

Christian Socialist, Austrian, 55
Cloakmaker, The, 246
Cloakmakers' Trial, 83
Closed Shop, 112
Clothing Industry, 15, 16
Clothing Industry, Women's, 24
Clothing Trades Department, 93
Cohn, Fannia, 1, 216
Cole, G. D. H., 6, 10
Collective Agreements, 124, 148, 154, 198, 199 (see also Protocol)
Collective Bargaining. See Collective Agreements
Coman, Prof. Katharine, 104
Committee on Grievances, 129
Committee on Immediate Action, 138
Competition, 30, 34, 38, 43
Consumers' League:
   National, 102
   New York, 103
Contractor, 18, 34, 107
Control of Production, 127, 136, 284
Convention, Union, 174, 189
Cooperatives, Labor Bank, etc., 248, 286
Council of Conciliation, 140
Craft Union, 162
Credit, 291
Credit Union, 249
Culture of Jewish Immigrants, 52
Custom Tailor, 17
Cutters, 164

Daily People, 167, 244
Daniel, Dr. A. S., 102
Darbas, 246
De Leon, Daniel, 244
Dental Clinic, 147
Deitsch, John, 209
Der Yiddisher Kempfer, 244
Die Naye Post, 246

341

INDEX

Die Naye Welt, 244
Die Naye Zeit, 240
Discharge, 30, 135, 136, 140, 143
Discrimination, 135
District Council, of Unions. See Joint Board
District Managers, of Union, 182
Dress and Waist Industry, 28

Education, Union, 205
Efficiency, 37
Employers' Associations, Attitude Towards, 195
Establishments, Number of, 37; size of, 33

Fashions, 30, 31 (see also Styles)
Filene, A. Lincoln, 115
Finnish Immigrants, 65
Fitzpatrick, John, 120
Fortschritt, 213, 246
Forty-eight Hour Week, 94
Forty-four Hour Week, 95, 152
Forward, Jewish Daily, 66, 70, 240, 241
Frey, William, 208
Friedland, Dr. Louis S., 216
Freie Arbeiter Stimme, 243
Fur Worker, 247
Fur Workers' Union. See International Fur Workers' Union

General Executive Board, 174, 188
General Officers, of Unions, 171, 174, 188
Gerechtigkeit, 246
German Immigrants
Giustizia, 246
Gompers, Samuel, Attitude on Secession, 89
Grievance Board, 145
Guild, Austrian, 55
Guild, National. See National Guild

Hamilton, Alice, 120
Hart, Schaffner and Marx, 120, 122, 123, 148
Headgear Worker, 245
Headgear Workers' Innstitute, 217
Hillman, Sidney, 2, 123
Hillquit, Morris, 66, 83

Hirsch, Emil G., 119
Holland, James P., 92
Home Work, 102, 106, 109, 120
Hoxie, Robert F., 8

Immigrant Workers, 46
Immigration, Altitude Towards, 193
Immigration, Italian, 66
Impartial Chairman, 145, 152
Industrial Council, 152
Industrial Democracy, 246
Industrial Workers of the World, 6, 78, 257
Industry, Clothing, 15 ff.; Control of, 36; Textile, 255 ff.; Women's Clothing, 24
Ingerman, A., 209
Initiation Fee, 192
Injunction, 115
Inside Shop, 21, 24, 34
Insurance, Attitude Towards, 196; unemployment, 280
International Fur Worker's Union of the United States and Canada, 95
International Ladies' Garment Workers Union, 80, 168, 215
Italian Immigrants, 63
Izold, Henrietta, 61

Jewish Workers' League, 209
Jews, Austro-Hungarian, 48; German, 48; Immigrant, 46 ff.; Rumanian, 48; Russian, 46
Joint Board of Sanitary Control, 129, 145
Joint Boards, of Union, 132, 174, 178, 179, 180
Joint Council, of Unions. See Joint Board
Jones, Jenkins Lloyd, 119
Journeyman Tailors' Union, 89, 96
Jurisdiction, Disputes About, 194
Justice, 246

Kaufman, Morris, 1
Knights of Labor, 71
Koldim, H., 2

Labor, Mobilizing, 39
Labor Party, 204

Labor Turnover, 28
Ladies' Hat Manufacturers' Protective Association, 79
Leadership of Unions, 171
Literacy of Jewish Immigrants, 52
Lithuanian Immigrants, 65
Local Union, 174, 175
Ladies' Garment Workers Union, *See* International Ladies Garment Workers Union.
Log System, 143

Mack, Julian W., 119, 151
Magnes, Judah L., 151
Marshall, Louis, 115
Mitchel, Mayor, 140
Monat, Peter, 1
Moste, Johann, 208
Muste, A. J., 1

Needle Trades Federation, 93
Nashville Convention, United Garment Workers, 87
Nathan, Mrs. Frederick, 103
National Consumers' League, 102, 115
National Guilds, 13
National Industrial Federation of Clothing Manufacturers, 153
New Members, Admission of, 191
New Post, The, 139
New Unionism, 4, 157 ff.
New York Call, 245
New Yorker Zeitung, 239

Officials, Union, 171
Old Unionism, 10, 158 ff.
Ordynski, Richard, 224
Overalls, 75

Part-time Work, 28, 38
People, Daily, 167, 249
Persecution of Jews in Russia, 53
Peskin, Dr., 209
Philosophy, of Unions, 156
Piece Prices, 136
Piece Work, 200
Pogroms, 56
Polish Immigrants, 65
Political Action, 203
Power, Mechanical, 32, 108

Poyntz, Juliet Stuart, 216
Preambles, to Union Constitutions, 168, 169
Preferential Shop, 116, 129
Press, Labor, 229 ff.
Price Committee, 136
Private Enterprise, 43
Production, Large-Scale, 19, 69
Productivity, 202, 274, 277
Protocol of Peace, 116, 128, 139
Pryor, Dr. John H., 103
Public, Representative of, 152

Rabochy Golos, 247
Radicalism, of Immigrants, 46
Rand School of Social Science, 210
Referendum, 174, 190
Robbins, Mrs. Raymond, 120
Russia, Economic Development of, 49
Russian Immigrants, 46, 65

Sabotage, 201
Safety, 108, 146
Sanatorium, 147
Sanitation, 108, 146
Schlesinger, Benjamin, 2, 140
Schlossberg, Joseph, 2, 213
Seasonal Unemployment, 27, 108, 279
Seattle Union Record, 235, 242
Shirtmakers, 94
Shop Chairmen, 174, 185
Shop Committees, 185
Skill, 40
Slacking on the Job, 201
Slovenian Immigrants, 65
Social Democrats, 71
Socialism, of Jewish Immigrants, 57, 71
Socialism, Italian, 64
Socialist Labor Party, 71
Socialist Party, 204
Socialist Propaganda, 60, 71
Socialist Trade and Labor Alliance, 71
Socialist Unionism, 67
Stone, I. N., 209
Stoppage of Work, 135
Strategy, of Unions, 191
Strike, General, 288; Shop, 135, 145; Use of, 196
Strike Promoters, 72

INDEX

Strikes:
  Chicago Men's Industry, 1910, 118
  Cloakmakers, 1890, 72
  Cloakmakers, 1910, 83, 111
  Cloakmakers, 1916, 84
  Fur Workers, 95
  N. Y. Men's Industry, 1912, 85
  N. Y. Men's Industry, 1916, 94
  N. Y. Women's Industry, 1919, 142
  Reefermakers, 1905, 81
  Suspender Makers, 98
  Textile in Lawrence, 1919, 260
  Textile in Passaic, 1919, 262
  Textile in Paterson, 1919, 262
  Waist and Dressmakers, 1909, 82
Structure, of Unions, 170
Styles, 30, 281
Subcontracting, 111, 129
Sub-Manufactures, 35
Sweatshops, 39, 102

Tailor-to-the-Trade, 22, 31
Tailors' Industrial Union, 89
Taxation, Union Systems, 184
Tenement House Act of 1892, 21
Tenement, Typical, 102
Textile Industry, 252 ff.
Trade Board, 149
Triangle Fire, 146
Trousers, Separate, 22
Turnover, Labor. *See* Labor Turnover

Unemployment, 38; Insurance, 280; Seasonal, *see* Seasonal Unemployment
Union Label, 75, 194
Union Made Garment Manufacturers Association, 75
Union Shop, 107, 116
Unionism. For New Unionism, Old Unionism, Socialist Unionism, etc., *see under separate heads*
Unions, Clothing Trade, History, 68
United Cloth Hat and Cap Makers, 76, 168
United Garment Workers, 74, 87, 166
United Hatters, 79
United Hebrew Charities, 59
United Hebrew Trades, 66, 71, 91, 209
United Labor Education Committee, 219
United Neckwear Makers, 97
United Textile Workers of America, 256
Unity Centers, 216

Volks Zeitung, 167

Wages, Guarantee of, 107; Iron Law of, 277; Relation to Profits, 37; Rise of, 110; Standardization of, 107
Waist and Dressmakers Union, 84
Warehouse, 18
Week Work, 200
Women, Difficulty of Organizing, 40
Women Workers, Italian, 64
Women's Trade Union League, 120
Workers' Educational League, 209
Workers' International Industrial Union, 257
Workers' School, 209
Workmen's Circle, 59, 210

Yiddische Gazetten, 239
Yiddishe Volks Zeitung, 240

Zuckerman, Max, 2, 212
Zigman, Morris, 1